Joseph W. Taylor

BORN TO BIRD

Joseph W. Taylor
BORN TO BIRD

Written and compiled by Ann Taylor

Edited by Alyssa Taylor Wendt

ImagoPress

Copyright © 2023 Ann Taylor

Alyssa Taylor Wendt, editor

First Edition 2023

Manufactured in the United States of America

Library of Congress Cataloguing in Publication Data
Taylor, Ann
    Joseph W. Taylor BORN TO BIRD

     1. Joseph W. Taylor 2. United States – Biography 3. Birdwatching
     ISBN 979-8-218-14485-2

"Following your bliss is not self-indulgent, but vital; your whole physical system knows that this is the way to be alive in this world and the way to give to the world the very best that you have to offer. There IS a track just waiting for each of us and once on it, doors will open that were not open before and would not open for anyone else."

— Joseph Campbell

CONTENTS

Joe's favorite bird was a Henslow's Sparrow.
Ordinary, it does not even have a song, it just hiccoughs!

FOREWORD

Joseph William Taylor was at the forefront of the conservation movement in the mid-twentieth century. Climate change, pesticide use, species extinction, environmental adversity and global warming weighed heavily upon his thoughts. A traditionally-educated scholar, an inclusive thinker and experienced naturalist, he retired at the age of fifty-four to pursue lifelong goals in the careful management of our natural world.

Since early childhood, birding was a true passion for my father. He never could articulate why his fascination with birds evolved. Still, he admitted that his quest to achieve the most extensive "life list" of North American wild birds allowed him to witness the majesty, wonder and excitement of the natural world both on this continent and abroad. It also brought him a notoriety which led many to an awareness of changes necessary for the preservation of birds and their habitats.

Long before the internet, cell phones and GPS-assisted directions, he journeyed with our mother Helen to the remote birding areas of North America and distant continents. Pouring over maps, reading guide books and seeking the advice and wisdom of lifelong birding friends, he finally attained his goals. As well as becoming the foremost bird lister in the United States, he also gained a deep reverence for the wildness of our natural world and worked tirelessly toward its conservation.

Joe was also the hub around which many ecological causes revolved as longtime president of Hawk Mountain Sanctuary in Pennsylvania and a founder of the American Birding Association. His leadership prevailed and his dedication to the love of birding is revealed in *BORN TO BIRD*, a compilation of his own writing and articles by those who admired and loved him.

Ann Taylor
2022

Curlew Mountain, Alaska - 1967

FOREWORD

Joseph William Taylor was at the forefront of the conservation movement in the mid-twentieth century. Climate change, pesticide use, species extinction, environmental adversity and global warming weighed heavily upon his thoughts. A traditionally-educated scholar, an inclusive thinker and experienced naturalist, he retired at the age of fifty-four to pursue lifelong goals in the careful management of our natural world.

Since early childhood, birding was a true passion for my father. He never could articulate why his fascination with birds evolved. Still, he admitted that his quest to achieve the most extensive "life list" of North American wild birds allowed him to witness the majesty, wonder and excitement of the natural world both on this continent and abroad. It also brought him a notoriety which led many to an awareness of changes necessary for the preservation of birds and their habitats.

Long before the internet, cell phones and GPS-assisted directions, he journeyed with our mother Helen to the remote birding areas of North America and distant continents. Pouring over maps, reading guide books and seeking the advice and wisdom of lifelong birding friends, he finally attained his goals. As well as becoming the foremost bird lister in the United States, he also gained a deep reverence for the wildness of our natural world and worked tirelessly toward its conservation.

Joe was also the hub around which many ecological causes revolved as longtime president of Hawk Mountain Sanctuary in Pennsylvania and a founder of the American Birding Association. His leadership prevailed and his dedication to the love of birding is revealed in *BORN TO BIRD*, a compilation of his own writing and articles by those who admired and loved him.

Ann Taylor
2022

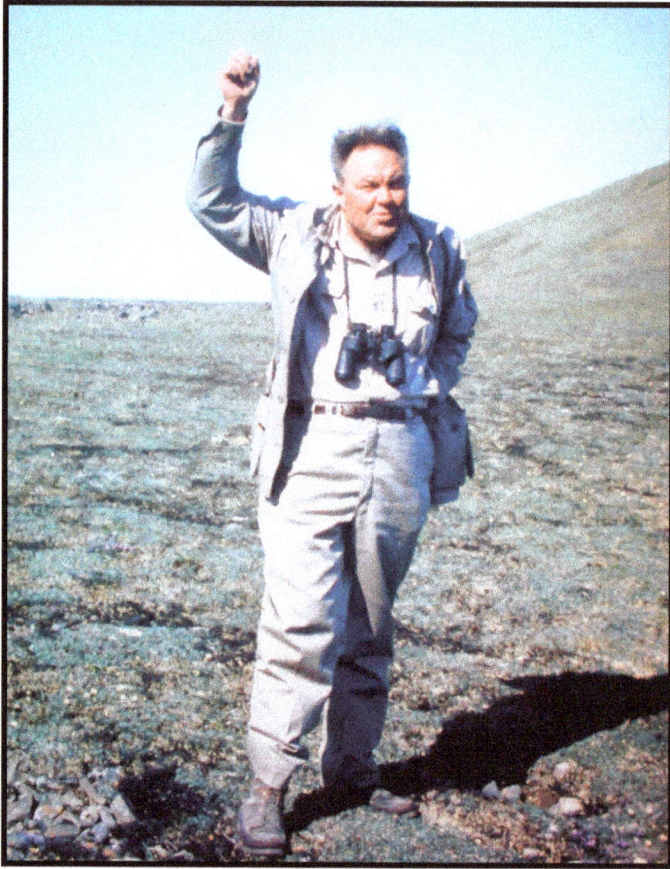

Curlew Mountain, Alaska - 1967

THE "600 CLUB"

The Bristle-thighed Curlew flew upwind. Joe Taylor had just augmented his membership in the "600 Club" with bird number 632! He and I had climbed Curlew Mountain which, by Alaskan standards, was more a steep hill than a mountain. Quietly walking through the high tundra and alpine flowers, we had startled the shorebird from its summer nest. Father was ecstatic, dancing around on the tundra in his heavy boots.

Summer in the Arctic is the time for sleepy grizzlies, molting caribou, tumescent salmon, and gigantic mosquitoes. Many unusual birds come there from their winter quarters and the Bristle-thighed Curlew was one. We toasted with whiskey back at our campsite.

Since his youth, Joe Taylor's only primal passion had been ornithology, although his work had been as an executive for the Bausch & Lomb Optical Company, the family business. As part of an informal and friendly competition with the renowned field guide author Roger Tory Peterson among others, he sought to attain the most extensive "life list" of North American birds. The members of this birding elite were all nearing or over six hundred individual bird species which they had identified in the wild.

Stuart Keith, a British ornithology associate at the American Museum of Natural History, started the "600 Club" when he published the first list of nineteen members in the December 1963 issue of *Audubon* magazine, laying the ground rules for future nominees. To qualify, it was necessary to see 600 species named in the 1957 American Ornithologists' Union checklist of some 700+ species of possible North American birds. All species had to be seen

1

Red-tailed Hawk

within the boundaries of the United States, Canada, Bermuda, Greenland, and Baja California.[1] Life listing is an honor system, no eye witnesses are necessary. All serious birders know which sightings are authentic and which listers are trustworthy.

In the decades to follow, the pursuit of "life listing" North American birds along with accidental or irregular appearances of strays was made more difficult by the AOU checklist changes. Joe repeatedly had to eliminate a bird from his list because certain subspecies were lumped together under one species. Ironically, he became a "new" member of the "600 Club" multiple times.

The quest of "life listing" was for Joe Taylor not only an amicable competition, but also one of aesthetics — the nature of beauty and the beauty of nature. "There's just an attraction for me," he explained to a local reporter in Rochester, New York, "I have no real feel for what it is. It's not the attraction of finding new and different birds. It's just the attraction of *seeing* birds. I sit in my house, and we have a pair of Red-tailed Hawks which live in the woods behind us. Whenever they fly by, three or four times a day, I'll walk out on the porch and watch them till they disappear. I truly enjoy it."[2]

From the 1960s to his passing in 1992, Joe would eventually add more than one hundred other North American birds to his life list, totaling 729 qualifying species. This was a remarkable and difficult achievement. Even with the highest score in the national game, he continued to seek out more, primarily challenging himself. Birding was his life.

OVERVIEW

To comprehend the significance Joe Taylor's life, *BORN TO BIRD* examines his life path as a journey toward his true self. This transformation came slowly, along with the complexities of a structured, formal upbringing. It is important to consider that initially there were expectations from his family and their upper middle-class status. He was born to economic and social privilege which was a rarity during the first half of the twentieth century. Neither the two world wars nor the Great Depression affected his life. Yet, an unexpected destiny with the natural world awaited him.

For the first fifty years of his life, he conformed to a rather traditional pattern, following the paths of education and employment which were, to large extent, dictated to him. Inherited wealth, high-ranking work at his family's business and social acceptance into the elite circles of Rochester, New York confirmed his success within these bounds. Nevertheless, beneath his apparent comfort with this formal exterior lay the beginnings of a developing obsession with birds and the natural world.

Birdwatching began for Joe at an early age. Quietly following his father on Sunday morning expeditions, his skill with bird identification blossomed, as did his private curiosity about birds and their habitats. Soon, he joined others in local bird censuses and gained memberships to birding associations. By the time he was an adult, Joe had become a serious birder with an authoritative presence – tall, heavy-set and remarkably self-assured.

Beginning in the 1950s, he and his wife Helen began to take their vacations alone, camping and visiting wildlife refuges around the United States. Often in near solitude and away from the pressures of family and commercial obligations, he created plans for bolstering the national pursuit of birdwatching. At the same time, he began to compile a list of the numerous bird species which he had personally identified. By the mid-sixties, with the means to continue "life listing," he joined the newly formed "600 Club," a group dedicated to the identification of North American bird species.

As his awareness about various problems facing our global environment grew, Joe made a pivotal decision to break with all traditional expectations and begin a new life. In his mid-fifties and full of energy, he abruptly retired from business and began to embrace naturalist pursuits wholeheartedly. With their children grown, he and Helen sold the family home, bought acreage for a house in the open countryside and followed his birding dream while he worked on numerous ornithological boards and publications.

Joe Taylor's significant contributions to the study of birds and the natural world, his tenure on many conservation boards, the twenty-six-years as president of Hawk Mountain Sanctuary in Pennsylvania and the collaborative formation of the American Birding Association are evidence of his dedication. As his primary focus eventually became the preservation of wildness and the crucial habitats in our natural world, the manifest transformation of his life was complete.

This monomythical journey is something we all have the potential to realize within ourselves. Are we living out our dreams, choosing our true passion over safe decisions or expected demands? The experience of one's life contains infinite choices, some planned, others circumstantial. A life transformed from expectation into passionate dedication is an inspiration, not only to birders. This compilation of biographical narrative, quotations and transcribed journals illuminates the powerful positivity of finding one's true path.

1966

The Taylor Children - 1921
Joseph, Robert, Hilda Ann and Thomas

BEGINNINGS

In 1978, I independently published All of Us, *a biographical history of John Jacob Bausch and his descendants from 1830 to 1978. The following text is excerpted from Joe's autobiographical contribution, as well as some published observations and my own recollections.*

"I was born on May 2, 1914, the first child of Hilda Drescher and Joseph Fillmore Taylor, in Rochester, New York in an apartment house at the northwest corner of Westminster Road and Thayer Street. In the following year, we moved to 1166 Clover Street."

In the late summer of 1920 at the age of six, Joe, his parents, sister and two brothers all traveled to Phoenix where they remained until June 1921. He recalled: "There, I got my first taste and love of the desert. Beyond the house, north and east, there was only desert, cactus and wildlife. Often, we drove out in the Model-T Ford on a wagon tract to the foot of Camelback Mountain watching for birds and other fauna. This was usually close to an all-day trip because we frequently got stuck in the sand for there were virtually no roads." These excursions would prove to be prophetic early life experiences. Joe's love of the desert and other wild habitats was grounded in Arizona. Throughout his life, he journeyed on extensive birding expeditions into unexplored reaches throughout the country.

When the family returned to Rochester, his schooling began in a one-room, eight-grade schoolhouse. In 1926, he enrolled in the Allendale School where he stayed through the tenth grade. At Allendale, he well remembered his history teacher, "Pop" Sims, who maintained discipline with swiftly and incredibly accurately thrown blackboard erasers which he kept stacked up on his desk.

Clarence Robinson, his French teacher, was an Englishman who had been a Boy Scout under Sir Robert Baden-Powell, the founder of the scouting movement. Consequently, there was considerable emphasis on scouting at Allendale and, although Joe never got beyond the rank of Star Scout, he did become the leader of the Moose Patrol.

In a 1992 recount of Joe's early years, *Bird Watcher's Digest* reported: "Young Joe Taylor took to birds with a passion. He was an official counselor for the Boy Scout bird study merit badge at age eleven. 'But nobody ever came to me to get the merit badge because I was too tough,' Joe added, 'As I remember, you had to know forty birds, and I would make them know forty – what they looked like, how they sang. With the other two examiners, all the boys had to do was go on two spring morning walks, and they'd give them the badge.'"[3] Joe had no sympathy for anyone who couldn't learn to identify birds as fast as he could.

1924

Joe had been regularly and seriously birding since childhood. Paradoxically, although he possessed an enduring passion for birds, he was remarkabky modest, even inarticulate, when he tried to explain it. "Bird-watching began as an excuse to accompany his father, always silently, on his birding trips. 'It was just being outdoors,' Joe said. 'Maybe it meant I didn't have to clean up the dog messes, fill the coal furnace, or shine shoes.'

"Perhaps the moment of truth and destiny came when he was eight-years-old and spotted a Golden-crowned Kinglet in front of their house. 'My father was, as many of his generation, a Doubting Thomas,' he explained, 'He would have none of it. "Nonsense! Wrong season! Pure nonsense!" I must have had a natural aptitude for bird identification for I recall

8

dragging my most unbelieving and reluctant father out of the house to confirm my identification in the front barberry hedge, at a time of year when these birds should have been nesting way to the north. He did. I was immediately hooked.'"[4]

When he was ten-years-old, he and his neighbor Tom Finucane did a National Audubon Society Christmas Bird Census in Highland Park in Rochester. They saw a Cardinal, an extraordinary discovery in 1924 since it marked one of the first northern records for this bird. "On another census, we were a little more venturesome and took a trolley to Summerville at Lake Ontario to see what gulls were there. Other than that, my transportation was always by bicycle."

Even though he often went birding with Tom, Joe actually spent more time with Tom's brother Dan chasing butterflies. They were enterprising, and together they created the Danjo Butterfly Company in a shed behind the garage. They sold butterflies and moths to Ward's Natural Science Establishment. They caught many of the moths by painting trees in the nearby woodlots with a mixture of sugar, molasses and "near" beer and then picking the moths off at night when they came to feed.

Sailing to Europe with the Boy Scouts - 1929

As Joe began to spend more time birding, this early butterfly craze dissipated, but butterflies remained as one of his real loves.

After Allendale, he boarded at the Taft School in Watertown, Connecticut. "I graduated *cum laude* from Taft in 1932, standing scholastically second in what must have been the least intellectually talented class in Taft's history. The boy who ranked first had an average of about ninety-five, and I was next at eighty-two, not high enough to even be on the honor roll in a normal year."

9

Home from Yale University - 1932

In the fall, Joe entered Yale University majoring in history and graduating with an A.B. degree in June 1936. "During freshman year, I took the one course in biology which was required, but from the vantage point of forty-odd years later, it was a sincere regret that I did not pursue this subject further. It is almost essential to a real knowledge of some aspects of bird behavior. I believe that we must know more about such behavior if we are to save our bird populations in this time of shrinking habitats and environmental changes."

Other than birding, his other lifelong passion was for Helen Taggart. "I met Joseph William Taylor when I was fifteen-years-old," she wrote for *All of Us* in 1978, "He was attentive from the very first, carrying my suitcases into my friend's house. I was so excited, I gave him the five-pound box of chocolates which was intended for my friend's mother. Joe broke off every date of that week to be with me. This was a delight for me but dismay for his former girls. He sent me a gardenia every day."[5] They were smitten, and this love lasted throughout their lifetimes.

During his four years at Yale, he had less time for birding as college activities and familial responsibilities took precedence. "In those days, even though you were old enough to be on your own in college, so long as you were primarily living under your family's roof, you did pretty much as you were told." Partly because he had a law office job readily available and partly because a legal training was an excellent background for a business career, he went to Harvard Law School and graduated in 1939.

On July 15 that same year, Joe and Helen Taggart were married at her family's home in Indianapolis, Indiana. When they were first married, they lived in an old farmhouse,

10

wonderfully redone for them as a wedding present from his parents. He "clerked" at his paternal grandfather's law firm, then Hubbell, Taylor, Goodwin, Nixon and Hargrave and finally, after two dismal failures, passed the bar exam in 1941.

"When the war came, I made no attempt to get in or stay out of the armed services, but with a growing number of children: Ann Drescher, Joseph Alexander and Henry Taggart and a medical history of hypertension, I was not called up in the draft until after mid-year in 1945. Then, this was canceled with the surrender of the Japanese. I did, however, join the New York State Guard and served for two years, achieving the distinction of being the only member of the guard who never advanced even one grade in rank. I entered as a private and was discharged as a private, not even private first class." During two weeks spent at Camp Smith in Peekskill, New York, he did receive verbal commendation for his rifle marksmanship. "This was a hangover, no doubt, from the days when Tom, Dan and I used to shoot at kites high in the air, aiming to break the sticks where they crossed."

During the war, Joe became engrossed with his work at the law office. As many of the other young men were away in military service, he was given responsibility for more cases sooner, including trying relatively major lawsuits which were usually reserved for more seasoned attorneys.

Joe and Helen - 1939

When his father became president of Bausch & Lomb, he asked Joe to abandon his law practice and come work at the factory. After much troubled deliberation, he acquiesced to his father's wishes and started to work there in the legal department in 1946. Dapper in a lightweight seersucker blazer and straw boater, he drove to work in his convertible with the top down regardless of the season. On snowy, freezing mornings, he would still be seen driving in style, wearing a long raccoon coat and a beaver hat.

11

Helen - 1948

The multi-storied B & L buildings resembled a gated fortress with a wide, well-lighted tunnel connecting the two office buildings on either side of St. Paul Street. At lunch time, literally hundreds of people would pass back and forth. Joe not only knew everyone, but also greeted them by name as he passed.

"On August 17, 1947 our fourth child, Mary Curtiss, was born, just a few months after we bought and moved into the Ward-Bentley house at the top of the Allen's Creek Road five-acre hill. It was a sprawling colonial house bordered by a dogleg golf course fairway on two sides with woods and fields on the others. This was a magnificently perfect house for bringing up a family, big and rambling." This conventionality was tempting. Still, for Joe the siren call of birds and the greater outdoors was omnipresent.

Joe and Helen decorated the house in an eclectic amalgam of styles: early American and English antiques, oriental rugs, softly upholstered chairs and couches and borrowed relics from friends and family. Until they became collectors of contemporary art decades later,

The Family of Hilda and Joseph Taylor, Joe's parents - 1949

12

the downstairs was practically papered with their collection of original Havell engravings from Audubon's "elephant folio." 590 was the crown of the neighborhood with Joe and Helen as its willing guardians.

This wondrous house was the family hub, but birding was still Joe's primary focus. On one of his rare non-birding weekends in the summer, he would be found tending to his large rose garden. He was a self-styled handyman with many projects all going on simultaneously. The house was in a constant state of change. Winters, he painted rooms while quietly singing *soto voce* to Gilbert and Sullivan, Rogers & Hammerstein and Ethel Merman. He loved music, loud music, from bagpipes and brass to Beethoven's "Ninth" and Copland's "Billy the Kid." In addition to raising her flock of four, Helen volunteered at several charitable organizations and often invited lady friends over for a luncheon. For the children, there were trees to climb, forts to build and bicycles to master. The age of television, shopping plazas and supermarkets had not arrived. Instead, the vegetable man, the egg lady, the butcher, the milkman and even the barber came directly to the house.

590 Allen's Creek Road

13

1951

1952

1956

1955

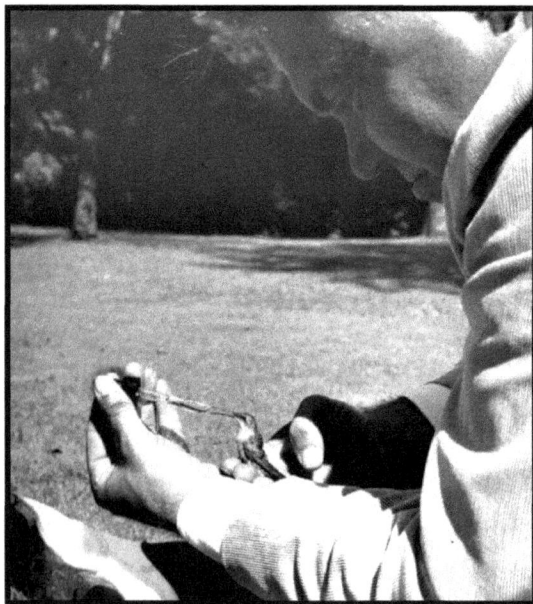
Feeding a baby hummingbird in 1955

Joe and his mother, Hilda - 1947

With his daughter, Mary - 1950

Joe and Helen found much of their social entertainment with neighbors and friends. They gave numerous cocktail and dinner parties, many "tea dances" and an annual New Year's Day open house. Multicolored Japanese lanterns were hung outside on some occasions, giving a special glow to the guests in their formal black or white-tie attire. The children watched spellbound from the second floor as a small orchestra played the dance tunes of the thirties and forties. The halcyon atmosphere was light and warm; no world events appeared troubling. Joe delighted in being an affable, welcoming host.

At the Bausch & Lomb Christmas party for all the employees' families, Joe dressed as the factory's Santa Claus. He was carried aloft into the room on a grand throne and listened carefully to the children's wishes as they sat on his ample lap.

Joe had a notably deep devotion to his mother Hilda. Before his father died and certainly every day afterward, he stopped to see her for a visit en route home from work. Weekends, she often joined his family at 590. Joe had a lifelong dedication to her well-being.

For decades, the extended family gathered for Sunday noon dinners and holiday celebrations at Joe's parents' home on Clover Street. On Christmas Day, his family dressed formally. Joe wore his morning suit, dove gray vest and spats, Helen a fashionable new dress. The children were gilded to the nines. Traditions were strong and the family united.

15

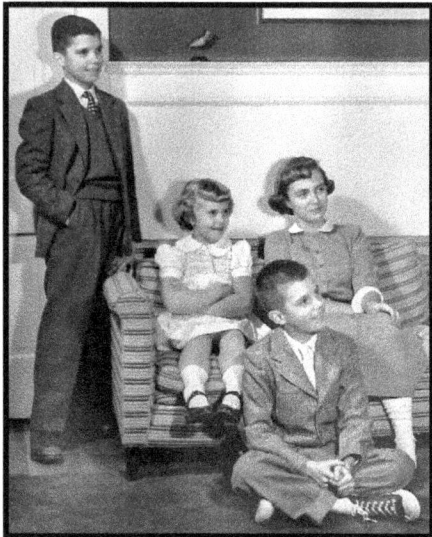
Joe, Mary, Ann and Hank - 1953

These times were also marked by a life-altering tragedy. In 1963, shortly before his eighteenth birthday, their son Hank died in a mountain climbing accident in Colorado. The ensuing sorrow profoundly affected every member of the family. Their idyllic life was shattered but, in time, the family grew even closer. Joe's participation with his other children became stronger as they were more precious to him after Hank's death.

———————————————————

From the 1940s through the 1960s, Joe and Helen began birding expeditions, near and far. They took annual trips in the spring to Oak Orchard refuge to see the great flocks of Canada Geese and in the fall to Hawk Mountain Sanctuary in Pennsylvania to watch the procession of southern-migrating raptors. In 1952, they began to combine their love of birding and camping. First, they drove to Florida, then to the Southwest, Nova Scotia and Newfoundland and other wilderness areas. "As a result, I saw much of the great natural beauty of North America and many of its spectacular scenic wonders. At the same time and because of all of this wandering, I also saw very many of the North American bird species so that when life lists of identified birds were published on a formal basis, I found myself at first near and, then, at the top of the list."

During Joe's tenure at Bausch & Lomb, he served as secretary and, subsequently, as treasurer. Still, he was never completely happy with this work. After his father's death, he became the likely candidate to accede to the presidency as he was very popular among the workers at the factory. In 1969, uncharacteristically, he called a family conference. The children gathered at 590, and Joe explained that he had no desire for this job and planned to retire. It was a moment of critical reflection and change — a pivotal point which elucidated his reach for personal autonomy. This decision not only changed his and Helen's life but also his relationships with his children, his lifestyle, his purpose and his outlook on the world.

16

BIRDING EXCURSIONS

A typical day of camping for Joe and Helen began at sunrise with a hot shower from a porous five-gallon bucket attached to the roof of the car, followed by breakfast cooked on their propane stove. Joe checked over the day's proposed itinerary notes with a library of guide books and maps. He often birded at their campsite while Helen made sandwiches, usually peanut butter and jelly, to take along for lunch. Often, in the excitement of viewing a bird, peanut butter would smear atop his binoculars.

They carefully repacked their camping equipment into the car and set off to wildlife refuges and reserves, noting all the birds along the way. After arriving at the next campsite in the late afternoon, they would always pause for a cocktail hour, relaxing with several drinks before preparing a dinner of fresh or freeze-dried food.

Joe also packed a tape recorder. Every evening after dinner, he would pour a highball and record their location, the weather and the birds they saw that day. Sometimes, if their birding had gone on late into the evening, he would get up before dawn to record the previous day's sightings.

The tapes themselves are long gone, but transcriptions of some of them remain. His words are not just listings, they are also testament to his joyous appreciation of the world of nature.

1952

BIRDING AND CAMPING
IN THE 1950S AND 1960S

FLORIDA - 1952

In the late winter of 1952, Joe and Helen planned the first of many birding and camping vacations – to Florida and elsewhere. The itinerary was mapped using A Guide to Bird Finding *by Olin Sewall Pettingill. Instead of pitching a tent, their station wagon was cleverly outfitted with a raised sleeping platform behind the front seats which held air mattresses and sleeping bags. A Coleman stove, the telescope, cameras and other camping gear could be stowed beneath it. They left in early March. Here are his journal entries for their trip.*

Mach 2: We left Rochester a little before noon and spent the night with Maurice and Irma Broun at Hawk Mountain Sanctuary. The next morning, we watched Maurice feed his flock of at least one-hundred-fifty Evening Grosbeaks. The weather became worse as we went south, but it finally stopped snowing and raining in southern Virginia. From then on, it was mostly sunny, although a little windy at times.

There were thousands of migrating bluebirds along the telephone wires in North Carolina. Following Pettingill, Wrightsville Beach outside of Wilmington, North Carolina, produced, as predicted, two American Oystercatchers and several Wilson's Plovers. We were particularly pleased with the oystercatchers because almost a hundred percent of those on the east coast winter at Bull's Island, South Carolina, and there wasn't going to be time to get out there.

1952

March 6: At the bridge over the Combahee River between Charleston and Savannah were our first Snowy Egrets, Louisiana and Little Blue Herons and Fish Crows. We camped that night for the first time at Ft. Clinch State Park north of Jacksonville, sleeping in the car. The next morning, driving south along the ocean we saw our first Brown Pelicans and Northern Gannets. Birding was wonderful on the old Kingsley Plantation on Ft. George Island east of Jacksonville: Pileated Woodpeckers, Blue-headed Vireos, flickers, waxwings, robins, gnatcatchers by the dozens and Myrtle, Yellow-throated and Palm Warblers. At Mantanzas Inlet south of St. Augustine, we saw our first Forster's, Royal and Caspian Terns and Black Skimmers and watched a Bald Eagle after an Osprey for almost ten minutes.

The number of Sparrow Hawks on the wires was amazing, particularly between St. Augustine and Daytona Beach, about twelve to a mile. Many of these small hawks must have been migrating.

Brown Pelicans

20

March 7: Flying over the St. Johns River marshes west of Melbourne were our first Ibises, White, Wood and Glossy, and an Anhinga. Clouds of egrets rose up from their roost or rookery across Lake Washington.

On Maurice and Irma's recommendation, we spent that night and the next sleeping on the beach at Sebastian Inlet on the outer reef east of Wabasso. A road runs out to the inlet through the scrub and sand dunes for about five miles. We picked a spot to camp near the end of the point where it was only about seventy-five feet wide and did nothing for two days but watch the pelicans and, surprisingly, one Man-O'-War coast by. We only left for a few hours to drive back north to Merritt Island and Canaveral Peninsula where we were lucky enough to squeak out the Dusky Seaside Sparrow and catch up, finally, with a pair of Florida Scrub Jays.

March 10: During the morning and early afternoon, the Audubon warden Glenn Chandler drove us in his jeep around the Kissimmee Prairie. We were amazed at the way he could spot the Sandhill Cranes over half a mile away. At that distance, they looked to us just like the saw palmettos. Every so often, he would turn off what they call roads on the prairie and go cross-country over trees and through ponds to get nearer to the forty or so cranes or to show us the Burrowing Owls. We saw four of the owls standing guard on their mounds, staring at us with their enormous yellow eyes.

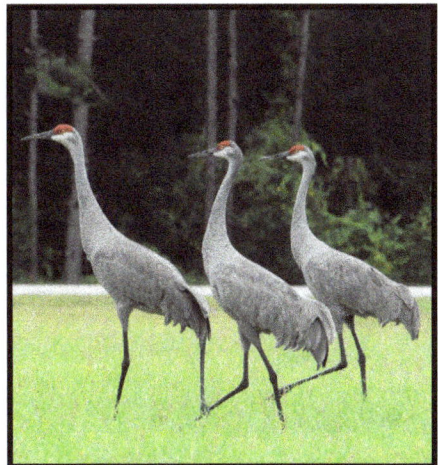
Sandhill Cranes

Pancake flat as the prairie may be, it is actually full of variety. We hated to leave this part of Florida. We stopped for lunch at Glenn's favorite hummock and picked wild grapefruit as our first course. On the way back, our one and only Audubon's Caracara was perched in a tree near Chandler's Slough. Later in the afternoon driving along the west shore of Lake Okeechobee, we found four Black-necked Stilts along with many other shorebirds, particularly large flocks of Short-billed Dowitchers.

21

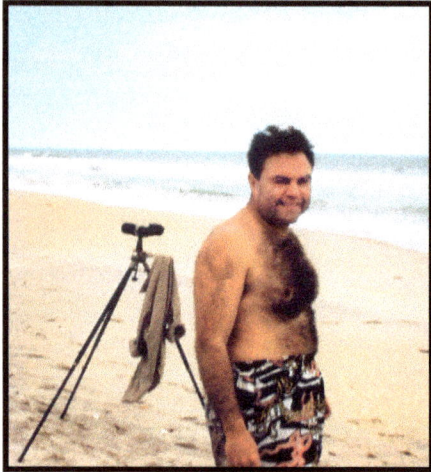
1952

March 11: We headed for Clewiston to find the Smooth-billed Ani. After covering the town and countryside with a fine-toothed comb without success, we followed Pettingill's advice and found Mrs. Jack Merritt who showed us one within five minutes. The ani was a most loose-jointed appearing bird, especially in high wind, and superficially a little like the Boat-tailed Grackles which, of course, were everywhere. On Key Largo late in the afternoon, we saw the first of several Insular Red-shouldered Hawks which are much smaller and very much paler than our northern birds.

March 12: The next morning on Florida Bay out from Tavernier, we joined the Audubon Tour led by Charlie Brookfield and Sandy Sprunt. The water itself is incredibly beautiful – azure blue and brilliant emerald green in streaks, accentuated by the sparkling beige of the sandbars which stretched out from the numerous mangrove islands. We found Great White Herons, Reddish Egrets in both color phases, characteristically flapping their wings and crouching down as they stalked their fish. American Egrets, Royal and a few Caspian Terns and a Yellow-crowned Night Heron perched about fifteen feet away. Ospreys nested nearby. As we came around the point of one mangrove island, over two hundred Man-O'-War birds took off and circled overhead. But the Roseate Spoonbills surpass everything. The rich, strawberry-ice-cream pink of the full-plumaged birds against the blues and greens of the water was really from another world. They belonged in "Alice in Wonderland."

After a morning like that, we couldn't feel too badly at not finding Gray Kingbirds or Scissor-tailed Flycatchers on the way to Key West. The season was too early for them anyway. We camped that night in Torch Key. This was, fortunately, one of the keys where there were practically no mosquitoes.

March 13: We wandered around Islamorada on Plantation Key looking for White-crowned Pigeons with no luck, although they had been seen earlier that day. Shortly after leaving

22

there, however, we pulled the car over to the side of the road and watched two Swallow-tailed Kites for over half an hour, some of the time not more than ten feet away. They are certainly neat, handsome birds with amazing flying abilities. At the north end of Key Largo, following Roger Peterson's directions, we saw the Short-tailed Hawk which was especially gratifying because none had been seen on the keys that year.

March 14: We camped at Flamingo, the deserted village at the tip of Cape Sable. On our way, we stepped into the Everglades to see Purple Gallinules at the Anhinga Trail. A wooden ramp had been built about two hundred yards into the slough so that birds and alligators, having become a little used to people, are relatively unafraid. That was the only night on which we had bad bug trouble, but it made up for the others!

March 15: We drove around the Everglades which, incidentally, is largely a flat, sawgrass prairie and not the dismal swamp which we had believed it to be. There were White Pelicans, Least, Semipalmated and Western Sandpipers near Flamingo and, at Snake Bight, thousands of Caspian Terns, Black Skimmers and a Wurdemann's Heron.

We had not been able to get reservations for the Audubon Everglades Tour, but Charlie Brookfield was kind enough to slide us in on a trip that afternoon to the famous Cuthbert Lake rookery. The ibis nests had been completely destroyed by a bad storm in February, but there were hundreds of egrets which seemed to be getting ready to nest in the island rookery, so we gave it a wide berth.

This turned out to be our biggest day, at least if you base it on accidentals. We drove across the Tamiami Trail very slowly, hardly ever out of low gear, watching the flocks of Wood and White Ibises, Florida and Purple Gallinules, egrets and herons. Just before we were going to turn off the trail onto the so-called Loop Road which ran back into the Everglades, we spotted a Black-Bellied Tree Duck standing in the shallow water with two Florida Black Ducks about twenty feet away. We watched it for a long time with binoculars and the 30X telescope. It could not be mistaken for any other bird. Flying once for about thirty feet, I could see the large white wing patches. Peterson says it had never been authenticated in Florida, so we were a little breathless for the rest of the day. The shower in a motel in Homestead that night felt wonderful after two days and nights in 85 degree weather.

March 16: We had to cover the west coast much too fast, although we did stop long enough at Sarasota to see a Least Tern.

March 17: We stopped at Wakulla Springs outside of Tallahassee principally too see the Limpkins and then went on to the St. Marks Wildlife Refuge and camped at its edge for the night. Most of the birds which winter there had gone north, but there were still many ducks and shorebirds including Marbled Godwits and Hudsonian Curlews. At night, we heard a Great Horned Owl hoot. This was our last birding except for an hour early the next morning in Kingsport, Tennessee where a friend found us a Bewick's Wren.

It was a wonderful trip, 185 species, inexpensive because we were able to sleep in the car and, if anyone should want to hear more about it, we can still talk for hours.

——————————————————————————————

Joe and Helen returned to Florida in 1972. *The Key West Citizen* reported: "Is bird watching a hobby, scientific research or a sport? In the realm of nature, a modern-day Audubon, viewing the world with a telephoto lens, the tycoon of birdwatchers has arrived for a few days of 'fishing.' Why is he so special? He has just seen his 693rd North American bird. Not Peterson, not Pettingill, but Joseph W. Taylor from New York.

"How does one measure success in life anyway? The name of the game is a nation-wide, extra-exclusive group named the '600 Club.' In the brief interim since its organization, the club has acquired more than sixty members. Joe Taylor is now in first place. However, the motto of the club is "Cooperation, not Competition." In a recent birding field guide, the number of permanent residents and migrants totaled about 645 and another 50 or so were listed as migratory or casual visitors. Joe Taylor has been known to travel extensively to where a particular bird has been reported. He says he is going fishing, but the chances are he's going out to the reef to look for the Bridled Tern which, if seen, would be number 694. He is a pro!"[6]

THE SOUTHWEST - 1954

In the spring of 1954, birding and camping continued. Joe and Helen's wide-ranging itinerary crossed four southwestern states. Beginning in southern Texas at the Laguna Atascosa Refuge, Joe hoped to find the rare Aplomado Falcon, but it eluded him. So, they drove on through the Rio Grande Valley into Arizona and camped at Madera Canyon, a riparian woodland which hosts more than 250 bird species in the Santa Rita Mountains. Birding there was exciting, producing several new species. Farther west in California, they stopped at the Salton Sea Refuge, a crucial feeding grounds for birds migrating from the Arctic to South America. This marine and freshwater wetland oasis in the desert attracts over 400 bird species with its varied habitats.

Turning back into Arizona, they birded at Oak Creek Canyon, a spectacular red-rock gorge north of Sedona and looked for the tiny Canyon Wren. When they reached New Mexico, Bosque del Apache Refuge produced tens of thousands of wintering cranes, geese and ducks. Although Joe and Helen birded as they traveled along the roads, the wildlife refuges fostered the most comprehensive bird life.

Oak Creek Canyon

1954

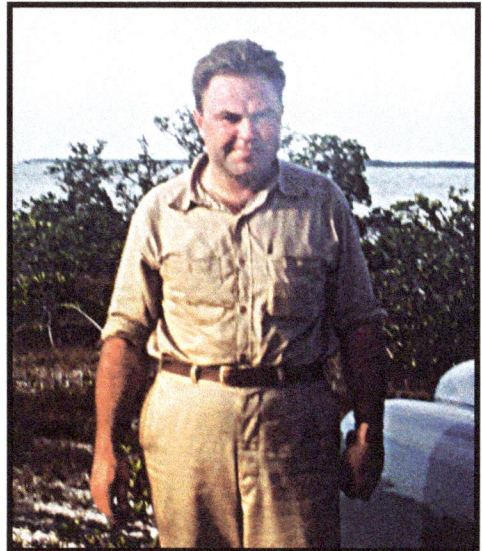

25

Following their trip to the Southwest, Floyd King, editor of Rochester's *Democrat and Chronicle* wrote: "While backyard birding can be entirely satisfactory, every birder dreams of a vacation trip to some far-off place where there are no cares and the birds are strange and beautiful. Joe Taylor and his wife Helen have just returned from such a vacation, a trip so rewarding that it will be with them always as an experience of a lifetime.

"The Taylors drove 8,500 miles in one month. On the road, they averaged 400 miles a day. They slept in sleeping bags in their station wagon, cooked coffee on a propane stove and lived on peanut butter and jelly sandwiches. They ran into terrific hail storms and dust storms, shivered in mountain cold and suffered in desert heat. But their enthusiastic verdict at the end was 'the best vacation we ever had.'

"Seeing the rare Whooping Cranes in their wintering grounds is an opportunity that comes to few. Birders will spend a lifetime in the field without ever recording a Green Jay, Derby Flycatcher, Williamson's Sapsucker, New Mexican Duck or Lewis's Woodpecker. The Taylors saw all of these and more.

"One of their first stops was at Moon Lake, Mississippi, the wintering ground of the Ruddy Duck. This lake, a backwash of the Mississippi River during flood stages, was literally covered with Ruddy Ducks, thousands upon thousands. They saw a similar site at the Sabine Wildlife Refuge in southern Louisiana, the wintering ground for Blue Geese, Snow Geese and a sprinkling of White-fronteds.

Ruddy Duck

"Observing the Whooping Cranes on the Aransas Refuge in Texas was a real feat of diplomacy. Taylor had gone to Washington seeking permission to visit these birds, but had gotten nowhere. There are only twenty-four of the cranes in the entire world, and they are guarded as carefully as the British crown jewels.

"At the refuge, the Taylors went directly to the manager who was so impressed with their sincerity and interest, he agreed to take them out in his boat to see the cranes. And telling of this kindness, Taylor added that they had camped at many bird sanctuaries and wildlife refuges on the trip and invariably found the resident managers to be, in his own words, 'incredibly nice guys.'

"The Whooping Cranes he described as 'beautiful things, nearly five feet tall and with tails like ostriches. They are simply tremendous in the air. The birds have a regal dignity that is in sharp contrast to the hoarse cry which gave them their name.'

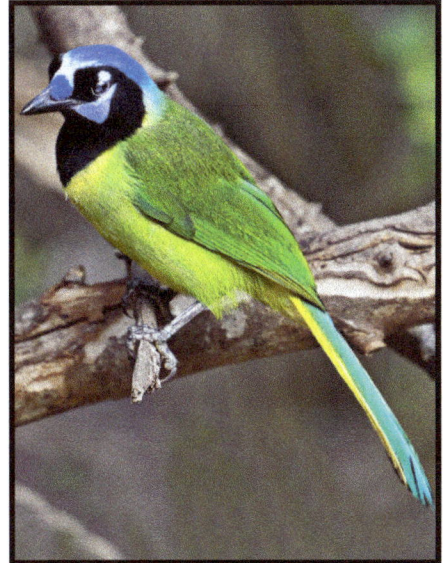

Green Jay

"The Taylors got another real thrill while camped in the Santa Ana Refuge beside the Rio Grande River. This is in tropical country and a warm rain was falling when Helen, who was peering through a dripping spotting scope, suddenly exclaimed, 'Heavens, what am I seeing?' It was a Green Jay, a bird that looks like an escaped inmate of a zoo. In fact, a peacock could take a lesson in styling from a Green Jay. Its back and tail are a handsome Kelly green. The head is iridescent royal blue with black face and throat. Rounding out the feather dress are bright yellow under parts and outer tail feathers. 'Part of the fascination of a trip like ours is that the unexpected is always happening,' said Taylor, 'Just after Helen saw the Green Jay, I spotted a Derby Flycatcher, an equally spectacular specimen.'

'Another time we were riding along near the Grand Canyon when I happened to glance up and saw a Golden Eagle, the only one of our trip. In the Bosque del Apache Refuge in Socorro, New Mexico, we saw the New Mexican Duck, the only place in the world that bird can be seen.'

In preparation for their trip, the Taylors did a great deal of reading about western birds. They were continually interested to see how closely their experiences tallied with the books.

27

'You read about something and wonder if it is so,' said Taylor, 'Then you find out that is exactly the way it is. Birds live in life zones and these zones can change rapidly when driving from the desert to the top of a mountain. The book says you stopped seeing Arizona Jays at 3,500 feet and then start seeing Scrub Jays. It was just like magic. We have an altimeter on the car. At 3,500 feet, we would see our last Arizona Jay, and it 3,600 feet, we would see our first Scrub Jay. Roger Tory Peterson told us not to miss the Madera Canyon in Arizona because, at 6,500 feet, we would see the Acorn Woodpecker. And just like he said, at 6,500 feet, we saw the Acorn Woodpecker.'

"The story of the Taylors' vacation is not complete without mention of one adventure only indirectly connected with birding. In mountainous Arizona, they explored many canyons because these are favorite birding sites. At the end of one of these canyons, they ran into a dirt road winding up the mountain. The road looked inviting, and they decided to follow it to the top. Before long, they began to doubt the wisdom of their decision. The road had narrowed to just room for their car. On one side the rocks went straight up and on the other straight down. Guardrails are unknown in the West and Joe, peering over the edge, remarked idly that one could fall a thousand feet without ever bumping a rock.

"By this time, Helen, particularly, had lost her enthusiasm, but there was no way to turn back. Rounding a curve about halfway up, they met another automobile bumper to bumper at a spot where a mountain goat couldn't have passed. Obviously, the other driver was a native of the area. Joe set the brake, got out and walked over. 'What is the etiquette in a situation like this?' he inquired. 'The etiquette,' drawled the native, 'is that *you* back down.' The trip back down the mountain was one the Taylors will never forget. But they still wonder if there might have been a rare bird at the top of the mountain.

"Later, after being caught in a dust storm so thick they could not see the ornament on the hood of their car for hours at a time, the couple had to drive 730 miles in one day to keep their schedule and get home on time. They lunched late in the day beside Lake Erie where they saw a Common Goldeneye duck, the first of their trip. Then as they drove into the yard of their home, they were greeted by the cherry call of a Black-capped Chickadee, a bird they had not seen in 8,500 hundred miles of driving during which they had identified 240 species. That is life for a birder."[7]

1955

NEW MEXICO TO BIG BEND - 1955

On the road again in the spring, Joe and Helen drove to Palo Duro Canyon in the Texas panhandle. A birding blind near the trading post provided an unparalleled opportunity to see hundreds of the park's birds from a single location. They drove on to Bitter Lake Refuge in New Mexico, another desert wetland for migrating waterfowl, shorebirds and a staging area for Sandhill Cranes. Taking a scenic route through the Huachuca Mountains into Arizona, they camped again at Madera Canyon. Although the birding was spectacular there, the elusive Coppery-tailed Trogan had yet to be found.

In the last week of their trip, they reached Big Bend National Park on the Rio Grande in Texas. The park has a variety of excellent birding locations: the riparian river corridor, desert springs, open desert, grasslands, pinyon, oak and juniper woodlands and moist forested canyons. Spring is the most popular period for birding with numerous rare migrants being reported. Finding rare migrants was their principal reason for visiting.

NATIONAL PARKS - 1956

Driving west through Colorado, they stopped at Mesa Verde National Park. Established by President Theodore Roosevelt in 1906, the park occupies more than 50,000 acres near the Four Corners region of the Southwest. With more than five thousand sites, including six hundred cliff dwellings, it is the largest archaeological preserve in the United States.

Fifty miles northwest of the Four Corners, they visited Natural Bridges National Park. The natural bridges were formed through erosion by water flowing in the stream bed of the canyons. Beyond the park in Utah, the San Juan River formed the Goosenecks. Similar meandering streams flow throughout the world, but specific conditions must be met for them to cut such deep, winding ravines.

On the border of Arizona and Utah, Monument Valley, renowned for its vast sandstone buttes, lies within the territory of the Navajo Nation. They camped there before going on to the Vermillion Cliffs where more than twenty species of raptors, including Bald and Golden Eagles, Peregrine Falcons, and other hawk species, could be seen.

This trip concluded with visits to Zion and Bryce Canyon National Parks in Utah. At Zion, they found Golden Eagles, Red-tailed Hawks, Pinyon Jays and White-throated Swifts. A plethora of songbirds and raptors inhabited the "hoodoos," irregular pinnacles of red and orange rock formations, at Bryce. This vacation was Helen's introduction to the West.

Goosenecks of the San Juan River

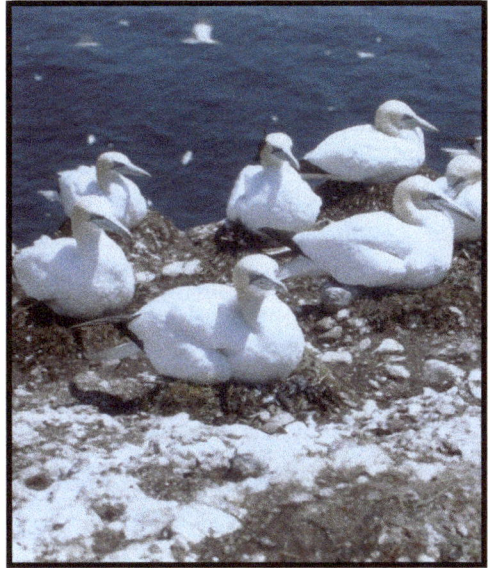

Northern Gannets

NOVA SCOTIA - 1957

The maritime province of Nova Scotia in eastern Canada is a birder's paradise. Joe and Helen drove and camped along its shores and into its interior. There was excellent birding in the Margaree Valley. The prime habitat centered around the Margaree River, its tributaries and the valleys surrounding it. All were alive with shorebirds, pelagic birds, waterfowl, songbirds and raptors. The cacophonic din delighted them both.

31

CHINCOTEAGUE AND THE OUTER BANKS - 1958

This trip focused largely on shorebirds and waterfowl along the Atlantic coast of Delaware, Virginia and North and South Carolina. Their first stop was Bombay Hook Wildlife Refuge in Delaware, a refuge and breeding ground for migratory and wintering birds along the Atlantic flyway. Tidal salt marsh water levels in the refuge were manipulated to produce desirable emergent and underwater plants for waterfowl. When the pools were drawn down, large populations of shore and wading birds fed on the mudflats.

Chincoteague Wildlife Refuge off the coast of Virginia includes more than 14,000 acres of beach, dunes, marsh and maritime forest. It was established in 1943 to provide habitat for migrating waterfowl, wading birds, shorebirds and songbirds as well as other wildlife and plants. More than 320 species of birds are known to occur in the haven of the refuge. Joe and Helen drove and walked the six well-maintained trails finding several new birds to augment their lists.

Next, they went on to the Outer Banks, a 200-mile string of barrier islands and spits off the coast of North Carolina. These islands protect the coastal barrier ecosystem. Sandy

1958

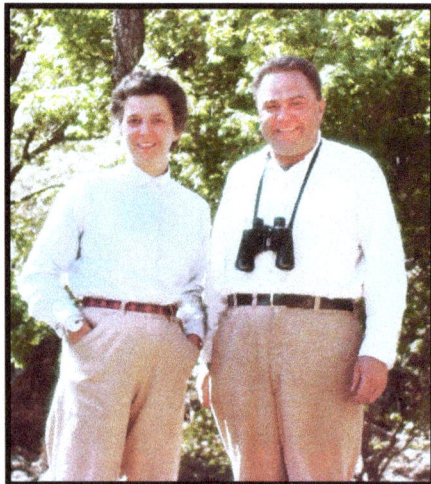

beaches, grassy dunes, wetlands, maritime forests and shrub thickets also provide wintering habitat for waterfowl. They especially hoped to find the endangered Piping Plover.

Moving farther south, Joe and Helen boarded a boat to Bird Key Sanctuary on Folly Island. The sanctuary itself varies in size from year to year with its ever-shifting sands. Its isolation and the absence of mammalian predators makes it an ideal place for ground-nesting birds such as Brown Pelicans, Laughing Gulls, Royal Terns, American Oystercatchers and Snowy Egrets.

32

THE PACIFIC NORTHWEST - 1962

After a brief sojourn back to the west coast in 1960, the next birding adventure took Joe and Helen to the Pacific Northwest. They left on a train from Toronto, crossing the prairies of Ontario, the wide plains of Manitoba, Saskatchewan and Alberta, stopping briefly in the Rocky Mountains at Jasper in British Columbia before reaching the Pacific coast at Vancouver.

After exploring Vancouver Island, they drove to the Olympic Peninsula. Because of a wide range of precipitation and elevation, salt and fresh water, forest, prairie and rock, it has a multitude of different habitats and supports amazing biodiversity. The peninsula has the perfect temperature to host mid-migration waterfowl. Surf Scoters, Buffleheads, Common Loons and Horned Grebes stop there along the Pacific flyway as they move south from Alaska and Canada for the winter. Wilson's Warblers, Black-throated Gray Warblers, Swainson's Thrushes and Western Wood Pewees which fly north in the early days of summer also pause at Olympic to refresh.

Clark's Nutcrackers

Following the avian migrations, Joe and Helen drove into the Cascade Range. Many species, including raptors which breed further north, pass through this area in the spring. Over half of the species breeding there are migratory. Vireos, swallows, nutcrackers, grosbeaks, thrushes, warblers and tanagers are among the many species which return annually in spring.

Finally, Joe and Helen's well-planned itinerary took them into the magnificent Glacier National Park in Montana. With the great abundance of bird life in the park, their birding lists were bulging, making this a remarkably memorable journey.

NEWFOUNDLAND - 1961

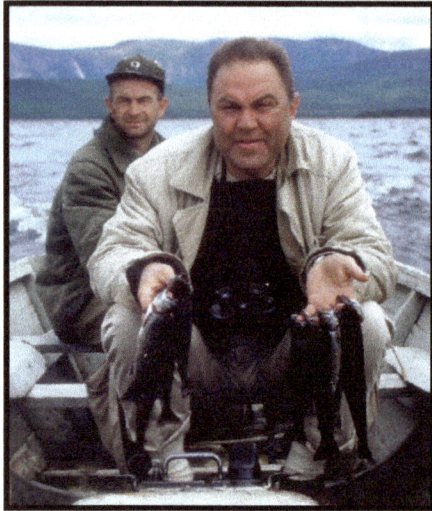
1961

Setting their birding sites to the north, Joe and Helen's next foray was to the rugged island of Newfoundland in Canada's Atlantic region. This easternmost province is considered to be the seabird capital of North America. They flew into St. John's, the capital. After a bit of successful fishing, they went out to Witless Bay Ecological Reserve. Immense numbers of birds nest on this four island archipelago during the seabird breeding season.

They were very excited to be birding in an unfamiliar location. North America's largest Atlantic Puffin colony, which includes more than 260,000 pairs, breeds there each year. The reserve also hosts the world's second-largest colony of Leach's Storm Petrels and thousands of Black-legged Kittiwakes.

After camping at Trepassey Bay surrounded by colorful lichens and soft caribou moss, they boarded a ferry to Cape St. Mary's Reserve. After birding there, they continued on to Terra Nova Park, a boreal forest of mostly old growth trees, where they witnessed a vast wildfire.

They later learned from the local ranger that fire is one of the mechanisms which is necessary to renew that type of mixed forest.

Atlantic Puffin

To further traverse this archipelago, yet another ferry took them to Bonne Bay, a fjord on the west side of the islands. Birding from the boat, they saw many Great Black-backed Gulls sporting over five-foot wingspans. During this two-week journey around Newfoundland, both Joe and Helen added several new bird species to their life lists.

34

BAJA CALIFORNIA - 1965

Baja is a peninsula situated between the Pacific Ocean and the Sea of Cortez bounded on the north by California and Arizona. A paved two-lane road runs about 1,000 miles from north to south. Side roads pass through tiny villages and wind along the eastern mountainsides and western coastal beaches.

Joe and Helen entered Baja through Mexicali in Arizona. Birding the length of the peninsula through desert peppered with boojum trees was spectacular. They saw Red-billed Tropicbirds, Blue-footed and Masked Boobies, Man-O'-Wars, Roadrunners and Elf Owls. At the village of Guerrero Negro on its western edge, they watched nesting Ospreys and marveled at gray whales breaching off the Pacific coast. After they reached La Paz, near its tip, they spent a few days deep-sea fishing with always an eye out for pelagic fliers.

With several indigenous and vagrant species, the Baja peninsula contributes much to the rich Mexican avifauna. Learning that the region has 529 regularly occurring species, Joe and Helen vowed to return in the near future.

Dunes at Mexicali

Osprey

ETYMOLOGY

J oe was curious about all aspects of birds: identification, behavior, diet and survival. Surprisingly, he also studied the evolution of their nomenclature. In 1972, he wrote:

Often, I have wondered how birds got their names.

Why, for instance, is a loon called a loon? Certainly "loony" comes from loon, and not loon from "loony." Now the answers to questions like these are provided in a new book *Words for Birds* by Edward S. Gruson. "Loon" is derived from the Scandinavian word "lomr" for "diving bird," and back of that from the Indo-European language, which contains the basic elements of many of our modern words. There, the root word was "la" which is also the source of our word "lament." So a loon is a diving bird which laments, and surely its mournful call can be taken for that.

To take some other names at random, "pheasant" comes, in the first instance, from the Greek "phasianos," A bird from the region of the River Phasis. In Latin, it was "phasiana avis," Literally a phasian bird and from there, it became "fesaunt" in French and then today's "pheasant."

Myths gave the rise to "plover." Shorebirds were, incorrectly, thought to be easier to capture in the rain, or to herald the rainy season. The name derives from "pluvia," Latin for rain, and the bird was called "pluvarius," or "rain-bird," which became "plovier" in Old French and the English "plover" is easy from that.

Many names are, directly or indirectly, imitative or echoic. "Gull" comes from the Celtic and came into English as "gwilan" from the Breton word "gwel-a," "to weep or wail," obviously a reference to the bird's cries. Similarly, "auk," coming from the Old Norse "alka" is imitative of the call. And "cuckoo" is plainly echoic, the earliest English form of the word being "cuccu." Remember the very Old English poem from around the year 1230 which begins "Sumer is icumen in, lhude sing cuccu." "Owl" and "howl" are derived from the same basic root and are also from the call. In Old English, it was "ule" and in Scandinavian "uggla," both of which, if you can pronounce them, sound like an owl.

Many names are plainly indicative of behavior – for example, woodpecker, flycatcher, creeper and nuthatch. "Nuthatch" is a corruption of "nuthack" which is what these birds often do. They wedge a nut into a crevice in the bark of a tree and hack away at it until the shell is broken. To a somewhat lesser extent are some other names derived from behavior. The wings of hummingbirds hum when they fly, and a warbler does not really "warble," i.e. sing with trills. But the so-called Old World warblers really do warble in the strictest sense. Doubtless, the first settlers on this continent saw some similarity between the North American warblers and the familiar birds they had left at home, even though our birds are brightly colored, and the European ones are terribly drab.

An intriguing one is "wren." It comes from the Middle English "wrenne" and the Old English "wraenne" which mean "lascivious." Why did the old Angles and Saxons believe these birds to be more lecherous than any others? And is this possibly where "Jenny-wren" came from?

Some names are very easy. "Blackbird" and "meadowlark" are obviously descriptive. "Oriole" is also and isn't too hard to fathom. Coming from the old Latin "aureolus," contracted in Medieval Latin to "oriolus," they both mean "golden bird." "Kinglet" is, of course, "little king" denoting the red or gold patch on its crown. "Longspur" is a reference to the claw on the bird's hind toe which is longer than the toe itself. Interestingly, the scientific name for the closely-related Snow Bunting, "plectrophenax," indicates that the bird is not a longspur. The word is derived from the Greek "plectron," a long claw-like tool and "phenax," to cheat or fake. The Snow Bunting, not having a long claw, is a "fake' longspur.

If you're good at German, "jaeger" is simple. It means hunter, which this bird certainly is. And "hawk" also comes from the basic Teutonic "hab" meaning to seize or hold, which was "hauk" in Middle English. And I think my favorite is "petrel," a direct allusion to St. Peter. Like him, these birds do sometimes actually seem to walk on water."[8]

Alaska 1967

ALASKA 1967

In June and July of 1967, Joe, Helen, my first husband Peter Wendt and I camped all over Alaska for nearly six weeks. All seasoned campers and lovers of untamed nature, we also traveled with the hope of augmenting Joe's life list of North American bird species. This chapter is extracted from the taped recordings he made each day of our journey.

June 9: We drove out of Edmonton, B. C. in a rented Pontiac station wagon. Snow covered the ground and continued to swirl around us until mid-afternoon and then gradually began to clear. By the time we arrived in Dawson Creek, the weather was really quite good.

During the last half of the day, when we finally came out of forest country and back onto the prairies, there were endless potholes, at least one every quarter of a mile along the unpaved AlCan Highway. Every one had at least one pair of ducks in it, mostly Bluebills. The holes appear to have steep banks which are obviously, to some extent, man-made. I wonder whether there is some conservation work done to make the potholes so the water will not evaporate. We got to Dawson Creek at 9:30. Along the way, with the sun still above the horizon. we saw two Short-eared Owls.

June 10: Up at 5:30, an absolutely brilliant, clear day with the temperature about 52 degrees. The AlCan highway is in really good shape here. This afternoon, we drove for an hour without seeing a car going either way. We are camped at Muncho Lake. So far as the birds go, Tennessee Warblers are all over. I heard a Chestnut-sided and a Myrtle. There are also Tree and Violet-green Swallows, Western Bluebirds and a Spotted Sandpiper flying up and down the lake.

Muncho Lake is absolutely beautiful. The water is aquamarine, and, with the sun on it, it looks more like Florida Bay than a big, deep lake in northern British Columbia. The lake runs north and south and, with the sun to the west of us behind a high ridge of mountains, we can't tell when the sun goes down. At a quarter to nine, it's still broad daylight although the sun disappeared behind the mountains quite some time ago.

There are lots of little low-growing wildflowers. I have no idea what any of them are except a few beautiful yellow lady slippers, three to four inches high. Today, we saw Canada Jays and a couple of ravens. Of course, we ran out of magpies early as we started to get into the woods.

June 11: Helen and I woke up around 3:00. It was raining like crazy – cold and windy. Everything was soaking wet, so we just stuffed everything into the car and finally got off around 6:30. We drove through a lot of tremendously sickening areas which were burned over by forest fires, forty-fifty-sixty miles long.

At Mile 550, we saw a cow moose. Every bridge has Cliff Swallows under it. We are camped about fifty miles outside Alaska on the west side of Whitehorse. We saw a Hawk Owl and also some Red-tailed Hawks. It was a lovely evening, even with the giant mosquitoes. My beard is at least an eighth of an inch long because obviously we didn't get to shave this morning, and we probably couldn't even get into a motel because we stink!

June 12: Up at 4:30, with the temperature about 34 degrees. Olive-backed Thrushes sang all night long. There are a lot of Pine Siskins, Boreal Chickadees and Western Pewees. I'm surprised the warblers are Myrtles, not Audubon's.

After we left our camp, the mountain scenery coming in to Haines Junction was absolutely spectacular, even more so as we drove north. At Kluane Lake which was still quite covered in ice, the open water was absolutely dead calm. The reflections in it were incredible. We saw the first Harlan's Hawk along Kluane Lake, which was my number 622, and a Bald Eagle, flying, shortly after that.

The whole St. Elias Range was absolutely cloudless which was truly rare. Mt. Logan is almost 20,000 feet, a spectacular sight. Sitting in the top of a black spruce was another Bald Eagle, about as tame as anything could be, like in a zoo. And about a quarter of a mile down the road, sitting in the top of another tree, we found another Hawk Owl.

Finally, we drove into Alaska off the dusty road and onto the paved one. We camped on the

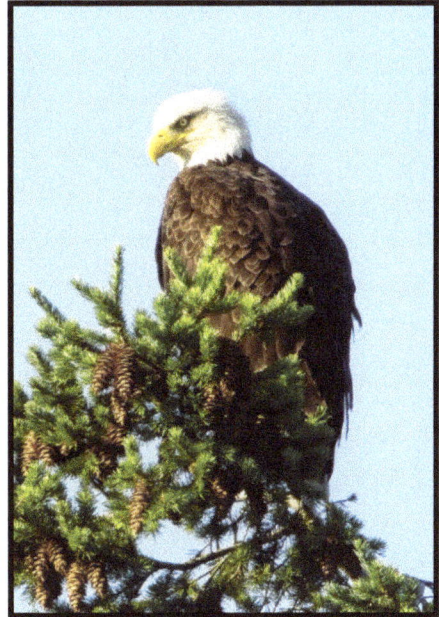
Bald Eagle

Tok River, not far off the main road. The most exciting thing about the whole day was seeing Mt. Denali, né Mt. McKinley, for the first time. Even with a little cloud cover, it was absolutely spectacular. We took very many pictures. The only problem was when it finally cleared, it turned out not to be Mt. Denali at all, it's Mt. Sanford!

We tried fishing in the river, but the river is very muddy with the spring runoff, and there were no fish. At the first bridge crossing, there were Grey-cheeked and Olive-backed Thrushes, and Northern Waterthrushes, all singing. We didn't need to stop for ice today as there was glacial ice upstream.

June 13: Up about 4:30, very warm and clear as a bell. We are in Mt. Denali Park and birds abound: Mallards, Snipes, Blackpolls, Black-capped Chickadees, Varied Thrushes, Fox and White-crowned Sparrows.

At the Savage River Campground, I thought I heard an Arctic Warbler singing across the road, but it turned out to be a Wilson's. About three-quarters of a mile down the highway, a Gray-headed Chickadee flew across the road and lit in a bush on the northside. It was obviously bigger than a Boreal or a Black-capped and had no chestnut on its flanks, a very timid, secretive bird. A little farther, we heard another Arctic Warbler which we didn't see. We stopped at McLaren Summit and wandered around the tundra to see a Lapland Longspur, an American Pipit, Bank Swallows, a Whimbrel and a pair of eagles being chased by a Mew Gull.

The weather has been cloudy, and we have yet to see Mt. Denali although something like it looms on the horizon every so often. The old McKinley Hotel is a wonder. The average age must be ninety-eight, reduced down by a young guy and his wife who came in with about six three-year-olds. Still, they nicely provided us with ice for free. We were disappointed that the road to Wonder Lake was still snowbound and only open to Mile 61. We were hoping to see Mt. Denali from across the lake.

June 14: A tremendously exciting day. Just as we were ready for breakfast, strolling through our camp came a great big black wolf. His fur was in absolutely prime condition. About twenty feet away, he lay down and rubbed his ears on the ground like a dog and rolled on his back before he strolled away. At first, I thought it was a dog, so we neglected to get our cameras. It was just unbelievable. We chatted later with the ranger, and he said "yes,"

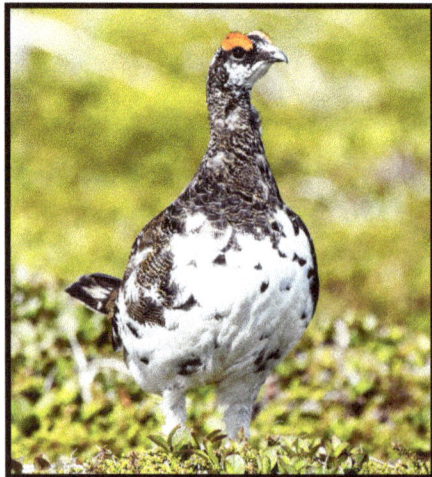
Rock Ptarmigan

without any question, it was the alpha wolf, leader of the Savage River pack. An extraordinarily beautiful animal.

Later, we drove west along the park road and came across a moose, several hoary marmots and a big herd of caribou very close to the road. We continued to Igloo Creek trying to find Arctic Warblers. I heard one a little farther up the road, got out and finally did find him – number 624.

We stopped to see Dr. Adolph Murie, one of the country's top naturalists. Graciously, he told us

where to find the Rock Ptarmigans and the
Northern Wheatears near the ranger cabin at
the East Fork of the Toklat River. Now raining,
we drove across Polychrome Pass hoping to see
Wheatears and Gyrfalcons, but the rain was
quite hard, and we didn't see them.

We stopped for lunch at Sable Pass. Against the
dark sky over the mountains we saw at least
two Golden Eagles, maybe three. We spotted
Rock and Willow Ptarmigans and numbers of
Golden Plovers. I saw one doing his courtship
flight which is rather fantastic. He flew on very

Whimbrel

stiff wings almost gliding, moving his wings up and down very slowly. In this way, he made
a great circle about half a mile across and then plunged back down to the ground.

Lapland Longspurs were singing in the air like skylarks. There were American Pipits,
Whimbrels, Common Redpolls and, of course, Mew Gulls. It is real odd to see the gulls in
the middle of the tundra and up on top of the pine trees. For the first time, I saw Snow
Buntings in their full summer plumage — absolutely beautiful, bright white and stark black.

Coming back across the Toklat, a grizzly bear was just kind of ambling along until he heard
or saw or sensed our car. Then he started running. As we got abreast of him, he took off
across the river in deep water. He was going like a tank with water splashing all over so
we could hardly see him.

We are now camped on the Sanctuary River. A cow caribou just went wading downstream.
I don't know whether she's wading or swimming or a little of both. None of us realized
that caribou have big black rings around their eyes, like spectacles. We didn't get back from
birding until about 8:30. It isn't bright daylight, but it's bright and the sun will be up again
at 3:00. Helen and Ann are just starting to cook dinner. This really has been a wonderfully
great day.

43

Mt. Denali

June 15: We got up about 6:30, the temperature was 49 degrees. The weather wasn't clear as we had hoped. Actually, in the high passes, rain was pouring. Along with many other birds, we finally saw the Arctic Warbler again, singing and I assumed nesting. There are apparently more of them than ever before, at least in Dr. Murie's memory.

Driving back to our Savage River camp, the same place we were night before last, we watched a mother grizzly and her small cub. We hoped that by some weird chance the wolf would come by again, but it didn't. Peter learned that at 8:00 tomorrow morning, the road will have been cleared of snow and the gate to Wonder Lake will be open.

June 16: We were up this morning at 4:30, the temperature was 34 degrees. It was crystal clear. We could finally see what was obviously Mt. Denali off to the southwest. I had seen the same hunk of ice earlier and wondered why we hadn't noticed it before. Assuming it was clouds, I hadn't really paid much attention to it.

From Ellison's at the gate, Mt. Denali was almost totally clear in all of its magnificence with only a few clouds hanging about halfway up. Driving the eighteen miles from Ellison's

44

to Wonder Lake was really like being in a new place. We had covered much of the park, but this was totally new. Within the first few miles, we saw a big old grizzly not doing much of anything except sitting on his rear end. We stopped at a couple of lakes and saw some Barrow's Goldeneyes, Oldsquaws and a whole bunch of little Northern Phalaropes spinning on top of the water.

Arriving at Wonder Lake, we drove the car track down to the campground and flushed a Great Gray Owl which was sitting in an alpine meadow alongside the road. It took a bit of convincing for me to believe it was a Great Gray. A Common Loon was nesting on a point in the lake and also a Green-winged Teal. From this spot, we could not see the summit of the mountain because there were a lot of clouds above us. So, we went back and stopped at Stony Hill overlook where you could see Mt. Denali plainly. Spectacular!

June 18: We drove all day yesterday to Fairbanks where it was about 80 degrees and dusty. We stayed at the old, pink, clapboard hotel on a dirt street. We did laundry, had a tire fixed, bought food and were off about noon up the Steese Highway. We had planned to camp at the Chatanika River but there were too many bugs, and it was a mess. So, we kept going. On the way, we saw a Hawk Owl and a Snipe sitting on top of a dead stump just at the tree line before the tundra. I wondered if they nested up this high.

At Eagle Summit, we finally found a road going off up the hill with a little bulldozed spot at the top where we camped. We were curious as to why this spot was leveled. Shortly after we went to bed, we found out. This was where everybody came to watch the Midnight Sun. It was like Grand Central Station, even with tour buses!

Strangers peered into our tents, small children and dogs ran around. Bedlam! Fortunately, they were gone by morning. We spent an hour or so photographing wildflowers at the summit and back along the whole crest of the ridge. We found a pair of Baird's Sandpipers and got back into Fairbanks in the mid-afternoon. It was very hot, at least 94 degrees.

June 19: We were up about 5:00 and flew to Anchorage on one of Alaskan Airways Golden Nugget flights. We checked into a very fancy hotel. We're not used to that. I did a little

Bonaparte's Gull

birding and took some pictures of a Red-necked Grebe on Spenard Lake or Hood Lake – they are both connected. I heard a Hammond's Flycatcher and saw an Arctic Loon. Some Bonaparte's Gulls swooped down at me, I expect because they had young nearby.

June 20: Up very early because we had to be at the airport at 5:15 to fly to Hooper Bay via Bethel. By noon, we were on the tundra, and it reminded all of us of the Nantucket moors. We were right on the shore of the Bering Sea in the sand dunes. It was foggy but alive with birds, all in their real spring plumage. None of us, of course, had ever seen real breeding plumage.

I was so excited. The Dunlins' calls were all over. There were lots of Northern Phalaropes, Lapland Longspurs and a great many Red Phalaropes. The Reds in flight were about as pretty as anything I've ever seen with their real broad, white wing stripes. At a distance were Emperor Geese sitting on one of the ponds, some Black Brant, a couple of full plumage Oldsquaws looking a lot like Eiders, a number of Pintails and a couple of Common Eiders, but no others so far. We saw at least one full plumage Long-billed Dowitcher which was almost bright red. Sabine Gulls, with their brilliant black and white wing pattern, were spectacular. The shore also hosted Black Turnstones, Black-Bellied Plovers, and we saw Sandhill Cranes flying.

Arctic Mountain Heather

Mountain Harebell

46

Hooper Bay

It was pretty foggy with a north wind. I would guess the temperature was around 50 degrees. The Bering Sea doesn't really look any different then any other cold piece of ocean. We were actually camped about two-thirds of the way down the airstrip, and it was really a very pleasant place to be. The airstrip is about three miles from Hooper Bay village. When we got here, the truck which met the planes was stuck in the mud so for quite a while nothing happened. But when the driver finally came, he agreed to cart our stuff down the airstrip. Peter and Helen took the airplane bus into the village and found Teddy Hunter, our native guide. They had to walk the whole three miles back. In the afternoon, Teddy came down to our camp. He is going to take us out birding tomorrow morning.

Teddy Hunter, our Eskimo guide

June 21: It's the longest day of the year. We could have stayed up all night and seen the Midnight Sun, but we have already been seeing it for days now. So, we didn't.

We were late getting up this morning. The truck was supposed to pick us up at 6:30. Fortunately, it didn't.

47

Actually, it never came so we walked to the village. There wasn't any hurry because the tide was out. We loaded all of our stuff onto Teddy Hunter's boat. He said it would be at least an hour before the tide would come in, and he could get the boat off the flats.

Waiting for the tide, we visited the local school and met Bob Clark, a teacher who is leaving after being there for two years. He told us, among other things, that the snowmobiles have almost totally replaced the dog teams. The problem is that the Eskimos are not mechanics. When they get a snowmobile, there is only one way to run it, and that's at top speed. They chase foxes on the tundra and over the ice flows. Eventually, the machine quits, and that's the end of it. It's abandoned.

Yesterday, when we were in Bethel waiting for our next flight, there were cars from various government bureaus: the Bureau of Indian Affairs, the Department of the Interior, the Department of Health, Education and Welfare, the Inter-Agency pool. All separate new cars – government waste. When we arrived at Hooper Bay, we found three large pieces of snow removal equipment. There was no mechanic there, and the people do not know how to run it. So, it sat up on a hill. The tires were flat, and it was all rusted. They do not care about plowing the roads. Instead, they just travel with snowmobiles or dog sleds.

Just before 10:00, the tide came in enough so we were off with Teddy about fifteen miles across to the far side of Hooper Bay. At this place, the kids shoot everything that flies or moves, first with bow and arrows before they are able to use guns, and later with guns. Teddy told us if we could get two or three miles from there, the birding would be fabulous.

We moved to the far side of Hooper Bay, and the air was alive with birds: Emperor geese, Canada geese, Black Brandt, at least three Steller's Eiders – number 629, two pairs of Bar-tailed Godwits – number 630, one female Spectacled Eider, with a distinctive circle around her eye – number 631. There are lots of Dunlins which are quite musical, sounding like peepers in the spring except, at the end of their songs, they start to descend instead of stop. We saw many Black Turnstones, a few Canvasbacks, mostly Sabine Gulls and one gull which was probably a Herring, although I'm not sure, because nobody said it came up here. The weather was incredible. It was calm all the way across the bay and, when we were coming back into the wind, it was hardly choppy.

June 22: We were all complaining because we didn't sleep well with the Canada and Emperor Geese flying over all night and yakking. Still, we were up reasonably early and flew in a pontoon plane out onto Curlew Lake. It was a big lake with very little vegetation around it, just tundra. The willows were only around three feet high, and then you hit real soggy tundra.

I was looking for the Bristle-thighed Curlew. Ann and I thought we could walk around Curlew Mountain and find the easy way to get to the top, but the tundra was so soggy, we sank down about a foot with every step. Instead, we went straight up. The climb was long and steep with four fake summits. It took us over an hour to get top. There was a broad ridge on top so I took

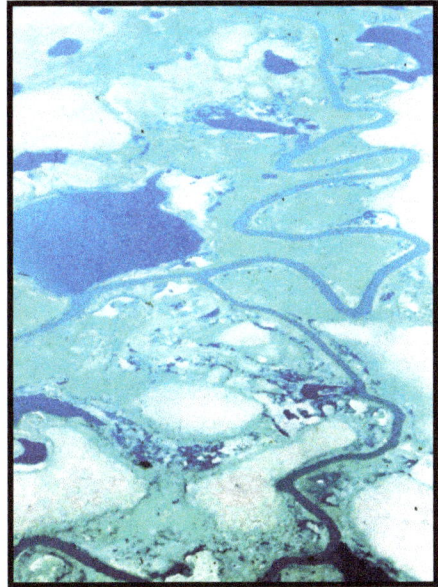

Flying to Curlew Lake

one side and Ann took the other. I was considerably ahead when I heard an odd call that sounded like a curlew. Presently, one came flying by and settled down on the side away from the lake. I could see it sitting on a rock. Just before it took off again, its rusty-red tail was very obvious. It flew toward Ann so she could identify it, and then it circled back – number 632.

We hiked back down and boarded the plane. The pilot flew us back to our camp at Hooper Bay. We saw lots of birds fly below us as we came back over Curlew Lake. Sandhill Cranes flew with the quick upbeat of their wings. A fair amount of geese and swans dotted all over.

The plane couldn't land on the Bering Sea so the pilot landed on one of the ponds by the end of the runway. As we circled to land, Hooper Bay itself must have had a hundred swans on it. The weather was an absolutely incredible 72 degrees, totally clear and a little breezy which kept the mosquitos away. There were a few small hazy clouds here and there, but almost all day it had been just lovely. It was almost impossible to believe that this was really Alaska!

1967

June 23: After shipping our camping stuff back to Anchorage, we flew on to Nome. We are ensconced in lovely quarters at the Northstar Hotel. It isn't quite the Regency, but it's very well done in pine paneling. We have a big picture window that looks out over Norton Sound, only fifty feet away.

The weather was almost cloudless and warm. Late in the afternoon, we went out and did a little birding and found a Rufous-necked Sandpiper – number 633 – in with a big bunch of Semi-palms. Out at Safety Lagoon, we also found Dunlins and Long-tailed Jaegers. We were looking for Slaty-backed Gulls which we didn't find, but there were kittiwakes and a lot of Yellow Wagtails and Red-throated Loons as well as Glaucous Gulls.

June 24: Ann and I got off about 9:00 and left Helen and Peter fishing at the mouth of the Nome River. We drove the whole length of Safety Lagoon. It was blowing hard enough so that fifteen or twenty jaegers were sitting tight to the ground.

On a sand strip into Norton Sound, there were sixty or seventy Glaucous Gulls, one kittiwake and one Slaty-backed Gull – number 634. We could pick out his red feet very plainly with the telescope. He was much bigger than the kittiwake and smaller than a Glaucous Gull and his black back really stood out. When we started back, we put up a Short-eared Owl and saw an Aleutian Tern – number 635.

We drove north out of Nome. While Helen and Peter fished the Snake River, Ann and I found ravens, a lot of Pintails, a flock of about ten Whistling Swans and a fair number of Greater Scaup and a Whimbrel as well as some gray whales spouting off the coast. Wandering around, we also saw Wilson's and Arctic Warblers and some Golden Plovers

50

and one bird I could not identify, but Helen later correctly identified it as a female or maybe a male Orange-crowned Warbler. Crossing the Penny River, we saw two adult, absolutely white, beautiful Snowy Owls. One flew against a snow patch. You just could not see him plainly because he was almost invisible. Here, our birding produced three new birds.

All through this Alaskan trip, we had seen fifty or more gold dredges, none of which were operating except one outside Nome. At the end of Safety Lagoon, there were two old steam engines and some flat cars just sitting in the sand. When the gold mining stopped, the Eskimos just left things where they were and walked away. It will be another hundred years before they totally rust to nothing.

June 25: We drove out to Safety Lagoon again, principally in hopes of getting a better look at the Aleutian Tern, which I did. It's appreciably smaller and darker than the Arctic Tern and flies quite differently.

In Nome, we bought a case of booze and decanted it into eleven plastic fifths in preparation for our next sojourn into the wilderness.. It looked like Coca-Cola syrup.

June 26: The four of us drove about twenty-five miles north of Nome through very nice country following the Nome River upstream. After seeing a Gyrfalcon with a White-tailed Ptarmigan in its clutches, Gray-cheeked Thrushes and Arctic Warblers, we returned in time to lunch with Bud Helmericks and his son Jim, our bush pilots for the next leg of our trip. We discussed the logistics of moving the six of us and our baggage in Bud's float plane and Jim's little Super Cub. It was decided that Ann and Peter would fly on Wien Airlines to Kotzebue with the luggage, and we would fly in the two planes out around Cape Prince of Wales and meet them in Kotzebue in the evening.

It was a lovely flight up the south side the Seward Peninsula. Kotzebue is on the north end of the peninsula. Bud decided he didn't have enough gas for the float plane so he landed and sent Jim back for gasoline. It took him an hour or so to get it. With the delay, we didn't get to Kotzebue until midnight. The sun was still up. Ann and Peter had arrived, but nobody had had any supper. We went to bed about 1:00, without supper.

In the morning, we went into town and had a really excellent breakfast at the only restaurant which was amazingly clean, neat and made very good food. In the meantime, Bud had hired Nelson Walker, another bush pilot, to fly in some of our stuff.

We flew to Shishmaref about halfway out the north side of the Seward Peninsula between Kotzebue and Wales and set up camp. From the air, we saw finback whales and a big herd of reindeer. A thirty-mile-an-hour gale was blowing, but our camp was on the lee side of a hill, and it was very clear, sunny and pleasant.

June 27: By 9:30, after ten hours of sleep, Bud, Peter and I were ready to fly to Wales. But the damn float plane was stuck in the mud at low tide. The three of us finally turned it around and, with Jim's help, we finally freed it. We arrived at Wales around noon. We flew in a zigzag pattern near the village and saw a Red-throated Pipit, but not much else. Then, unbelievably, we both saw a McKay's Bunting, absolutely pure white with none of the black on its back like a Snow Bunting. We tried to figure out what else it could be and came to the conclusion that it could be nothing but McKay's, even though it should not be there – number 639.

Wales Mountain was tremendously exciting and relatively easy to climb. We could see both Little and Big Diomede and the Siberian mainland very plainly. There were Semi-

Eskimo children of Shishmaref

palms and Western Sandpipers, longspurs and redpolls. On the north end of the Wales range was a rounded knob where one would expect a bird to perch. A pair of ravens was sitting there. One would fly off and then the other would fly on. They were really playing above the mountain all day long.

Flying back to Shishmaref, there were seventeen dead walruses on the beach, most of them with their tusks, and one dead whale. Arriving back in the village, we heard Golden-crowned Sparrows singing "Three Blind Mice." It was an unbelievably clear song, even clearer

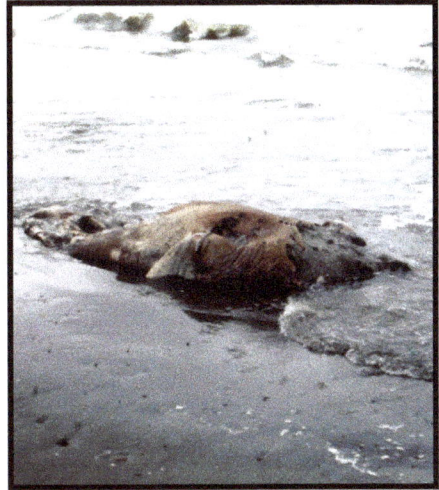

Dead walruses

than the White-throated Sparrows. I couldn't try to whistle it because I have never been a very good whistler.

It was cold, overcast and windy here, well under 50 degrees. In Shishmaref, the people are artistic, extremely nice and helpful, clean and neat and, surprisingly, so was the town. The houses have lawns, having dug out the tundra to bring in grass. Wales was not as good, but it was still a neat, clean village. Compared to Hooper Bay which was littered with tin cans and Kotzebue which was a terrible tourist town, Shishmaref was the best.

June 28: We left Shishmaref about noon, Ann in Jim's plane, Peter still in the village and Helen and me with Bud. Bud went back to get Peter and our gear after dropping us on the beach at Kivalina. We were planning to go on to Point Hope. The wind was blowing like crazy. Jim's plane couldn't get off in strong wind because it was likely to turn over backwards, and that would be an unpleasant experience.

Unbelievably, when Bud flew to Shishmaref for gas, he wandered into town and ate dinner while we were sitting on the beach at Kivalina with no food, and Peter was stranded with no way to cook. Bud didn't pick him up until after 9:00. Fortunately, a local boy gave Jim a char fish. We cooked it for dinner and waited until 11:30 for Peter and Bud to get back.

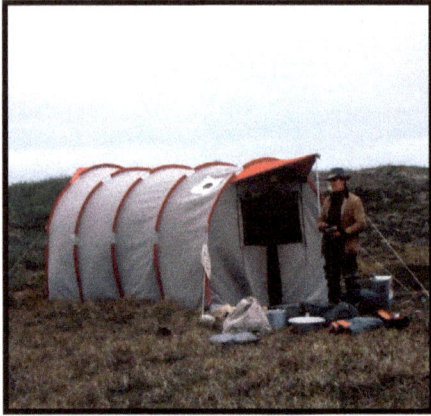
One tent for four of us

While we waited, Jim asked one of the Eskimos to take us across the Lopp Lagoon, and we had about three hours of good birding. We were hoping for Spoon-billed Sandpipers, but didn't find them. But we saw Sharp-tailed Sandpipers – number 640 – and watched them for half an hour. I could see the chestnut on their heads and their buffy breasts, breaking off like Pectorals, but much lighter. Their scaly backs are kind of like a Baird's, with very little wing stripes and a ruddy overall cast. While there are no breeding records for Sharp-tails in Alaska, they are common in the fall, and I was sure this was what they were.

The lagoon also produced a Bar-tailed Godwit which hovered into the wind right over my head about ten feet up, some Golden Plovers and a Long-billed Dowitcher. Our Eskimo friend took us up the Walik River in his outboard. A lovely river, it winds across the tundra where we saw Surf and Common Scoters, a lot of Yellow Wagtails, Sandhill Cranes, a Red-breasted Merganser and a pair of Steller's Eiders. Over the tundra Long-tailed Jaegers soared. We came back very wet and cold. One wave actually broke into my pocket!

June 29: Up again around 7:30. Bud dawdled around and slightly warmed up what was left of the char for breakfast, and that was all. An argument ensued about our plans. Bud wanted to leave one of us at Kivalina as he had left Peter the day before, fly the rest to Barrow and then come back for Peter. We just said, "No." We were all going to fly together. Finally, Jim said he could take two people in his plane if he took all our luggage out. Bud could take Helen and me if we only took only a little baggage. Then he admitted he was very low on gas. Nelson Walker had told him there was government gasoline at Cape Thompson. Jim flew there and retrieved the gas. Finally, we took off late in the morning.

Landing at Point Hope in the early afternoon, we wandered around on the rocky tundra near the village and did not see much. Still, there were several Snowy Owls, Semi-palm

Sandpipers, Golden Plovers, longspurs and a great many Ruddy Turnstones. For the first time, we saw knots among the plovers. Jim had flown back for our duffels, the telescope with the big lens, the tripod, our fishing rods, Bud's tent as well as most of the food, but not our booze.

We took off in the late afternoon. Bud had decided not to fly to Barrow, as planned, but to Wainwright. We could not fly around Cape Lisburne because it was foggy, and there were a great many seabirds nesting on it. It would have been very dangerous if the plane had to fly below the fog and the frightened birds flew up. So, we took off inland across the cape with most of the ground under fog. Finally, Bud landed about 9:30 at the Kuk River, thirty miles south of Wainwright. He was nearly out of gas, again! Fortunately, Jim had picked up three cans of spaghetti and meatballs which Bud finally got around to heating after we set up his very small – four by five feet – tent. This tent was intended for all four of us. He had brought along two sleeping bags and three air mattresses which just filled the inside of the tent. How we crammed all of us into that tiny tent I do not know, but we did.

June 30: The next morning, we were up by 7:00. There was no breakfast because Bud's emergency rations did not include breakfast. Freeze-dried food, which we used ourselves, was available, but he didn't subscribe to it. It was a lovely morning, and the fog was lifting. When Bud came walking up from his plane, I said, "Bud, it is a beautiful morning." He said, "Yes, but we won't be able to take off because there is no wind." This was typical. Going out to the plane, Bud carried only one gas can and left the rest of us to take everything else about half a mile through the mud. Finally, with enough breeze but no breakfast, we did take off. Both of his gas gauges read below the red mark where it says "No Take Off." Still, we made it to Wainwright and, fortunately, found more gas.

We finally got off from Wainwright around noon with instructions to Bud to land at Barrow. He said he could not tell about the foggy weather at Barrow because there was no

Snowy Owl

55

Bluethroat

weather station north of Kotzebue and no way to reach Barrow on his radio. Obviously, he had no intention of going to Barrow. He did head north a little, but mostly headed east right for the Colville River Delta where he lived, like a horse going home to the barn. We stopped at an Eskimo fish camp on the Niglick River, and they gave us tea and caribou meat. All of us were madder than hell at Bud.

Except for the snack at the fishing camp, we had had no breakfast and no lunch. Bud and Jim were always eating sardines out of tin cans, but they didn't offer us any. Jim brought out six O'Henry bars. He and Bud each ate two and gave each of us half of one. We left the fishing camp and got to his house on the Colville River delta late in the afternoon.

Around his house were lots of tin cans and other trash. Not quite as bad as an Eskimo village, but bordering on it. We did have a good caribou stew dinner made by Bud's wife Martha. We were bedded in basement rooms of the Helmericks' house with one comb, only one toothbrush for the four of us and no shaving equipment. As Bud had left most of our equipment and our booze at Point Hope, I asked him if he had any whiskey. He said, "No, it is illegal." That was about as phony as a three dollar bill!

July 1: In the late morning, Ann and I flew north to Umiat on the Coville River to try to find Bluethroats. We found them – number 641– after a walk of about a mile through some boggy country. Returning to the house, we all decided that we had to get the hell out of there right away. Somehow, we would get into Barrow, be on our own and get ourselves back to Anchorage.

Bud and I argued. He said that it was impossible to leave the next day because the ice pack was still in at Barrow. I said this was unacceptable. There was no reason why the two of them couldn't fly us into Barrow. If it was foggy, he could land on a pond, and Jim could

56

ferry us in. He countered, if it was too foggy to land, we just plain would have to come back. I reluctantly agreed. It didn't make sense for us to continue if we let him run things. As it was, we were lucky that one of us was not still back at Kivalina with the luggage.

July 2: We labeled this "Escape Day." After Bud's usual dawdling because "there's always fog in Barrow in the morning," we got off around 11:00. We landed about two miles south of town, and Jim ferried us in. The first thing we did was check the weather for the 30th. It had been fine, no fog. Bud was just a plain, unmitigated liar.

We called Tom Brower who runs Brower's Arctic Hotel. He took us to the hotel. Tom told us even though Barrow was dry, maybe we could get some booze at the Arctic Research Laboratory which was about three miles down the road. Thirsty, we made the long walk on a reasonable sandy road. We arrived to find that everything but the coffee shop was closed on Sunday.

Helen started flashing her eyes and, presently, she found a young man named Frank. He was our first savior. He went to his quarters and brought out five cans of cold Budweiser which tasted great. Before we had finished our beers, we were introduced to a guy named Smitty, a real character. W. C. Smith, half-crocked, said there was a bar at the DEW Line Station three miles farther down the road. "Come with me," he said – our second savior.

We hopped aboard a big four-door pickup, and Smitty took off like a jet. At the DEW Line Station, we entered a mobile unit with "Authorized Personnel Only" on the little door. Inside was a perfectly lovely dark bar, replete with a Myna bird and a pool table. There was no bartender, but Smitty picked up the phone and presently along came a temporary bartender. Helen asked for some pretzels or potato chips. Smitty disappeared and came back with a large platter loaded with shrimp, cold steak, pepperoni, cheese, melon, celery, crackers, carrots – just great hors d'oeuvres. The six of us really dug in.

We found out that Smitty was not one of the mechanics, instead he was in charge of this DEW Line Station. He knew Bud and thought as little of him as we did. Bud flew a fifteen-year-old Cessna float plane which had a top speed of eighty-miles-per-hour and, if there was any headwind, his speed was about fifty. If there wasn't a strong wind, he could not get take off from the water. The plane had only one passenger seat – mine – next to Bud and his incessant talk about himself. Helen had to sit in the back on the luggage and camping gear. The flights were never short, so this was pretty uncomfortable.

Jim was a pretty good guy, but he never called his father on any of the numerous lies he told us. His Super Cub was a real nice plane although it couldn't carry much. With great big tires, it only needed a hundred yards to land. In that plane, Ann sat on the floor with Peter's legs wrapped around her waist. The Helmerick duo was in no way able to handle the trip we had planned.

Smitty gave us an extraordinarily pleasant evening at the DEW Line bar after the pretty grim trip with Bud. That night, we didn't have to pay for any of the booze or any of the food, a real lifesaving deal. Interesting, though, that when we had our film developed of the many photographs we had taken at the bar, there were none. Smitty was a very smart man, indeed.

July 3: Barrow itself was a very messy town. Some of it was new, but most of it was old. There were natural gas lines running all over which heated all the houses. We had breakfast at Tom Brower's Café. In the meantime, we had made arrangements with Max Brower at the Arctic Research Lab to pick us up and take us out on the tundra in one of his Weasels.

In the afternoon, we went birding in the Weasel. It was very rough going. We couldn't get out far enough to get away from the Barrow kids who shoot birds on the tundra. Still, we saw Snowy Owls, Snow Buntings, Golden Plovers, Semi-palm Plovers, Red Phalaropes, Long-tailed Jaegers, a couple of Common Eiders, some Oldsquaws and a Common Loon.

We went back out to the DEW Line bar for cocktails, this time as paying guests. Smitty arranged for us to be driven to the airport for our flight to Anchorage. After landing in Anchorage, we found out that our baggage had not come in, as Bud had promised. Checking the Wien cargo area, we found that our baggage had not even made it as far north as Kotzebue.

July 4: We called Nelson Walker – our third savior. He agreed to fly out to retrieve it, take it to Kotzebue and get it shipped so we would have it in Anchorage before we went out to the Pribilof Islands. Sure enough, Nelson did just that, and our gear arrived at the Anchorage airport in time. We were really glad to see it.

July 5: Up early, we rented some fishing tackle and headed for the Kenai Peninsula to fish but had no luck. As we drove along the shore of the Cook Inlet, the weather turned bad. In the evening, we reached the little town of Ninilchik, found a gravel pit and camped.

Earlier, we had gone to Portage Glacier which was brilliantly blue. At the lodge, we asked for ice, and they told us to just go and pick up what falls off the glacier. This was what the lodge used in their bar. So we did, and it was excellent ice. It lasted for forty-eight hours and was still unmelted when we threw it out.

In the little town of Sterling at the Moose River Bar, we ran into an itinerant fish peddler and asked him where to fish because he had a trunk full of silver salmon. He wasn't very much help, but he did suggest either the Ninilchik or Anchor Rivers.

Portage Glacier

The rain stopped, and we drove on to where the Anchor River comes close to the road and did a little fishing. I wandered back a little farther to a pool and very presently hooked a large king salmon which I finally landed. As it was about three feet long and must have weighed over thirty pounds, I was exhausted.

We continued to fish there the rest of the day without catching anything except a few Dolly Varden trout which we threw back. Ann and I found a reasonably good place to camp in a public camping ground on the river. While Ann cooked dinner, Helen and Peter fished but had no luck at all.

We drove on to our campside east of Ninilchik and found that we had forgotten to bring water. The girls volunteered to drive back for it when we discovered the car was stuck. After pushing and placing rocks and branches under it, we finally got it out. They left for water, and Peter and I hauled everything we had taken out of the car to higher ground.

July 6: It rained last evening. We were able to use the big plastic sheet which Ann and Peter had brought. It was strung between Helen's and my tent and the back of the car

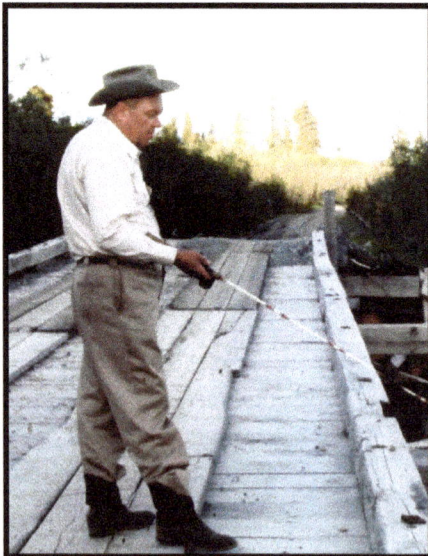
Fishing on the Anchor River

creating a space of about twenty feet in between. It worked out beautifully. We were dry, and it was much more pleasant than trying to cook in the rain.

Early in the day, I saw an Oregon Junco and some Boreal Chickadees. Hermit Thrushes sang pretty near all night long.

Being on the Alaskan mainland had been both enlightening and harrowing. Driving from B.C. up the AlCan Highway to Denali Park, flying out to Hooper Bay and Curlew Mountain, birding, fishing and camping had, except for the Helmericks' bungle, been splendid. We were excitedly anticipating Pribilof Islands' birding.

60

Kenai Lake

July 7: We taped up the boxes with our camping gear in preparation for our trip to the Pribilof Islands. Our last drive on the mainland was down to Homer, the farthest point south on the Kenai. The mountains at Cook Inlet were spectacular, but the birding was not. Driving back to the successful fishing spot, Peter hooked into another king salmon which he battled for a while. Then his line snapped like a bow string. Apparently, the fish turned around and whacked it with his tail, and that was it.

July 8: Although we almost missed our flight, we made it to the Pribilofs. Howard Baltzo, the guy in charge of Government House, opened up the canteen for us so we could buy food. Sitting on the southwest corner of St. Paul Island, the weather was incredibly great. Our campsite was below a little rise just back from the steep, high cliffs and was mostly out of the wind. The village of St. Paul was remarkably neat. Howard told us this was because it had been run entirely by our government for years, and before that by the Russians. The Aleuts had had nothing to say about how it was managed. Then, in the early 1960s, the government had begun to turn it over to the natives and were doing it gradually.

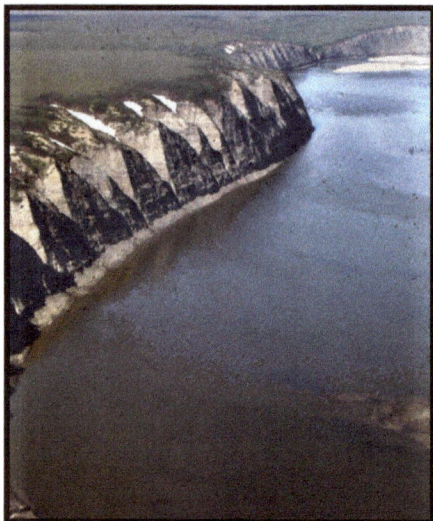
Bird cliffs at St. John's, Pribilof Islands

Too excited, we did not set up the tents right away. We went birding instead.

The birding was absolutely spectacular! I have never seen cliffs with seabirds like this; they are just packed in shoulder to shoulder. I got nine new birds: Northern Fulmar, Red-faced Cormorant, Rock Sandpiper, Red-legged Kittiwake, Parakeet Auklet, Crested Auklet, Least Auklet and Horned Puffin in addition to the Pribilof Winter Wren – now at number 650. In addition, there were a lot of Brunnich's Guillemots, Thick-billed Murres, very few Common Murres and four or five Harlequin Ducks in the ocean. Pribilof Gray-Crowned Rosy Finches were an inch bigger than usual, almost as big as a robin. Kind of like English Sparrows, they were all over the island and the village.

62

Parakeet Auklets

Horned Puuffins

Thick-billed Murres

Crested Auklet

Harlequin Duck

Red-faced Cormorant

63

The Aleuts and the government employees were very friendly. Apparently, we were the first people ever to camp on the island. We were definitely a curiosity for the natives. Each evening, a large crowd would gather in a line about fifty yards away and quietly watch us cook dinner.

July 9: After breakfast, we meandered out to the Finhogsto Bluffs. It was only a mile away and a mild climb, but we took four hours to get there. The bluffs were quite interesting because the top two-thirds sloped steeply but not enough to have been precipitous. Wherever there was a bare spot in the grass, there were birds, mostly murres and kittiwakes. The only new bird for today was a Glaucous-winged Gull – number 651. We saw several blue foxes and heard their very hollow barking. Helen picked up several murre's egg shells on the tundra which undoubtedly had been stolen by foxes and eaten.

July 10: Peter and I walked into town and rented a Chevy Sportsvan so that we could explore more of the island. We drove out to Northeast Point to bird, and saw nothing new. Helen told us she had identified twenty varieties of wildflowers in the tundra. She was becoming quite the expert. Coming back, we veered off the road and got stuck in the sand – soft, volcanic sand. We heaved and pushed and lifted and got out reasonably easily.

July 11: The weather was not great, and we had not slept well because Snow Buntings kept sliding down the dew on our tent roofs. We drove out to North Point in the morning

after each of us made his or her own pancakes. Peter made a large one, I made some small ones, Ann made a heart-shaped one and Helen made a big "J." We did not see much on the way to the point but, once there, there were Harlequin Ducks, Red-legged and Black-legged Kittiwakes, Glaucous-winged Gulls, Red-faced Cormorants, occasional murres and a few fulmars. I saw two grayish-brown geese with long necks and frontal shields. All I could think of was Gray-legged Geese, but I will have to check this one out when we get home.

July 12: We went "sealing" early, having had an excellent sealing breakfast with the native sealers at 4:30. We watched as the men rounded the seals up from various points on the beach and herded them up beyond the road. These were all little two-to-three-year-old male fur seals which hung out with the big bachelor seals.

When they were all together, the men began the seal kill. This was an extraordinarily efficient, systematic operation. About ten seals were separated from the herd at a time. First, the noise-makers, who had five-gallon tin cans on the end of sticks, rattled them which made the seals raise their heads. Next, the clubbers whacked them on their heads with huge, long bats, killing them instantly. Then came the skinners who slit them down the middle, followed by the skin pullers who pulled the pelts off. And finally the skin throwers threw the skins to the skin piler-uppers who stacked them into neat rows. This subsistence harvest was all very quick and very orderly.

There were men who collected "seal sticks" from the carcasses. You could only get them from male seals, and I don't think this needs any more description. They hung them up outside buildings, dried them and sold them to a factory in Brooklyn. There, they were mixed with herbs and sold as a potion for something – you guess what.

The carcasses went into a grinding plant where they were ground and used for mink food. The skins went into a skin-processing plant where the blubber was scraped off. Then they were brined and packed off to Greenville, South Carolina to be processed. When that was finished, the skins became the soft, velvety fur used for garments.

In the afternoon, we went out to Lukanna Lookout and watched several huge bull seals with their harems. Driving to North Point again, we hoped to find the unidentified geese, unfortunately without any luck.

July 13: Packing up took all morning. In town, we brought our gear to Reeves Airways and then had lunch at the Company House. Ann had seal liver which she said was fine except that it was green! We flew back to Anchorage via Cold Bay and Port Heiden and planned our final days in this magnificent territory.

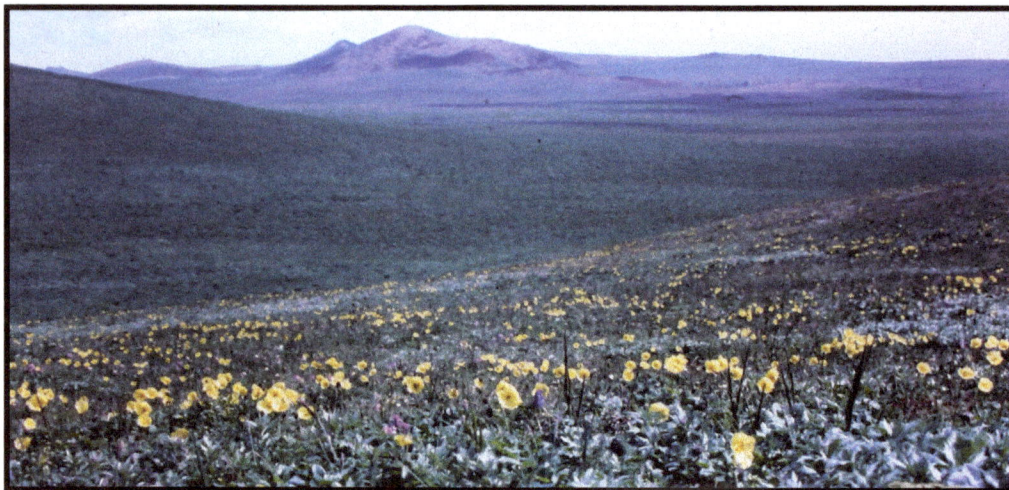
Arctic poppies on St. John's, Pribilof Islands

July 14: Helen, Ann and Peter met with Don Sheldon in Talkeetna, and he flew them out to Stephan Lake where Nick Bottner, a Dutchman, ran a fishing lodge. They had a little rain but, with the sun out again, finally began fishing in the early evening. They caught more than thirty-five Graylings in two-and-a-half hours! It was just too easy; no need for strategy. It was midnight before they left the lake, so they didn't arrive back until three o'clock in the morning.

I was due to fly out to Adak on the Aleutians, but the plane was canceled. So, I drove around the countryside and came back to wait for the rest of the crew.

July 15: This was our last day in Alaska, also our twenty-eighth anniversary. We drove to Seward – a lovely, lovely drive until we came to the town. It looked like an old movie set with false fronts and very little behind them. For some reason which no one understood, Seward was voted one of the eleven All-American Cities in 1963 and 1965.

We drove back to our hotel in Anchorage. Ann and Peter took us out for a fine anniversary dinner. And we all flew home. I guess that endeth the tale.

Flying home over the Alaskan range

Roger Tory Peterson, Joe and his father, Joseph Fillmore Taylor
Hawk Mountain Sanctuary - 1950

HAWK MOUNTAIN SANCTUARY

Joe was introduced to Hawk Mountain Sanctuary by his father in 1944. He definitely concurred with its premise of protecting birds of prey. Invited onto the board of directors in 1948, he assumed its presidency in 1966 and, twenty-six years later, retired in 1992. He was dedicated both to its causes and to the mountain itself. He and Helen annually journeyed there in the fall with birding friends, young and old, and often simply went on their own to oversee and enjoy. I was privileged to be with them from time to time. Joe's love of the mountain and its conservation goals remained foremost in his commitment.

In 1992, Dyan Zaslowsky wrote the following article for the *New York Times*: "Hawks and eagles have been migrating for eons along the stony spine of the Kittatinny Ridge in northeastern Pennsylvania. But it is only since 1934, when a section of the rocks became a bird refuge, that people have gone there to marvel. Every year more than 50,000 people are drawn to Hawk Mountain Sanctuary, a 2,200 acre private nature preserve in a dot of a town called Kempton, about an hour north of Allentown. The sanctuary is on a thickly wooded 1,300-foot-high promontory above the farm lands of the Pennsylvania Dutch.

"This autumnal migration, which runs August 15th to early December, is particularly notable because sometime during this season, the sanctuary will count its millionth bird of

The North Lookout[9]

prey since it started keeping records in 1934. Birds arrive in their greatest numbers when the foliage turns, offering two excuses for a visit in the fall. Hawk watchers typically head for the exposed sandstone spine of the sanctuary's North or South Lookout, and settle for the day on the jumbled stony couches with their binoculars, books, sketch pads, picnics and blankets. An impromptu assembly can number one thousand on a bright, warm weekend in October. All face the stage, which is what the sky becomes when the birds are flying.

"On my first visit to Hawk Mountain, I was struck by the crowd's reverence for the birds as much as by the birds themselves. North Lookout was positively serene despite the number of people who had gathered. The crowd – many of them Mennonites from the nearby farming communities, judging by their apparel – talked in whispers if at all. Throughout the day, one of the Hawk Mountain guides, or 'counters' as they are known, calmly narrated the changing scene. 'Sharpie coming up on the right!' one counter announced, pivoting in the direction of the Sharp-shinned Hawk. The counter acknowledged the arrival of a Chimney Swift – 'a cigar with wings,' she called it. At the same moment, an Osprey rose higher in our sphere of vision, backlit by the sun. Binoculars tilted upward, and the congregants murmured approval.

70

"Such worshipful human behavior is one remarkable indication of how the attitude toward hawks and eagles has changed. It was hunters, at the end of the nineteenth century, who first discovered the advantages of Hawk Mountain's location. With their pump and shotguns, they blasted hawks and eagles out of the sky as they flew into firing range. It was a civic duty to do this. Wishing to eradicate predatory birds from the face of the Keystone State, if not the earth, the Pennsylvania Game Commission at one point even paid a $5 bounty for each dead Goshawk.

"Hawks of all kinds were despised because they preyed upon smaller birds and, now and then, hens and chicks. Popular folk wisdom held that Bald Eagles attacked lambs and untended infants and carried them off to their aeries to devour. Thousands of birds both wounded and dead were left to rot where they dropped. The rocks on this section of the Kittatinny Ridge fell silent in the autumn of 1934, when an ardent bird lover named Rosalie Edge wrested the high killing ground from a failing tombstone company and established the first hawk sanctuary in the world.

Rosalie Edge and Maurice Broun

"Mrs. Edge, who earlier in life had been a New York suffragist and socialite, was justifiably held in her middle age as 'the only woman in conservation.' Her one-woman Emergency Conservation Committee successfully agitated for numerous environmental reforms. She did manage to change the local conduct toward hawks. She hired an armed caretaker named Maurice Broun, who felt about hawk protection as she did, and together they rigorously enforced the new Kittatinny code: 'Watch, don't shoot.' She became the birds' outspoken champion and led national efforts to educate the public about their right to exist. The ridge was transformed into what Mrs. Edge called 'a citadel of peace.' The transformation was an

71

economic one as well. Hawk-related tourism has replaced hawk hunting as a primary source of Schuykill County's income.

"The land Mrs. Edge optioned to buy for her sanctuary had been skinned off its timber, but she let nature resume its course. Hawk Mountain is dense with second-growth: chestnut oaks, an understory of red maples, sassafras, sweet gums and witch hazel, brilliant in autumn. Hawk Mountain is known as one of the best natural vantage points in the world from which to see large numbers of birds of prey. From the sanctuary's North and South Lookouts, visitors can see twenty of North America's thirty raptorial species, including Bald Eagles, Golden Eagles, Osprey, Peregrine Falcons, Broad-winged Hawks and American Kestrels. October is a month of quantity as well as diversity. A week after my visit, Cooper's Hawks, Sharp-shinneds, kestrels and others were streaking by at a rate of one-hundred-fifty an hour, riding the brisk currents of west-northwest winds that presage good hawk watching.

"Hawk Mountain counters (both volunteers and paid staff) assiduously track the number and species of birds and the weather conditions. There is even a phone line to find out about the preceding days highlights. Since Hawk Mountain's inception not a single day has passed when birds – raptors and others – were not tallied and, as a result, the sanctuary willingly supplies ornithologists with the longest running record of raptor migration patterns in the world.

"Rachel Carson found Hawk Mountain's data is extremely useful when she was conducting her research for *Silent Spring*, and she frequented the lookouts. The counters are a blessing to fledgling bird watchers. Their friendly expertise is dispensed to anyone who doesn't know a peregrine from a pigeon and, as one of the nation's top bird education centers, Hawk Mountain is a good place to start learning the difference.

"Ornithologists believe that hawks migrating from eastern Canada and New England fly over the ridge because they are trying to conserve their energy by supplementing their wing power with the updrafts from the ridge, oriented in the same direction the birds are heading on their trip to South America. They take advantage of thermals, which are bubbles

The Board of Directors - 1950
Joe Taylor, Roger Tory Peterson, Marion Ingersoll, Maurice Broun, Francis Trembley, Peter and Rosalie Edge

of warm air that rise as cooler mountain air mixes in from below. Flying at a speed of forty miles an hour, the hawks can cover about two-hundred-fifty miles on a good day.

"At Hawk Mountain, flocks of Broad-winged Hawks typically arrive in September, when they can be seen churning within a single thermal, looking as though the birds are boiling in a kettle. In fact, when the hawks appear in this sort of configuration, they are said to be 'kettling.' Even for non-birders, hawks are thrilling to watch because of their dramatic flights. The chance to see sky-kettles boiling with hundreds of hawks is something watchers hope for when they spend a day at the lookout. And yet, sighting a solitary immature Bald Eagle, as I did, can be quite exhilarating as well.

"Hawk Mountain Sanctuary includes about eight miles of hiking trails that wind through the woods toward lush brows of rhododendrons at several scenic outcrops. A few minutes from the parking lot, one trail up to the lookout is accessible to the handicapped. All other trails, some of which connect with the Appalachian Trail, are rocky but easy enough for children to negotiate. From the South Lookout you can see a curious geologic formation called the River of Rocks, a mile-long gash of boulders left by the last ice age. Those who get restless just sitting at the lookout can always hike down to it.

73

Conserving raptors worldwide

"Outside the Visitors Center is an outdoor exhibit about how to landscape to encourage wildlife and a sculpture of a Golden Eagle, once thought to be extinct in the region. The center itself features a bookstore, murals explaining the relationship between birds and winds and their predator-prey cycle and two windows from which visitors can view birds at feeding areas. The sanctuary has a staff of fourteen and is supported by an association of thousands members nationwide.

"While Hawk Mountain's efforts concentrate on birds of prey, it has also preserved a remnant of colonial history in the form of a white stone cottage called Schaumboch's, a private residence for sanctuary staff members. Built shortly before the Revolutionary War as an unprotected outpost in hostile Delaware Indian country, the cottage stood practically at the edge of the world as then known by the settlers. In the mid-eighteen hundreds, Schaumboch's became an important stop for wayfarers on the rough mountain road between Drehersville and Eckville. The building is named for its most sinister occupant, a man reputed to have murdered and robbed at least twenty travelers after plying them with his homemade whiskey. Residents attest to so many paranormal incidents that the notion that the house, and maybe the ridge, is haunted is very much alive."[10]

"Joe and Helen Taylor are birds of a rare feather. Whether rubbing shoulders in the board room or sharing a fire with campers on the Alaska tundra, they are singularly at home. Though unpretentious and unassuming about their accomplishments, they have served the mountain with great strength and true dedication for twenty-six years as president and first lady.

"Joe's birding career began very early, when he was allowed to birdwatch along with his father, and climaxed in June 1972 when he became the world's first birder to reach 700 North American species.

"He first came to Hawk Mountain in 1944 with a group of five other birders. The thrill of seeing so many hawks at eye level drew them back along with others and, in 1948, Rosalie Edge its founder invited him to join the board. Eighteen years later, he assumed the presidency of the sanctuary. Over the years his vision has helped build it into an organization with nationally recognized education, research and conservation programs. To support this growth, both Taylors have given generously.

"Helen, his wife of fifty-three years, is a gracious, self-effacing woman, found at Joe's side during nearly all of his birding adventures. She met her husband-to-be when she was fifteen, on a trip to Rochester, New York from her home in Indianapolis. A seven-year courtship ensued, including a Vassar education for Helen and Harvard Law School for Joe. Within a few weeks of Helen's graduation, they married, settling on the edge of Rochester. After seven years in legal practice, Joe became a Bausch & Lomb corporate attorney, advancing to the office of treasurer, a position he held when he retired in 1969.

At the North Lookout - 1964

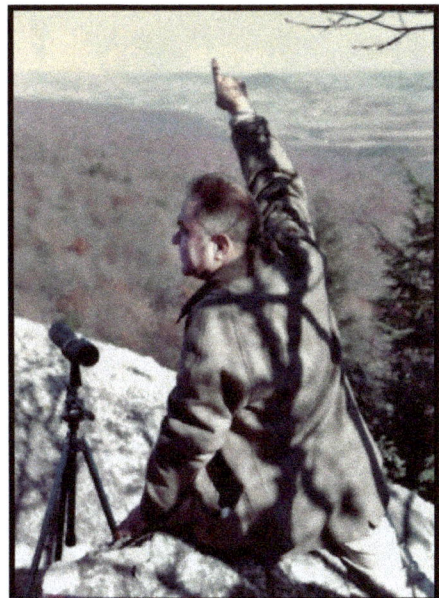

"Joe and Helen have made over three hundred trips to Hawk Mountain, keeping in touch with board, staff and events. Even though he is stepping down as president, Joe will continue to serve on the board and hopes to make many more trips with Helen to Hawk Mountain. 'Helen loves the mountain as much as I do,' explains Joe.

"'Hawk Mountain has become family to us,' Helen adds. 'Through the years, we've just enjoyed being there and knowing its people.'"[11]

75

Joe and Helen, c. 1980

In 1984, for the fiftieth anniversary of Hawk Mountain Sanctuary, Joe Taylor wrote, in part: "It was forty years ago that I came under the spell of Hawk Mountain, a spell from which, happily, I have never recovered.

"By mid-October of 1944, we had saved enough gasoline rationing coupons to get to that rumored new hawk watching place in Pennsylvania – Hawk Mountain – where hundreds of raptors were supposed to pass by in the fall. I remember that drive all too well. It was a terrible night: cold, pitch-black, over poorly-marked roads, with a driving rain that was coming down in buckets. Sometime after midnight, we reached the old Abraham Lincoln Hotel in Reading, the only place we could figure out to stay. Little did we realize that we had lucked into the perfect weather conditions – a passing strong cold front followed by brisk north-northwest winds. When, under clearing skies, we finally found our way to the North Lookout the next morning, hawks were already zipping by in a steady stream. We were enthralled – not only by the birds, but just as much by the breathtaking view. I expect my life changed then and there, for I can never totally leave the mountain behind. I have,

I think, been there every fall since then, certainly every fall since 1949, when I became officially connected with the sanctuary.

"Hawk Mountain means more to me than the hawks and the view. Its mystique has to include the great people who have been there, through tough times and easy, 'keeping the faith,' as it were.

"In the eastern United States, about a hundred miles inland from the Atlantic Ocean, the ancient Appalachian Mountains stretch from Central Maine to Central Georgia, generally paralleling the coast. In many parts of its range, particularly in Pennsylvania, the mountain chain is several miles wide. This is the Kittatinny Ridge, the 'endless mountain' of Pennsylvania's Lenapi Indians. Birds of prey on their southward fall migrations utilize this ridge perhaps for visual guidance. And certainly the birds make use of the air currents created by the upward deflection of the prevailing west and northwest winds and by the solar heating of the valleys between.

1984

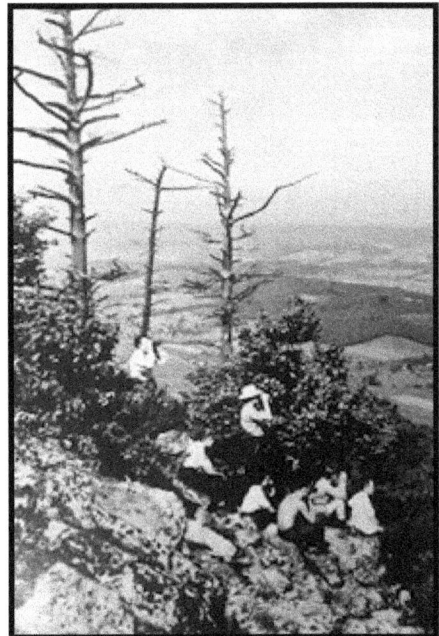

"Here, atop a ridge where in some ancient time a truly awesome force twisted it into a zigzag, is a bold sandstone outcropping, the famed North Lookout of Hawk Mountain Sanctuary. Observers can sit on the lookout, revel in a magnificent view of the countryside a thousand feet below and watch the parade of thousands of raptors passing by each fall. Many of the birds pass below eye level, a site which is a new experience for most of us. Many birds are so close that you can see the color of their eyes.

"This truly wonderful spectacle was not always thus. A hundred years or so ago, there was a sandstone quarry near the top of Hawk Mountain. The tough Pennsylvania Germans

77

Hawk slaughter - 1930s

who mined the sand must have seen the hawks passing by each fall and decided to have some sport in shooting them. By the early 1900s, shooting the raptors had become a highly organized operation. Hundreds of hunters were at the ridge tops shooting at anything and everything that flew by. They regarded this activity as excellent target practice in preparing for the small game season in November. When a hawk came into range, sometimes a hundred or more guns might go off at once, and the bird would disappear in a puff of feathers. Then, after six or seven seconds, there would be the patter of lead shot on the dry leaves in the valley below, sounding like a deluge of heavy tropical rain. Most of these men also believed they were performing a valid public service for hawks were generally looked upon as vermin which ought to be destroyed. Into the early 1930s, so many thousands of hawks were slaughtered along the ridge that several species were being driven close to extinction. No one seemed to care.

"Late in 1933, the shooting activities on the ridge were reported at a meeting of the national Audubon Society. Rosalie Edge was in the audience. A former ardent suffragette, she had turned her energies to conservation. In the fall of 1934, Mrs. Edge devised a way to buy the mountain. She purchased 1,200 acres at $2.50 an acre. Realizing that a warden was needed if the shooting was to be stopped, she persuaded Maurice Broun, a bright young ornithologist from New England, to take the job.

"Maurice and his wife Irma moved to the mountain. That fall and the first few to follow were rough and dangerous for them. But their efforts put an almost immediate stop to the shooting. Hawk Mountain Sanctuary began to exert its powerful influence on raptor conservation, both here and abroad, helping to spur local and national legislation to protect birds of prey.

78

"Maurice and Irma were not on the mountain that fall in 1944 when we were first there. He was overseas serving in the Navy, and she was staying with relatives on Cape Cod. The sanctuary was manned only on weekends by Francis Trembley who was, at the time, the Association's vice president. Fran was a professor of zoology at Lehigh University in Bethlehem and one of the greatest teachers of natural history I have ever known. He gave us our first lesson in identifying raptors at eye level. There were more than 1,200 that first day. In the 1960s, Fran conducted a teachers' summer course in ecology, using the mountain as a laboratory. In 1969, I had the unforgettable experience of taking his course.

"The Brouns came back immediately after the war. With the mountain secure, the sanctuary began operating year-round. When people again could use their cars to travel, a new phase of the Hawk Mountain story began. We have often said that 'Maurice made Hawk Mountain,' but that is only partly so. Hawk Mountain was there, not only physically, but spiritually. What Maurice did – and for this we all owe him an everlasting debt of gratitude – was to preserve, nurture and guarantee that spirit, that aura, that mystique of the mountain.

Irma and Maurice Broun - 1958

"There are many of us who still remember those early days on the North Lookout, when forty people was a big crowd, and Maurice talked about any phase of natural history which happened to occur to him – usually hawks and Hawk Mountain. We remember, too, those memorable evenings when we gathered at Shaumboch's, partly to talk about the day's events, but mostly just to sit at the feet of the 'master.' And then more and more people came to the mountain, and those lovely, quiet days and evenings became a thing of the past. But the Hawk Mountain spirit always remained.

"With this reminiscing, I would be severely taken to task if I did not describe Rosalie Edge.

Very simply, to me she was a splendid person – interesting, entertaining and tough. She was the first great conservationist I ever knew and still ranks among the greatest of all. I always looked forward to seeing her. I like best to think of her at the fall directors' meetings, all of which she ran on a no-nonsense basis. Roger Peterson and I were elected to the board in 1949 and, since these fall meetings were to begin at noon, the two of us would spend the mornings on the Lookout, coming down just in time for the meeting's start. (Peter Edge said we were always late, but he was wrong. It's just that we were never early.) Now and then, when discussions at the meetings became long and, to us, tiresome, Roger and I would quietly start our own conversation about birds – any birds. Suddenly, we would become aware that there was absolute silence in the room. We would look up to find Mrs Edge's imperious eagle-eyes staring down at us. No word was spoken, but our little 'subcommittee meeting' was over at once. I have fond memories of those times, for behind that imperious stare was a real twinkle. What a lady!

"These and many more wonderful people have kept the Hawk Mountain spirit alive and flourishing. Helen and I extend our sincere thanks to all of them. I have every confidence that fifty years into the future, the unique mystique that defines Hawk Mountain will still be there."[12]

Steve Oresman and Joe - 1981

Stephen Oresman, fellow birder, former Hawk Mountain Sanctuary board member and friend of Joe and Helen, wrote: "In October of 1958, my wife Enid and I were invited to join the Taylors on their regular fall trip to Hawk Mountain. We left in the morning in their Ford Country Squire for about a seven-hour drive depending on stops. Joe had special stops called 'Drinking Trees' strategically located along the route. These were places where one could pull off the road in a pleasant scenic spot, drop the tailgate, enjoy hors d'oeuvres and 'deep freeze' martinis.

"'Deep freeze' martinis were made by pouring off a shot from the top of the gin bottle, replacing it with dry vermouth, placing the bottle in the freezer overnight and an open empty thermos bottle in the refrigerator. In the morning the result was a viscous liquid which was poured into the chilled thermos. Since no ice was required, the martinis were served straight in small, elegant silver cups which came in a special fitted leather case.

"We arrived at Hawk Mountain in the afternoon and met with Maurice Broun, the curator for twenty-five years, and his wife Irma at Shaumboch's cabin, their residence on the mountain which they shared with a tame Screech Owl which flew loose. Maurice, a highly-strung individual, had developed a national reputation for the sanctuary. He was recognized as an ornithologist, author and the pioneer in the collection of data on migrating raptors. His rapport with the founder, Rosalie Edge, however, was tenuous, at best. Joe was there to lend a sympathetic ear and calm him down.

"The evening event was cocktails on the large uncovered porch of the Common Room, the only other building on the property. Saturday brought the hawk watch on the North Lookout followed by another cocktail party. Daily trips up the mountain could bring lovely weather and lots of birds flying close and providing exciting views or miserable weather and no birds or everything in between. As the youngest member of the group my role was that of sherpa carrying a big wicker pack basket of lunch, blankets, extra sweaters and the like up the steep trail.

"About three o'clock, the sun began to lower and the temperature dropped. Following hours sitting on the lookout rocks, a hearty lunch and a lot of fresh air, those not serious about hawk watching began to drift down the mountain toward cocktails at the Common Room. The die-hards hung on hoping for the proverbial four o'clock Golden Eagle, a rare sighting in those early years.

"Not all bird species migrate nor do necessarily all individuals of the same species. The distances traveled, timing and routes followed vary widely. It would seem that raptors, larger species evolved to rapidly pursue and capture prey, would be strong long distance fliers, but this is mostly not the case. The capability for sustained long distance flight is a function of the ratio of weight to wing loading and the ability to stock up and carry extra fuel. A Ruby-throated Hummingbird can fly non-stop from Florida across the Gulf of Mexico while a Broad-winged Hawk and many other hawks depend on thermals and wind and cannot fly far across water. They must stop each night to rest and feed when this assistance fades.

"Thermals are caused by the sun's heat warming the earth's surface creating rising air currents which provide lift to migrating hawks. Similarly, strong winds striking ridges create considerable additional lift. Hawk Mountain is a place where both these conditions occur in the fall and create excellent conditions to assist south migrating hawks.

"At Hawk Mountain what is now called North Lookout is a rocky outcrop that rises over a large gap in the ridge so the approaching hawks can be seen from a long distance. On some days they may come quite low over the lookout but, even when flying high up, hunters learned that hawks could be lured into shooting range with tethered live pigeons. Since hawks and owls were not protected by law, it became a popular local shooting spot.

"The slaughter was huge. On some days, hundreds of hawks were killed. The situation came to the attention of Richard Pough of the National Audubon Society, but they were not interested. National Audubon had been started by a coalition of northeast Audubon societies and created sanctuaries to prevent the killing of herons and egrets for feathers to decorate ladies' hats. By the 1930s, however, their constituency was principally interested in songbirds, and hawks ate songbirds.

"Hawk Mountain Sanctuary was founded by Rosalie Edge, a strong and difficult personality. The mountain was her personal fiefdom. The land was acquired simply to stop the shooting of hawks. That was the curator, Maurice Broun's, charter when Mrs. Edge hired him. The impetus for later creating a hawk count is not clear, but it certainly expanded the charter and, while its contribution to raptor conservation was not obvious then, it certainly proved its value later.

"After Maurice and Irma left in 1966, Alex Nagy became the new curator. He had been hired to assist Maurice in property maintenance and whatever else was needed. Alex was a husky, ruddy-faced cheerful person who over the many years working with Maurice became an expert hawk watcher.

"When Alex retired in 1981, Jim Brett who had been the education director became curator. Jim wanted to visit East Africa. Subsequent trips to Tanzania paid dividends in future years at Hawk Mountain because he internationally expanded an intern program which was locally focused. The program was highly successful, and a number of the graduates made significant contributions to international raptor conservation and research.

"Visitation to the mountain continued to grow. This growth forced change. For years the only parking was along the two-lane road that not only led to the sanctuary but also was the route for through traffic to the other side of the mountain. The congestion and the danger from the speeding through traffic impelled the township to ban parking on the road itself and forced the sanctuary to build a parking lot on the south side of the road.

"In addition to the parking problem there was the need to deal with visitors, so a Visitor Center was contemplated. While in the earliest years many of the visitors were birders and members, most of the newcomers were families there for an afternoon outing, a hike and mountaintop views of the changing foliage. These typically one-time visitors certainly did

Joseph and Helen Taylor Visitor Center

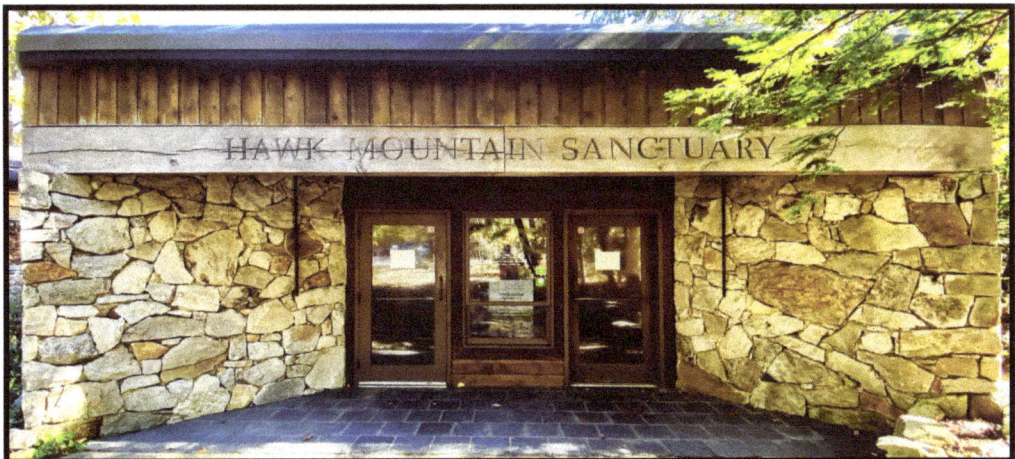

not know about or care about raptor conservation. On arriving at the North Lookout they were known to ask where were the hawks, expecting them to be perched in trees or in cages or whatever.

"The site of the new Visitor Center was contemplated in 1991 on the north side of the road between the entrance gate and the South Lookout. That way visitors could enter the center to go up the trail and could, thereby, be exposed to exhibits on the importance of raptor protection. The Board, however, decided to place it on the south side of the road.

"As president, Joe Taylor's style was to promote raptor conservation by taking action where he could act at virtually his own discretion. He recognized the importance of raptor research and created the position of Research Director, understanding that raptor conservation involved a census of raptors nationwide, not just at a few points like Hawk Mountain. This led him to be active in HMANA, the Hawk Migration Association of North America.

HMANA is an independent association with no paid staff. It struggled at first to establish standards for hawk counting for the numerous sites which had sprung up. It has evolved over the years with waxing and waning support from Hawk Mountain's board. Over thirty years after its founding, all the reports from the various count sites were finally consolidated at the Acopian Center for Conservation Learning at Hawk Mountain.

"Sarkis Acopian was a native Armenian and a highly successful Allentown entrepreneur. The idea of the science center was discussed with him. Mr. Acopian agreed to fund the entire center as long as it was named after him. But, there were those in the township and on the mountain who were opposed to any more building on the mountain. An alternate site was purchased just off the west side of the mountain. As this was in a different township a building permit was readily obtained for a multipurpose headquarters structure and a separate residence complex for Jim Brett's interns and visiting scientists.

"The most significant change that Joe initiated was to establish the position of Executive Director which took over some of the functions that Joe handled as president and CEO.

Jim Brett, curator, Joe and Stan Senner, executve director - 1990

"The operations of Hawk Mountain had grown sufficiently large and complex to require both a curator for day-to-day operations and an overall business manager as well as a fund-raiser. He brought on board Stan Senner who made significant contributions to the organization. His laid-back style and appearance hid a strong intelligence and excellent managerial and political skills. During his tenure as Executive Director, the internecine feuding that can arise in such small isolated organizations was subdued or at least disappeared from view, and the whole operation ran comparatively smoothly. When Stan retired, a board search committee hired Cynthia Lenhart. a 'policy analyst' for National Audubon in Washington, D.C.. In 1991, Joe decided to step down as president and was eventually succeeded by Minturn Wright, a Philadelphia lawyer.

"Hawk Mountain has significant recognition as a nature preserve and a place for family outdoor recreation and scenic vistas. This attracts tens of thousands of new visitors each year who can be exposed to ideas about conservation and raptor conservation in particular."[13]

"Spirit of the Heart" dedication - 1990
Helen, Jim Brett curator; Mary Taylor sculptor and Joe

In 1991, Joe Taylor, retiring president of the sanctuary, wrote: "I have for some time been concerned that those magnificent people who were responsible for starting the sanctuary and guiding it through its formative years would drift back into history and be forgotten. I felt that we needed a memorial to them – Rosalie Edge, Maurice and Irma Broun, and Alex Nagy – to serve as a constant reminder of their contributions to the mountain. And now, with the hearty approval and endorsement of the directors, we have such a memorial. At the entrance to the Habitat Garden, landing with wings outstretched atop a six-foot rock, is a magnificent Golden Eagle, 'Spirit of the Heart.' To me and to many others, it is truly awe inspiring. I am terribly proud to say that the sculptor is my daughter Mary Taylor.

"'Spirit of the Heart' was designed and executed by Mary, a nationally recognized, award-winning artist, recently honored by her acceptance in the prestigious Society of Animal Artists. The 300-pound sculpture, created over a period of nine months, is constructed of corten steel rod. The span between its wingtips is nine feet. The sculpture on its stone base is fourteen feet high and contains approximately 5,000 feathers. As the eagle weathers, it will rust to a golden patina."[14]

Nearing the final days of his tenure as president, Joe wrote: "When most of us think of Hawk Mountain, our thoughts turn to crisp fall days, multi-colored foliage, cool northwest winds and hawk flights. But Hawk Mountain does have more than one season. In winter, if you're lucky, there's snow and dramatic ice storms. Spring draws only a few hawks over the lookouts, but songbirds by the hundreds wing along both sides of the mountain.

"Spring also brings the blossoming of plants along the roadside and in nearby woods. In May, the dogwoods and redbuds flower, giving way in June to the delicate pale pink blossoms of the mountain laurel and then the large white blooms of the rhododendrons in early July. In the quiet of early morning when the dew is still sparkling, a subtle fragrance wafts through the forest.

"Early summer may be the most pleasant season of all. We haven't visited the mountain a lot in the summertime, only a day or so now and then, and once the whole summer. That occasion was a delight, even though particularly rainy. Because of the rain, the foliage and flowers were extraordinarily lush.

Mary Taylor with "Spirit of the Heart"

"Naturally many bird species – hawks and songbirds – nest on the mountain. American Redstarts, Red-eyed Vireos, Wood Thrushes, Ovenbirds and other woodland species raise their young in the forest. Cardinals, titmice, chickadees, nuthatches and hummingbirds are attracted by the feeders of the Visitor Center and by the ponds of the Habitat Garden.

"Wood Thrushes have become fairly scarce on the mountain in the last year or so, and Ovenbirds for longer than that. We are conducting research on the thrushes and Ovenbirds to determine whether fragmentation of the forest affects their breeding. Final results are not in, but it appears that even though the total acreage of our forests may remain the same, its breakup into small patches does decrease the breeding population.

"One of the summer finds which I'll never forget was the Worm-eating Warblers in the ravines off the Hawk Mountain road on the Drehersville side. I remember driving down the mountain road when I heard their call, 'Bzzbzzzzz,' like the sound of a fast Chipping Sparrow. Without any hesitation, I pulled the car off the road and chased down the ravine after them. They were the first Worm-eating Warblers I ever saw. Another memorable sighting was the Hooded Warblers near the rhododendrons along the old Copperhead Trail.

"I cannot write about all the insect species on the mountain, but I would be remiss if I didn't mention the gypsy moth – that nuisance, menace, blight or whatever you wish to call it. Problem though it is, the defoliation and the rapid refoliation by the forest are truly startling and dramatic phenomena.

"Lastly, I have to mention the arachnids. Every summer for many years, Fran Trembley, zoology professor and a director of Hawk Mountain from 1934 until 1978, taught a course on ecology for high school teachers before the word 'ecology' appeared in any but the biggest dictionaries. I attended his course one season and well remember the day I spent down at the River of Rocks searching for spiders. Crawling on those rocks on a hot, still summer day, one can find spiders all over the place. We found an almost unbelievable – to me, at least – twenty-eight species, and I'm sure there are more.

"For Maurice and Irma Broun, summer on the mountain was a quiet, peaceful time, a time to relax before the gang showed up in mid-August to hawk watch. Maurice worked at maintaining the sanctuary and its trails, posting boundaries, giving informal tours and talks, writing and politicking with neighbors. He explored the mountain woods in solitude, thoroughly enjoying opportunities to 'botanize' (his word) and most of all to 'fern.'

"Maurice was a real authority on ferns and in 1938 wrote *Index to North American Ferns,* considered a definitive guide on the subject. His book was the first listing of the forms, varieties and hybrids of ferns north of Mexico, and even included the garden escapees which had become naturalized. He assembled a collection of non-living and living specimens, tending a fern garden across the road from Schaumboch's cottage, the remnants of which can still be seen.

"Whether you like to bird, botanize or both, I hope to see you on the Mountain before fall."[15]

1971

––––––––––––––––––––––––––––

Joe's final report in 1992: "One traditional duty of the Hawk Mountain president has been to write semi-annual messages to members, and having been president since 1966, this is my fifty-second letter to you. This is also my last such message. I am stepping down as president on October 3rd, but I will remain as a director. Giving up all connection with the mountain after forty-four years on the board would be too hard.

"Looking back over the past twenty-six years, it seems to me that the sanctuary is quite a different place with different aims, but with the same wonderful spirit, although we had to get past a couple of serious crises to get here.

"In 1967, curator Alex Nagy became ill and had to retire. In the early 1970s, Pennsylvania finally passed the Model Hawk Law, protecting all raptors. We were then faced with a serious dilemma: our original mission fulfilled, what was our future? Should we remain simply a pleasant place to go in the fall and watch hawks? Or should we try to move ahead and become a more significant part of the general conservation movement?

"In hindsight, this may seem like an easy decision, but it wasn't. Several very able members of the board felt strongly that we had accomplished our purpose, and we should stay as we

89

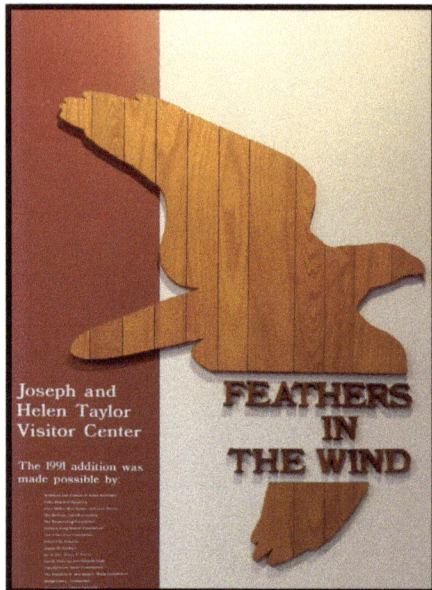

Joseph and Helen Taylor Visitor Center - 2021

were. To me, this meant Hawk Mountain would become just one more lookout on the Blue Mountain.

"Fortunately, other opinions prevailed. We would look to new horizons. Choosing Stan Senner as executive director started us on the path to a broader conservation approach. Then, with Cynthia Lenhart as his successor, we moved forward at a substantial pace. I am happy to step down with the future looking so very bright.

"The other dilemma had to do with our Visitor Center. By 1971, it was becoming increasingly apparent that our physical facilities were no longer able to handle the ever-increasing numbers of visitors. A new headquarters building was badly needed. The big question was where to put it. Should it be south of the road, or should it be on the escarpment near South Lookout? I felt that it should be on the escarpment. This was discussed at several board meetings, and all the directors seemed to agree. Then, we had one last meeting to confirm the details, and the board completely reversed itself and voted to locate the building south of the road. I was shocked, but the die was cast, and the Visitor Center stands where it does.

"On the whole, though, the past has been very smooth, and I personally have spent many happy times on the mountain. I recall the fun we had when Helen and I stayed at the vacant Common Room before I had the good luck and good sense to hire Jim Brett as resident assistant curator in 1971.

"I also remember when Arnie Waag from Iceland visited us there one fall. Suddenly one early morning, we awakened to discover we were in the middle of a major southern movement of songbirds. Arnie wrote me later to say it was the first time he had ever seen seventy-nine new birds while running around the woods in his undershorts.

"And there was the time I fell down the bank above Pine Creek and sliced up my hands quite badly on the shale, and Alex took me over to his family's farm where his mother washed out the cuts. It hurt like the devil, and she kept telling me to stop crying like a baby. Mr. Nagy brought out a bottle of his best Scotch to settle me (and him) down.

"And I remember too, the thrill of our fiftieth anniversary party in 1984. And the pride I felt at the unveiling of our daughter Mary's eagle sculpture and again at the formal opening of the new Visitor Center last year.

"I will always remember you – the members who have really made Hawk Mountain the unique place it is today, and the staff, past and present, who have never deviated in their loyalty to me or to the Mountain. None of all of this would have been possible without them and you."[16]

Last climb to the North Lookout - 1989

91

Late 1960s

THE SOUTHWEST
May 1968

After our very successful camping adventure to Alaska in 1967, Peter and I again joined Joe and Helen for another camping excursion to the magnificent Southwest. We saw about 182 species of birds in a little over two weeks. Joe added twelve new ones to his life list which was 664 when we returned. His journal reports this trip.

May 12: Leaving Denver, the weather was miserable. We passed towering Chimney Rock between Pagosa Springs and Durango. Birding along the roadside revealed a few Gray-headed Juncos, Mountain Bluebirds, Mexican Jays and Hammond's Flycatchers. We drove on to Mesa Verde National Park in southwestern Colorado where 4,000 archeological sites, cliff dwellings, pit houses, pueblos and masonry towers of the Pueblo peoples dating back to A.D. 550 are preserved.

May 13: Starting out, there was snow on the ground and heavy clouds almost down to the earth. Our destination was Chinle, Arizona, a few miles from Canyon de Chelly where we planned to camp. On our way there, we saw our first White-necked Ravens and lots of Horned Larks. But that could not compare with the fabulous birding in Chinle itself.

We found Violet-green Swallows, Yellow, Wilson's and Audubon's Warblers and, principally, two Gray Flycatchers – my first new bird – number 653. They were not in the piñon pines where they are supposed to be but down in the cottonwoods. A little bigger than our Least Flycatchers at home, they were very gray, faintly tinged with yellow underneath, and the back two-thirds of their lower mandible was abruptly flesh-colored. They were strongly wagging their tails, very phoebe-like.

The weather finally cleared. Canyon de Chelly was absolutely spectacular! Even photographs cannot do it justice. Looking down from the rim, its depth was tremendous. Riding with a Navajo guide down 600 feet or more into the interior in a four-wheel drive open truck, we marveled at the overhanging cliffs chiseled after eons of water and wind. No river runs through the canyon, instead a heavy wash which comes down from the countryside carved the walls as it came. The water this spring was quite deep and, when crossing it, we were nearly stuck several times. A few native sheep herder families still lived among the ancient cliff dwellings, ruins and petroglyphs which depict, among other things, antelope and early Spanish conquistadors on horseback.

May 14: Leaving Chinle, we drove through beautiful Oak Creek Canyon just north of Sedona and spotted the Red-faced Warbler – number 654 – just at the top of the canyon. I'd been looking for it high in the ponderosa pines although I know it nests on the ground. It was actually low down in the understory.

We camped about a third of the way between Prescott and Wickenburg on the west slope of the mountains. This was high chaparral country above the desert floor. At 6:00, the sun was still very high, The temperature is a warm 60 degrees, and there was enough breeze to blow our tents around.

May 15: We drove to Baja through Mexicali, and we are now sitting at Augie's Riviera Motel in San Felipe on the coast of the Sea of Cortez. On the way here, in the absolutely appallingly raw desert, we saw three Ferruginous Rough-legged Hawks and a Scott's Oriole about thirty miles west of Yuma. The desert was wide-open salt flats with nothing growing – flat as a pancake – caked salt and mirages, real grim.

Canyon de Chelly

95

Consag Rock

May 16: Today, Papa Lupé, our local guide, took us in his large tug-like boat to Consag Rock, a 300' island twenty-two miles off the coast. The boat was not very fast, but it was seaworthy. About a quarter of the way out, we saw a Least Petrel – number 655 – and farther out a Black Petrel. The Least is a small bird, rather like a sea-going Chimney Swift, except for the wing beat. It has a wedge-shaped tail unlike any other petrel and is totally black.

The birdlife on Consag Rock was incredibly alive with about 2,500 Brown Pelicans and maybe 2,000 Brown Boobies – number 656 – and six Blue-footed Boobies – number 657. A Red-footed Booby – number 658 – stood alone. I first noticed the large red bill and kind of pinkish feet. It was bigger than the gulls and smaller than the Browns. It was thrilling to see such a huge gathering of marine birds.

This huge, sheer rock was very white, not from the sun but from the guano of seabirds nesting there for centuries. Even if you could dock a boat, the climb would be almost vertical and certainly slippery. Consequently, we did all of our birding from the boat. Most of the day, a Man-O'-War bird hung over the top. There were two Red-billed Tropicbirds soaring near the rock – number 659. They were unmistakable with their long streamer-tails and bright red bills.

The island is also a breeding place for seals, probably fur seals. But the bulls were not nearly as large as those on the Pribilofs in Alaska and the cows were bigger. Counting their pups, there were probably five hundred in all.

We did some fishing. Helen had her line in for about thirty seconds when she caught a three-foot shark. After that, we began fishing for mackerel, called Sierras here, with hand lines. You let the line out behind the boat and – Wham! – you haul them in by hand. Very exciting! Doubly so because the sharks were trying to get them while you were bringing them in. We ended up with about sixteen.

It was a beautiful, cloudless, calm day and very hot when we left the rock, but pleasant when we returned to shore where there was a little breeze cooling us off.

May 17: Leaving San Felipe north toward Mexicali, we surprisingly saw a Ring-necked Pheasant. It was lovely farming country, neat and clean and apparently prosperous, but the houses were pretty poor. The road came into the States at Lukeville just south of the Organ Pipe Cactus National Monument. We stopped at the headquarters and received permission to camp there at the back end of Quito Baquito pond on the international border. There were lots of White-winged Doves. They sing "Who cooks for you, who cooks for you all."

Red-billed Tropicbirds
and Brown Boobies

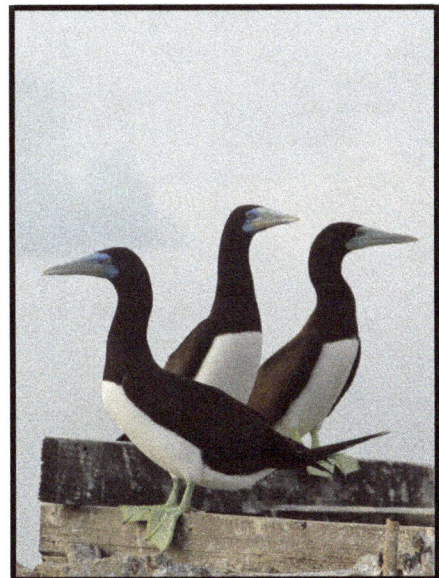

At Dripping Springs, a very outgoing Curve-billed Thrasher hopped up and picked bugs from our radiator. Noisy, ubiquitous Cactus Wrens were all over, but they didn't bother me.

May 19: We drove west to the Saguaro National Park which is peppered with multiple kinds of cacti. Saguaros, which flourish and are protected in the two districts of the park, grow at an exceptionally slow rate. The first arm typically grows from the trunk when the cactus is between fifty and seventy years old, although it may be longer in times when rainfall is very low. This cactus can live as long as two hundred years. A mature saguaro may grow up to sixty feet tall and weigh almost 5,000 pounds when fully filled with water. Many millions of these giants live in the park along with other species of cactus. Finally, to cool ourselves off, we drove north of Tucson to the top of Mt. Lemmon and relaxed.

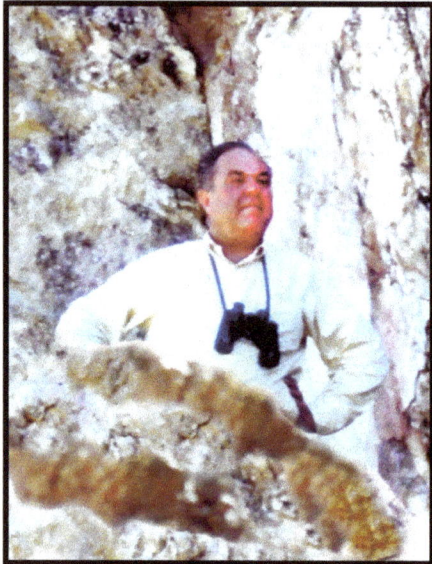

At Dripping Springs - 1968

May 20: In Patagonia, known for its astonishing variety of birds, we saw sixty-one different species. Notably, we found the Rose-throated Becard and the Thick-billed Kingbird – number 660. It really has a very thick bill and is much shorter and stubbier than the Gray Kingbird in Florida. There were many other southwestern species: Pyrrhuloxias, Phainopeplas, Vermilion Flycatchers, Western and Summer Tanagers and dozens more. Very exciting birding!

May 21: We camped at beautiful Madera Canyon in the Santa Rita Mountains south of Tucson. At the Santa Rita Lodge, we found Black-chinned and Broad-billed Hummingbirds and an Elf Owl again nesting in a hole in a telephone pole.

We are really eating well on this trip with Ann as the cook. Tonight, we had breast of chicken, noodles almondine and big petit pois. Delicious!

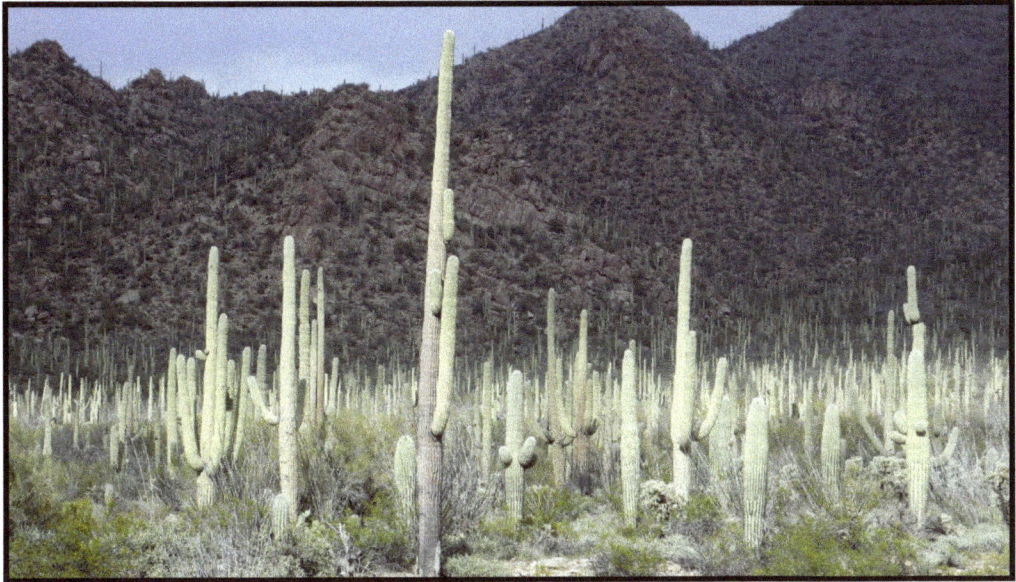
Saguaro National Park

May 22: I got up about 4:30 and went out to look for the Coppery-tailed Trogan. I didn't find it right away but, after breakfast, we found its nesting site and watched it come and go – number 661. The male is absolutely spectacular – brilliant deep scarlet in front and a bright iridescent green in back. Helen and I had looked for it for a long, long time. It was wonderful to see it so beautifully and to see it so beautiful.

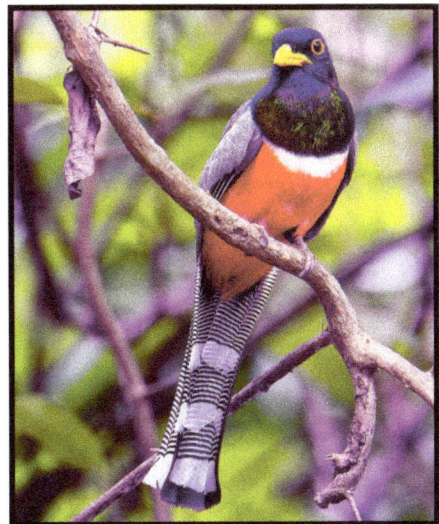
Coppery-tailed Trogan

Other birds in Madera were Painted Redstarts, Hutton's Vireos and Red-eyed Cowbirds doing a fantastic courtship display. The male got his feathers all puffed up, his wings fluttering and flew straight up in the air and turned slowly in circles about three feet in the air. Then, he came slowly down again, still all puffed up and wings still fluttering.

99

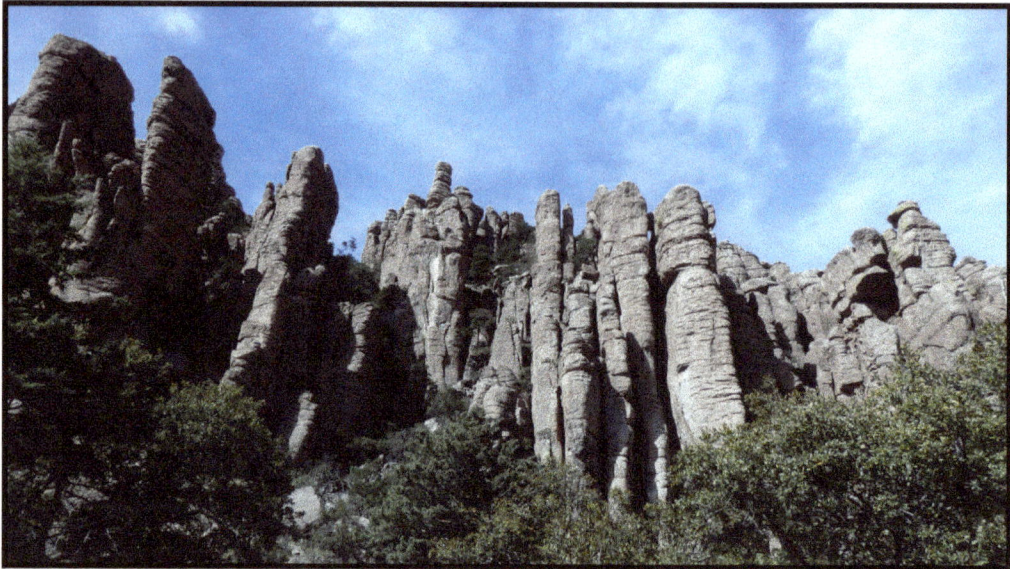
Chiricahua National Monument

May 23: Then we drove through Box Canyon and Sonoita to Ramsey Canyon to see the hummingbirds: Black-chinned, Broad-billed, Blue-throated and Rivoli's. Apparently a Violet-crowned had been there. I looked but, unfortunately, did not see it.

But I did see an amazing bird, a Parula Warbler. It had typical coloring with the light spot on its back and white wing-bars, a chestnut band across the chest, so it can't be a Sennett's Warbler.

May 24: We took off through the Chiricahua National Monument toward Big Bend in Texas, driving all day.

May 25: We camped near Boquillas Canyon in Big Bend. In the morning, we found Black-eared Bushtits – number 662 – east of Panther Pass. They were in a flock through the junipers and piñon pines. We were so close to them that we didn't even need binoculars.

Driving on to Santa Elena Canyon, we stopped at the Old Ranch where the rangers thought there might be hummingbirds. The ranch is an oasis in the middle of nowhere which still had one operating windmill so there was water and lots of birds. It was over 104 degrees and we had no air-conditioning – very hot! Fortunately, there was a faucet nearby. So, creating makeshift showers, we cooled off. Helen and Peter slept in their wet bathing suits!

May 26: I was up early looking for the Lucifer's Hummingbird without any luck. Last night, in addition to the Lesser Nighthawks, there were lots of bats. And all day today there was the high-pitched buzzing of cicadas up on the desert.

There were, of course, lots of butterflies. We got a good look at one whose underwings looked like a Monarch and the uppers were plain brown with white spots – the Queen.

May 27: Following very steep javelina trails up to a plateau, I found myself in a rock slide. I was just running in place because the rocks were spinning out under my feet. Ann and Peter made it up okay, but Helen got into some cactus. Peter had to go back down and pick the spines out of her. Eventually, we all made it up into the canyon where we found the Lucifer Hummingbird – number 663. It's very small, not much bigger than a Black-chinned, with a real decurved bill. Its throat, even in deep shadow, was a "V" of purple ink. It has a forked tail, which, no doubt, accounts for its descriptive name.

The Queen

We took a longer trail back to camp to avoid sliding down the steep, rocky path and got a good look at some lovely Painted Buntings.

May 28: On the way out of the park, we stopped at the fossil bone exhibit which was absolutely ghastly. There in the middle of nowhere was a glass house with some bones lying on the ground in it. All the bones are painted the color of dog messes. Who knows why? The temperature was 112, and we were very disappointed and very hot.

Texas Kingfisher

May 29: We drove to Garner State Park about thirty miles north of Uvalde to find the Texas, or Green, Kingfisher. The countryside changed markedly driving east, with flowers and grass instead of desert.

After asking about the kingfisher at headquarters, we drove to the Eric River as suggested and found it on a dead branch low down close to the water – number 664. It is a handsome small kingfisher with a very dark cap, a white line below the cap and a bright green, almost iridescent back. The male has a broad chestnut band across its white front. We're doing pretty well with a new bird almost every single day!

May 30: We left and went on to Laredo where both the temperature and the humidity were grim, and then on to McAllen to try to find the Ringed Kingfisher. Quite a few had been seen there, but you just had to be at the right place at the right time. We returned without any luck and stayed at the Holiday Inn in McAllen to keep cool.

Falcon Dam on the Rio Grande River, featuring a large variety of waterfowl and others, was built by the United States and Mexico to harness the river's variation in water level and flooding areas. There we found Tropical Kingbirds, White-fronted Doves, Lichtenstein's Orioles, Scissor-tailed Flycatchers, Chachalacas and lots of Black Vultures. It was a good way to end a splendid birding excursion.

June 1: Driving north from Houston on our way home, we passed the edge of the Big Thicket, known in Texas as the Big Ticket. It looked wild enough for the Ivory-billed Woodpeckers to still exist there. I wish ...

ROCHESTER MUSEUM AND SCIENCE CENTER

Rochester, New York, 1968

Citation of Joseph W. Taylor in the Field of Ornithology

From Kivalina on the Chukchi Sea in arctic Alaska to the Texas sand shores of the Gulf of Mexico, from Long Island's Montauk Point to Consag Rock in Baja, California, Joseph W. Taylor has searched the far corners of North America to find as many birds as possible that occur on the continent. His quest has been by auto, plane and boat, on horseback and afoot over thousands of miles, and in its course he has camped in the searing heat of the Arizona desert and on the frozen tundra at the edge of the Arctic Ocean.

Yet he is unimpressed by the fact that his list of 664 species of North American avifauna exceeds all but that of one other man, a professional ornithologist. For this is his hobby, and only one facet of a deep and abiding concern for the vital need for conservation. This concern has grown with an early interest in birds which continued through schooldays, through college at Yale University, through law school at Harvard and through a successful business career with Bausch & Lomb, of which he is now treasurer. It has led to his election as president of the world-famed Hawk Mountain Sanctuary Association. It is reflected in his election to the administrative board of the Laboratory of Ornithology at Cornell University, in his fellowship in the Rochester Academy of Science, in his trusteeships of the Seneca Zoological Society and Bird Refuges Inc., in his charter membership in the Genesee Ornithological Society and in his special interest, as a life member, in the habitat preservation efforts of the Wilson Ornithological Society and the American Ornithologists' Union.

His plans, soon, to devote all his time and energy to conservation are an expression of his deep feeling for nature's essential wilderness and a refusal to kneel before the forces bent upon its destruction.

For all these reasons, the Rochester Museum and Science Center is proud to greet him as a Fellow.[17]

1968

THE BIRD REPORT

Beginning in 1969, Joe wrote a weekly bird report for the Democrat and Chronicle, one of Rochester, New York's newspapers. Subjects ranged from local sites for good birding to his travels, both domestic and foreign, as well as his views on conservation and ecology. This narrative would become too long to include them all, therefore, ones with particular enthusiasm or philosophical views have been chosen from over six hundred essays.

ROCHESTER AREA AVIFAUNA

April 16, 1969: Recently driving to Ithaca on a beautiful morning was a delight. There had been a small dawn chorus of robins, giving a hint of what will come in May and June. Along the Thruway, a few "V"s of Canada Geese went overhead, heading for open water after their early morning feeding in the fields. A Red-tailed Hawk flew by, harried by three or four Red-winged Blackbirds. On the broad open plain between Waterloo and Ovid, Eastern Meadowlarks and Song Sparrows were in full song. Horned Larks flew up from the roadside gravel. An occasional Yellow-shafted Flicker flew alongside the car, its underwings bright in the morning sun. A few Sparrow Hawks were perched on the telephone wires. Grackles, many already paired, flew across the road, and every few hundred yards a male Red-winged Blackbird perched on the wires or on top of a small tree, his territory already staked out, awaiting the arrival of the noticeably smaller females which do not come north until two or three weeks after the males.

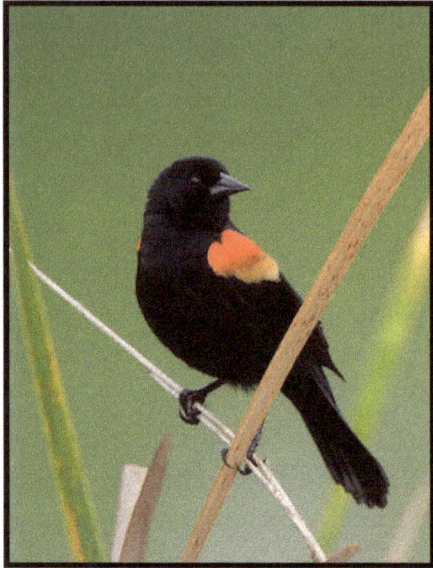
Red-winged Blackbird

It is interesting to note what has happened to the Red-wings nesting habits in the past ten years or so. In 1969, the manuscript for Arthur Cleveland Bent's *Life Histories of North American Blackbirds, Orioles, Tanagers and Allies* was completed. He said, with regard to their nesting habitat, that water is essential and that marshes with extensive growth of cattails and sedges are their favorite breeding ground.

This still may be true, but they have now spread into the upland areas where substantially no water exists. When they first return, they are common at bird feeders – a new development. Yet the numbers of marsh-nesting Red-wings do not seem to have declined. There apparently has been a sharp increase in their population, caused by what, we cannot be sure.

This has not been without its detrimental effects. With the increase in upland-nesting Red-wings, there has been a sharp decrease in nesting Bobolinks which inhabit the same areas. Apparently the much earlier arriving, more aggressive blackbirds are driving their black and white cousins out.

Dr. O. S. Pettingill, Jr., administrative director of the Cornell Laboratory, recently returned from Argentina where he had been studying the Bobolinks on their wintering grounds. The birds which breed here and to the north of us in Canada, start south in mid-summer but apparently do not reach Argentina until January, having migrated along the eastern edge of almost the whole Andean range. Dr. Pettingill found them by the thousands in northeast Argentina, well north of Buenos Aries where they are regarded as a real pest.

There, they descend in flocks on the rice fields just as the grain is reaching the "milk" stage and apparently cause much havoc. When not feeding, flocks will gather in one tree, in all stages of moult from their drab, brownish winter plumage to full black and white breeding plumage as we know them, and all sing at once, their pleasant tinkling songs being in chorus more like English Sparrows or Starlings.

At the Cornell Laboratory of Ornithology, the pond, as usual, was alive with waterfowl. The resident Canada, Blue and Snow Geese were, of course, there along with Trumpeter Swans. Some of the wintering Black Ducks and Mallards have scattered to breed elsewhere, but many still remain. The male Wood Ducks in full breeding plumage were magnificent. A pair of Redheads swam by and, while we were watching, half-a-dozen Pintails pitched in.

Wood Duck

But the hit of the show was a Hooded Merganser, his brilliant black-bordered white crest gleaming in the sun and sending a streak of reflection six or eight feet across the calm water.[18]

November 12, 1969: Driving about the countryside these fall days, you will see large compact flocks of blackbirds – these are Starlings. The flocks which sometimes contain hundreds of individuals expand and contract, elongate and shrink, and turn like a flash with all the birds in unison. It is a fine performance to watch.

The Starling was successfully introduced in this country – in Central Park in New York City – around 1800 after unsuccessful tries for about twenty years. It had been common in Europe for centuries, feeding chiefly in grassy meadows and with cattle in pasturelands, in relatively small numbers. Here, when it did take hold, it found an unfulfilled ecological gap, and the population expanded with a vengeance. I can remember my

Starling

107

Eastern Bluebird

father telling me that around 1910, he made a special trip to New York just to see these birds, but a few years later they had spread as far west as Ohio and south to Virginia. By 1923, they had covered the East to the Mississippi.

For many years, the Rocky Mountains kept them from the West Coast. They were rare there as late as 1954, but they have now crossed the mountain barrier and are everywhere in the Pacific United States. We saw none in Alaska two years ago, but I believe that they have now managed to get to the Hawaiian Islands.

Basically today, the Starling is a major nuisance as anyone who has the misfortune to live in an area where they have decided to take up a winter roost can testify. Their droppings deface the facades of beautiful buildings all over the country, and the noise produced by thousands on a night-time roost is quite unbearable.

There is little question in my mind that the Starling was the principal cause of the almost complete disappearance of the Eastern Bluebird. A strong, aggressive bird, it simply drove the bluebirds from their nesting holes. It has probably had a similar, although not so drastic, effect on Purple Martins and, in some areas, on Tree Swallows. Where they have become excessively numerous, which sometimes seems to be everywhere, they can cause extreme damage to grain and cereal crops and to orchards. They have been seen to settle like a black cloud on a vineyard and eat the entire fruit crop in an incredibly short time.

Actually, the Starling does do some good. It has certainly served in helping to bring the Japanese beetle under control. Also, a flock feeding on a lawn can quickly clean out the grubs which feed on roots. It eats other beetles and weevils which feed on such plants as clover and strawberries. Food studies have shown that in May almost ninety-five percent of their food is animal matter. This drops to somewhat under fifty percent in July when our cherry and other fruit crops come in. On the whole, they are at least as beneficial as many of our native birds. Their main problem is one of over-abundance.[19]

October 31, 1971: As a general rule, we do not see very many Canada Geese in this area in the fall. In the spring, we are on one of their flyways with probably close to 100,000 birds. They are concentrated at the Montezuma National Wildlife Refuge on the east and three state and federal refuges at Oak Orchard on the west, with scattered flocks in between.

In the fall, however, they bypass us, splitting north either to go down the Atlantic Coast or across Lake Erie and south by way of the Ohio River valley. But once in about every ten years, or maybe a little less, the geese come through here in good numbers in October. This is one of those years.

Quite likely this is a function of the weather. With a week of incredibly lovely autumn in the middle of the month, it seems probable that the Canadas, their biological clocks set to move them south, came down on a broad front, rather than being driven along their normal routes by the usual strong winds from the north.

Regardless of the reason, it is indeed good to have them here twice this year, for they are irresistible birds. Whether they bring the glad tidings of coming spring or the foreboding of the long winter ahead, I expect there is almost no one who doesn't look up at the sound of their honking overhead. Most of us, without thinking, count the numbers in their long "V"s as they pass.

Canada Goose

They are to all of us, instinctively, the true symbol of the wild and the longing to be in wild places. I let the lamb chops burn almost to a crisp over the charcoal one evening as I watched and listened to a big flock going down apparently to Mendon Ponds after a late afternoon foray to a nearby cornfield.

The Canada Goose is by far the most widespread of all our North American wild fowl,

109

breeding all the way from Alaska to Labrador and Newfoundland. They winter principally in the south from Florida along the Gulf Coast into Texas and southern California. Even before the advent of the national wildlife refuges, a few wintered north to Martha's Vineyard in the East and to the warmth of southern British Columbia in the West. Today, with great strings of refuges designed to provide both wintering grounds in the north and breeding grounds south of their normal habitats, large numbers of these birds can be seen year-round in the central United States from the Carolinas west.

Ten distinct subspecies of this bird are recognized by the American Ornithologists' Union, the scientific body which classifies all our birds. They differ somewhat in coloration, but chiefly in size. The smallest is the Cackling Goose, no bigger than a Mallard duck, which breeds in the Aleutians. I remember seeing one in January a couple of years ago on Vancouver Island where they sometimes winter. The largest is, or was, the Giant Canada of the Dakotas and southern Manitoba, which may now be extinct.

Our familiar goose is third from the top in size being about thirty-eight inches long. The White-cheeked Goose of central Alaska and the Giant are respectively about forty and forty-three inches. In weight, they range from two and a half pounds for the little Cackling, to fifteen for the Giant and an average of about thirteen for ours. Even within each subspecies, however, there is considerable size variation, which is apparent to anyone who looks over a flock with reasonable care.

These are magnificent birds. Thanks to the efforts of both state and federal agencies in providing refuges, they are more abundant now then they have probably ever been.[20]

June 1, 1975: Now it is truly spring, and a magnificent spring at that. Not every year do we have a real spring, but when we do, it certainly makes up for all the horrid weather which can happen in western New York. The fruit trees – apples, cherries and pears – are this year's objects of great splendor. Their full white blossoming is set off by the pinks of the flowering crabs, the varying shades of purple and lavender of the lilacs, magnolias and other ornamentals, the brilliance of the dogwood, the still bright yellow of the forsythia

Apple blossoms

and the greens of the leafing-out trees. Many of them are still not much more than iridescent, fragile lace.

And with all this loveliness about us, we have what to me is really the frosting on the cake. I do not know why I get so carried away by such a seemingly insignificant bird as the Henslow's Sparrow, but I do.

After a complete absence last year, now we have at least two pairs back in our fields. They are truly quite wonderful. Perhaps the bird's charm lies in its incredibly poor song which Roger Tory Peterson in his eastern field guide describes as follows: "The Henslow's perches atop a weed, from which it utters one of the poorest vocal efforts of any bird. Throwing back its head, it ejects a hiccoughing 'tsi- lick.'"

As if to practice this "song" so that it might not always remain at the bottom of the list, it often hiccoughs all night long. And not only is its song terribly poor, but the bird itself is not much to look at. It has a very short tail, streaked back with russet on the wings, with a large bill and a large, flat-topped, olive-yellow, striped head. When it is not singing from its weed top, it skulks through the dry, weedy meadows in which it likes to nest.

111

Henslow's Sparrow

And from our observations of these birds this year, it seems to us that they do not sing at all if there is any dampness in their fields. We first heard them in mid-May. Then, we had a deluge of a rain storm. For four days, there was no "hiccoughing." We were very afraid they had left the area or maybe even drowned in all the water. But when the fields finally dried out, they started up again, loud and jaunty as ever. I think they are truly fine birds. While they have become considerably scarcer in recent years, they do now seem to be holding their own, and we hope they will continue to do so.[21]

Post-birding drowsy relaxation - 1975

THE ADIRONDACKS

In the early 1900s, Camp Irondequoit on Lake Placid was purchased by Joe's grandparents, Anna and Willibald Drescher. Back then, it was without electric power. Oil and kerosene lamps lit the house by night. Several outbuildings housed ice blocks to preserve the summer pantry. In the twenties, Anna and the cook provided the meals while Joe, his siblings and cousins hiked and camped in the pristine Adirondack peaks. They learned to swim in the chilly waters and braved the ever-present biting no-see-ums.

Later, this mountain idyll became the summer domain of Hilda, Joe's mother. In the sixties and seventies, she welcomed the visiting family and friends. Peter and I met Joe and Helen there most summer weekends for congenial gatherings, birding and fishing. Off we would go in the misty dawn hoping to catch fish for breakfast, which we often did. Until the mid-eighties, Joe continued to bird there and in other Adirondack habitats.

September 17, 1969: A few miles west and north of Paul Smiths in the Adirondacks is a country known as the Madawaska, largely private land owned by the Rockefeller family and by the St. Regis Paper Company. It consists of sandy, blueberry-bracken barrens with occasional clumps of alders. Where the land drops down near the streams and is wetter, the forest is interspersed with balsam, spruce and white pine. On the Saturday before Labor Day, we spent a morning there. In the southern fringe of Canadian Zone

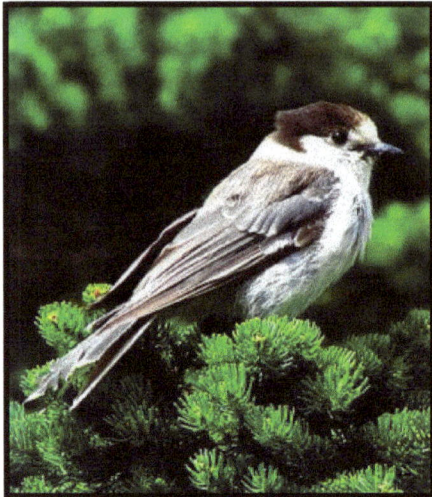
Canada Jay

four special birds are to be found. That day we saw all of them.

Gray, or Canada, Jays are generally unafraid, noisy birds but, here on the Madawaska, they are silent and glide through the woods on their broad wings, almost like owls. Perhaps this is because this is the extreme southern limit of their range.

Even harder to find are the Spruce Grouse, but when you do find them, they are extraordinarily tame. A male flew off into the woods as we drove by. We backed up and found a female about forty feet off the road on the ground. Walking in carefully, we soon saw the male up in the dead lower branches of a spruce. Presently, we came upon two fully grown birds feeding near their mother. In the north, these birds are known as "fool's hens" because of their total lack of fear. We had no trouble coming up to within a few feet of them on the ground. The male barely moved as we walked about under his perch. He is a handsome bird – slaty, blue-gray above and spotted black-and-white below, with a comb of bright red skin over each eye and a black ruff.

Boreal Chickadees are not uncommon in the higher elevations of the Adirondacks, but they are hard to find out of the mountains. Back in on the trail into the Madawaska River, we heard and saw a small flock of four or five. They sound like obvious chickadees, but their song is much slower, hoarser and buzzier than our Black-caps. And their brown caps are not easy to see as they crawl about high in the spruces.

A few years ago in this Canadian wilderness, a Goshawk was an unusual record. Today however, for reasons which we do not yet fully understand, they have become relatively numerous. We were pleased, nevertheless, to see one soaring high above us and then going into a dive after its prey.

114

It had been a very foggy morning, and the mist was still in the air as we turned onto the dirt road leading into Madawaska country. There were birds everywhere moving through the barrens on their way south. The air was alive with insects. A pair of Common Nighthawks flew over taking their last meal before retiring for the day. But the most interesting of all was a fly-catching Yellow-bellied Sapsucker. The bird was making no pretense at all of drilling holes in trees or a digging bugs out of their bark. It was sitting on top of a utility pole, its head tipped back and turning from side to side obviously watching what was going on around it. About once every thirty seconds, it would make a quick flight into the air, invariably

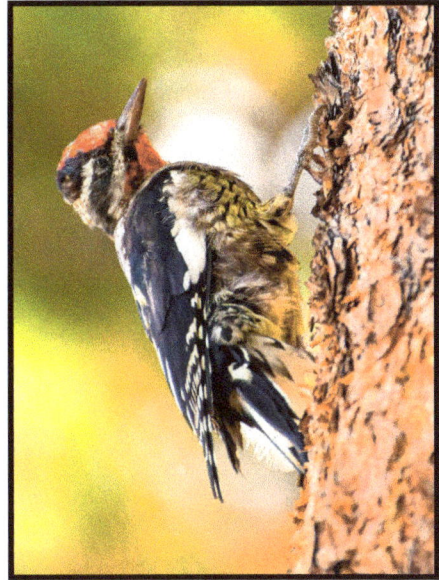

Yellow-bellied Sapsucker

catching an insect. Watching through binoculars, we could see the insects flying by and could almost be sure which one the bird would go for. It was as unerring in its accuracy as any flycatcher. We watched for a long time, fascinated, before leaving this remarkable performance.[22]

November 5, 1969: The Adirondacks in late October can produce surprisingly interesting birding. On a crisp, clear Saturday morning, the high peaks' ridges and valleys near Lake Placid were sharply outlined by the season's first snowfall. They looked like the Swiss Alps as we drove through the forest north from Saranac Lake almost to Malone.

Ordinarily, this trip on the main road can be done in less than an hour. Over back roads, sometimes not much more than leaf-covered wagon tracks, it took us almost four hours to reach Chasm Falls on Malone's southern outskirts. We passed through the old logging town of Onchiota, past the White Fathers retreat on Lake Kushaqua, originally established as a haven for tired businesswomen, principally telephone operators. Then we drove on through

Mountain View on the northern boundary of the Adirondack Preserve into Owl's Head, best known because it so frequently records the coldest winter temperatures in the country and then down into the St. Lawrence Valley to Chasm Falls.

The brilliance of the early fall foliage on the mountain and hillsides was gone. It was replaced by the pastel shades of grey and brown of bare trunks and branches and broken by patches of the soft yellows of birches and aspens. Occasionally, there was a late-turning maple, still almost flame-red. At the lower elevations, tamaracks, changing from green to pale green to yellow ochre to yellow, stood out in contrast to the dark green of the spruce and white pine forest.

Up on Norman's Ridge, a high windswept plateau just east of Vermontville, we put up a small flock late-migrating Eastern Meadowlarks. Two Horned Larks were working their way through a newly ploughed field, and overhead some American Crows were having trouble against a strong headwind.

Back down in the woods, it was soon apparent that this was going to be a Dark-eyed Junco day. Every few miles, large flocks of them feeding along the roadside flew up as we drove by. Mixed in with the juncos were a considerable numbers of immature Chipping Sparrows – surprisingly difficult to identify. They had very pronounced brown cheek patches and plainly visible median head stripes rather than the solid chestnut cap of the

Dark-eyed Junco

adult. Additionally their feathers were all puffed out as protection against the cold so that they appeared to be much larger than we thought they should be. Deep in the woods, we slammed on the brakes, excited, as a big Pileated Woodpecker flew across in front of the car. It paused momentarily on a tree trunk and then disappeared down the steep hill.[23]

January 28, 1970: Some time ago, it was my pleasure to take part in the releasing of two

116

Great-horned Owls. These birds had been caught in padded pole traps at a game farm where they had been allegedly poaching. They were carried in burlap bags far from the place where they had been trapped.

When the first owl was released, it sat on the ground in front of us for about a minute, staring with its great yellow eyes and snapping its beak. Then, it flew off to the stub of a dead elm where it was almost immediately attacked by a pair of Red-tailed Hawks which had not been in evidence before.

Great-horned Owls

The second bird was truly magnificent. When she (from the large size, I believe it was a female) came out of the bag, she turned to face us. Bending forward, fluffing out her feathers and half spreading her wings to increase her size, she snapped, hissed and snarled at her tormentors in absolute fearless defiance. I was able to approach to within about two feet of her before she took off.

The Great-horned Owl has no fear of man when her young are involved. There are numerous instances of people being struck by one as they were climbing a nest tree.

Last fall, a friend showed me two long scars on his back where he had been raked by an owl's long, sharp talons on its first pass at him. In the second pass, the bird hit him solidly driving one set of claws into his shoulder and the other into his scalp, it nearly knocked him out of the tree. He had to climb down the tree with the owl clinging to him before he could free himself. For the rest of the year that owl went unmolested.

The Great-horned Owl is without question the most savage, wild and fearsome of our birds of prey. Yet, it seems to have tremendous adaptability. "Civilization" has made little, if

117

any, dent in its numbers. It is a bird of the deep woodlands and, fortunately, we still have many of these. It lives in the same areas as the Red-tailed Hawk. These two birds complement each other. The owl hunts at night and the hawk in the day.

This owl is our earliest nester and starts to lay eggs in late January or early February. On any calm, fairly warm night, if these owls are around you can hear their deep, resonant calls – an unmistakable "who-whoo, who, who-whoo."

Many times the female must incubate her eggs when almost completely covered with snow. Only her ear tufts stick out of the white blanket. Since the eggs take twenty-eight days to incubate and the young birds are unable to shift for themselves for between ten and twelve weeks, they do not leave the nest until middle or late June. This may be the reason for the early nesting.

These birds are voracious eaters, feeding on skunks, rabbits, rats and mice. They rarely nest more than four years in one place as by that time the food supply is pretty well exhausted.[24]

Whiteface Mountain at the north end of Lake Placid

June 18, 1971: One of the places I find most delightful in the Adirondacks is a so-called floating or quaking bog just to the east of Paul Smiths. Here, the tightly-knit mass of vegetation floats on top of the water underneath, rising and falling as the water level changes. The mass is so tightly woven that it is walkable. As one steps across its somewhat soggy surface, the surrounding area trembles. The flowers and plants shake, sometimes as far away as fifty feet or more – a very eerie sensation.

The surface is composed mainly of various cranberries, huckleberries and blueberries and leatherleaf shrubs. Looking closely, we could also see the tiny pink, four-pointed, star-shaped flowers of the small-leafed cranberry hugging the ground.

The overall view of the bog was one of white flowers – Labrador tea. Here and there a dash of deep red of the pitcher plant was thrown in. The Labrador tea is a member of the laurel family and, in the Adirondack bogs, it grows to a height of almost two feet. We remembered having seen it on the Alaskan tundra where the blooms were only an inch or so off the ground.

While we were standing out in the middle of Paul Smiths bog – it's really quite a small one surrounded on all sides by the tall forest – a Broad-winged Hawk came into the opening and circled several times. His black-and-white striped tail seemed to shine in the sunlight until he was driven off by a pair of Blue Jays.

The feature of this excursion to the Adirondacks is the pre-sunrise trip up Whiteface Mountain, and it is always exciting. It was not as crystal clear this year as last. A cloud hung over the top 400 or 500 feet of the mountain but, from under the cloud, the view was as breathtaking as ever. I think the lakes and rivers take on a kind of ethereal quality when seen, far below, through the cloud's mist.

The reason for this drive up the mountain at 4:30 in the morning is to hear the singing of the Bicknell's Thrush, the subspecies of the Grey-cheeked, which breeds in the high mountains of the Northeast. We heard it several times – a much more weezy and slurred song than that of the other thrushes, with a series of descending whistles, usually rising at

119

Common Merganser female

the end. There were Boreal Chickadees at about 3,800 feet where the upper part of the mixture of spruce, birches, maples and other hardwoods gives way to almost pure spruce. Blackpoll Warblers were everywhere singing their high-pitched staccato songs.

But the bird of the day, and probably of the whole trip, was a Common Merganser. It flew back and forth somewhat aimlessly far out from the mountain itself and high over its ridges and shoulders, and certainly far from water. These mergansers are common breeders on the Adirondack lakes but, as soon as the eggs are laid, the drakes disappear, leaving the females to incubate and raise the young alone. Nobody is really sure where they go or why this lone one was flying about so very far from where we think of them. It was a mystery.[25]

Camp Irondequoit, the Taylor family compound on Lake Placid

120

MICHIGAN

The family cottage in Pinewoods on beautiful Higgins Lake was built in 1909 by Joe's in-laws, Lillian and Alexander Taggart. Helen and the family happily retreated there every summer to enjoy water sports, tennis, ping pong, butterflying, birding and the company of many relatives. After his retirement, Joe loved to join them for several weeks rather than just an occasional weekend.

A ugust 8, 1972: About one hundred miles south of the Straits of Mackinac in Michigan's lower peninsula is Higgins Lake. Here on the north shore is an association of private homes in a magnificent stand of woodland. Virgin white pines tower 120 feet and more overhead, and some of the old maples are almost as tall.

So high is this upper story that forty and fifty foot second and third growth timber lives below it without difficulty. In the hot days of summer, the light filtering down through the many layers of needles and leaves gives a truly cathedral-like quality. And the breezes through the trees provide a soft background of sound for the many bird songs.

When we were there in the latter part of July, Wood Thrushes and robins still sang in the early morning. Perula Warblers were everywhere – their buzzy trills went up the scale and tipped over at the top. American Redstarts were almost as numerous, and the soft, slow, Chipping Sparrow-like song of the Pine Warbler seemed perfectly in place. Red-eyed Vireos were high in the trees. When the day got hot, the Wood Pewees really sang.

121

Red-breasted Nuthatch

All throughout the day, Ovenbirds called loudly, although not really very often. Black-capped Chickadees and Red-breasted Nuthatches chirped and buzzed nasally as they worked through and around the tree trunks. Down by the lake shore, Cedar Waxwings, with high-pitched thin whistles, flew out from the fine old white birches, chasing after insects. A few Ring-billed Gulls soiled the boats and floats which they used as roosts. Near the fringe of the woods, Least Flycatchers loudly called "chebec," and where there is a small bog you can hear the "hic-three beers" of the Olive-sided Flycatcher every time you go by.[26]

August 27, 1969: At the turn of the century, the Ausable River in the upper half of Michigan's lower peninsula was one of the most famous trout streams in the country. Millionaires came to the old wooden hotel in the small lumber town of Lovells in their private railroad cars to fish the river's fast-running waters.

Today, the old hotel still stands, almost in ruins, but the shingle mill and the old general store are gone, replaced by modern markets and gasoline stations. The river, however, is lovelier than ever and is still good fishing. In 1900, the area had just been thoroughly lumbered, and old pictures show a pretty stark landscape. Now, a second-growth of trees has matured.

A few weeks ago, we canoed down the five-mile stretch in a restricted part of the river's North Branch. It is almost wholly untouched by man. No trash litters the area. We saw only two houses, far apart. The banks are covered with tamarack, black spruce and an occasional white pine, with here and there a clump of white birches or alders. There was a profusion of late summer wildflowers – ironweed, grass of Parnassus, blazing star and many others unidentified.

122

The birds had pretty much stopped singing except for an occasional Black-capped Chickadee, Wood Pewee or Red-eyed Vireo. But a pair of Bald Eagles soared overhead for a while. A Broad-winged Hawk flew out to take a quick look at us and then disappeared. We chased a Great Blue Heron downstream for about ten minutes until he came to the end of his territory and flew back up over us. A Belted Kingfisher preceded us almost halfway along.

We startled a couple of deer browsing along the bank. They bounded off, their white flags showing plainly through the underbrush. Once, a mink cut across right ahead of the canoe. Sometimes the river is wide and the current slow, and we drifted peacefully along with small trout jumping all about us. And then it would narrow, and we'd have to work a little to stay upright. What a most rewarding couple of hours!

This area is also the breeding ground of the Kirtland's Warbler. So far as anyone knows, this bird nests only here in the dry, hot jack pine stands, and then only in limited places. It builds its nest on the ground under a jack pine. Research has found that the ideal stands must cover at least eighty acres. The trees must be six to eighteen feet tall, eight to twenty

years old, with numerous openings to keep low limbs exposed to sunlight and, thus, alive. If the trees are too short, their lower limbs are too thick, and the ground is too damp. If they are too high, the lower limbs have died, and the nest would be too exposed.

Kirkland's Warbler

These jack pine barrens suit the Kirkland's needs exactly, but the key to maintaining the right habitat is fire. The jack pinecone is very light and will only pop open and scatter the seeds necessary for regeneration under intense heat. Before today's modern forest fighting techniques, there was no problem. Lightning did the trick. But our efficiency almost pushed the

123

Kirkland's Warbler out of its home and into extinction. Fortunately, the problem was recognized in time. Now the U. S. Forest Service with the cooperation of the Michigan Conservation Department is burning a mile square block of mature jack pines on a five-year cycle to keep a perpetual supply of young growth – an excellent example of practical conservation.

Let's hope it works. The Kirkland's is a fine bird – blue-gray above with a black mask and black streaks on the sides of its bright yellow breast. Its song has a rich, ringing quality. It migrates from its wintering grounds in the Bahamas principally through Ohio, although there are a few New York records. Only about one thousand of these birds exist in the world. As a curious statistic, assuming the adult birds weigh about half an ounce each, the total population constitutes only thirty pounds of very rare bird life.[27]

August 1, 1976: We spent the last two weeks of July in the northern part of Michigan's lower peninsula – the breeding ground of the Kirtland's Warbler. As so few of these warblers now are in existence, it's possible that their disappearance altogether is one of the things one thinks and talks about here. This brought to mind an article on species extinction which appeared some time ago in *The Bird Watch*, the publication of the Bird Population Institute.

Basically, the article points out, extinction of a species is not new in the bird world. It has apparently always gone on, irrespective of the acts of man. The Merriam Teratorn, a large vulture, became extinct a long time ago all on its own, as did the LaBrea Stork and the Mamcalla, a flightless auk. From what paleontologists have learned from excavations through layers and layers of bone and fossil fragments, they now believe that the average life of any given bird species is about 500,000 years, and then it is gone forever.

Man, as just another condition of the environment, seems to be able to speed up the extinction process, at least to some extent. Certainly, he seems to have done so in the case of several instances such as the Passenger Pigeon and the Great Auk, but quite probably he is only speeding up the natural process and not the real cause of extinction.

124

According to an associated paleontological theory, the primary cause lies in the birds themselves. As a species gets older, it gets larger in size, and just before it becomes extinct, it very often reaches its maximum. From the layers of dirt and bones in the diggings, it has been found that just before the large species disappears, a similar, but smaller, species first appears which, subsequently begins to increase in size as the extinct species did before it.

From these opinions of the paleontologists several very interesting observations, if not conclusions, can be drawn.

Certainly many of today's rare, endangered

Great Auk

species are the largest of their genera or families. The Whooping Crane is the biggest crane; the Ivory-billed is the biggest woodpecker; the California Condor is the biggest vulture. The Passenger Pigeon and the Great Auk were, respectively, the biggest doves and alcids. Even the Kirtland's Warbler is among the largest of the warblers.

There are exceptions, to be sure. I don't think, for instance, that the Labrador Duck was a very big duck. But there is certainly enough evidence as to size to justify considering some additional hypotheses.

Why do species get larger? Research being done on Harris's Sparrows is beginning to suggest as a species settles into its chosen environment, it begins to set up social rules, dominance hierarchies and territories and to evolve into a larger size to defend these social rights. Bright, showy plumage shows it off and advertises its aggressive potentials.

White is the showiest color, and the Ivory-billed, the Whooping Crane, and the California Condor show more white than their near relatives. The Labrador Duck was very white, and the Passenger Pigeon was much brighter than the Mourning Dove. But granted that all this is true, why does the larger bird become extinct? This may be because of the smaller

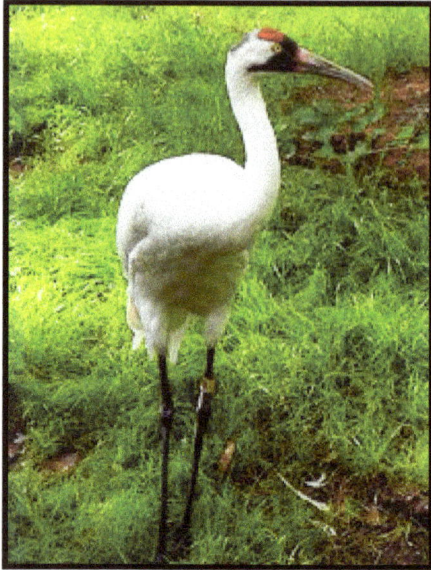
Whooping Crane

species which come in to fill the vacated niche. When the smaller bird can successfully settle in and maintain itself, it too will embark on its own evolutionary course of getting larger and showier to abet more aggressive advantage, thus amplifying the rate at which the older species evolves its larger size. Then, as the older species continues to grow larger, two things happen. It evolves into becoming more and more dependent on a narrower and narrower part of the food resource base available. The Ivory-billed Woodpecker became an insect-eating specialist on big, dead cypress trees in the middle of swamps. With this limitation, it also became more and more inflexible, narrow and inefficient so that it lost the ability to adapt to the changing environment. No longer could it adjust to rainfall or temperature changes or to the loss of its favorite food source. Since the environment is constantly changing with or without the help of man, the older, larger, showier species become extinct, and the young, quiet species take over. The meek inherit the earth.

All of this makes a good deal of sense to me, but even if these theories should prove to be entirely correct, they should not provide a complete salve for our consciences. For man, by his rapid changing of the environment, has brought several species close to extinction. The most notable of these is certainly the Peregrine Falcon, which now, maybe, is being rescued by the heroic efforts of just a few people. So even if we know why species die a natural death, we must still be very careful about making drastic changes in our environment.[28]

August 12, 1992: I wonder how many of us, other than the inveterate birdwatchers, were conscious of the almost complete absence of bird song at Pinewoods on Higgins Lake in Michigan this summer.

126

Particularly this summer, with its very late spring, there should have been even more than the usual number of birds singing when we arrived in mid-July, but there were almost none. It was a scarily real "silent summer." Away from the Higgins area, when we looked for wildflowers or just explored the sandy back roads, there were plenty of birds singing – Wood and Hermit Thrushes and four or five species of warblers and vireos. Downy Woodpeckers were drumming. Blue Jays were screaming their warnings that "man" was on the way. Yellow-shafted Flickers bounded down the road ahead of us. Swallows and others were after insects over the open fields.

But at Pinewoods, it was ominously quiet. One Great-crested Flycatcher called from the highest tree tops. Only two pairs of robins nested near our cottage and one other at the dining hall. There were two or three Black-capped Chickadees and one Palm Warbler and one Nuthatch, probably a White-breasted, and that was all. There were no other flycatchers or warblers, no woodpeckers or vireos, no thrushes singing off in the distance, no jays to wake us up in the morning. I sadly missed the delicate little "Where's Elizabeth?" song of the Brown Creepers. There were no Song Sparrows working through the weeds and grasses at the lake shore and now and then popping up to sing from a taller stalk and not a sign of the wonderful Pileated Woodpeckers which are such a thrill just to watch.

Cedar Waxwing

By early August a lone pewee wandered in to call plaintively from above, and three Cedar Waxwings. rather than the usual dozen or more, were hawking for insects out over the lake but, except for this, it remained quiet – very, very sad and frightening.

Is it possible that BT, that supposed "non-lethal except to gypsy moths" spray kills the birds outright and directly as well as indirectly by starvation?[29]

127

NANTUCKET

October 15, 1969: Nantucket Island in the fall can be very exciting. Small enough – fourteen miles long from east to west and between three and six miles wide – so that any part of it is readily accessible. Regardless of the weather, whether you are interested in birdwatching, scenery-viewing or fishing, there is never a dull moment.

One of the most interesting birding spots is what is known as The Mothball at the end of Hummock Pond Road on the south shore. On the maps, this area is designated as Cisco Beach. It was here in the old days, when whaling was Nantucket's principal activity, that a whale watching station was manned to alert the sea captains of the leviathans arrival.

Watching the ocean from there for shearwaters, we saw a sperm whale come to the surface to "blow" several times. Shearwaters are pelagic, gull-like birds which sail over the ocean surface with very little wing flapping, banking on stiff wings in the wave troughs. We saw a steady, although widely interspersed, flight of Cory's Shearwaters, the largest in the East, and at least one Banks, one of the smaller of this family and quite rare on the Atlantic coastal waters.

The Mothball itself is about two hundred yards back from the shore. An acre of Japanese black pine has been introduced to protect its exposed shorelines with many clearings, both large and small. As the only area of its size and kind on the south shore, in the fall the migrating songbirds seem to gather here in greater numbers than at any other place on the island. The birds coming across from the north have a natural tendency to congregate to restore their energies before heading out over the open ocean.

During the week we were there, we saw seventeen species of warblers, including a Mourning which is rare on Nantucket. The individual and species numbers varied from day to day, but there was never a time when we couldn't find at least a few. Almost every time we stopped, there would be Red-breasted Nuthatches, Brown Creepers and Golden-crowned Kinglets working around the branches.

A cold front which went through one night brought a big influx – White-throated Sparrows, many Baltimore Orioles, Brown Thrashers, Red-eyed and Solitary Vireos, Ruby-crowned Kinglets, Rose-breasted Grosbeaks and, very surprisingly to me, a Dickcissel. One doesn't really expect to find Dickcissels so far east of the Great Plains, but they are apparently gradually spreading this way.

Edith Andrews, Nantucket's foremost ornithologist, conducts an extensive bird banding operation at The Mothball. It is aimed to a large extent at determining what birds come there, how long they stay and their condition upon arrival and leaving. We spent the better part of one fascinating morning with her.

Rose-breasted Grosbeak

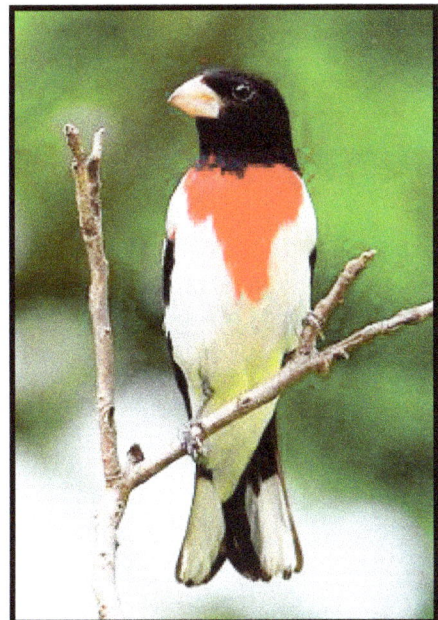

Mrs. Andrews has cut several narrow paths through the woods and along these she sets up her mist nets. The caught birds are transferred to carriers which she has made by sewing leather bottoms to mosquito head nets. They are just about the right size for the birds to move about without damaging themselves. All of her handling and record-keeping equipment is kept in the trunk of her car. The carriers are taken there and hung from a board, sometimes as many as a dozen at a time.

As each bird is taken from its carrier, it is first banded and then its plumage is examined to determine its sex, if this is not otherwise

129

Ruby-crowned Kinglet in a banding net

apparent. Next, its wing length is measured with calipers. This can help determine its sex and age. Then it is placed in a paper cone, head first, and weighed on extremely accurate scales. When it is taken out of the cone, Mrs. Andrews blows on its breasts and belly feathers to spread them apart to find how much fat the bird has. This is readily discernible as small yellowish globules under the skin. Lastly, she wets the feathers on its skull and spreads them apart to determine whether the skull has ossified. Then the bird is released. At one time during the morning, a young man who had been watching this whole examination, remarked, "That bird must think he's being drafted!"

The weighing and fat determination is important for Mrs. Andrews' primary purpose. When the birds arrive on the island, they are generally without fat and their weight is down. These both build up as they rest and eat in The Mothball.[30]

October 22, 1969: One of the things that surprised me most on this trip was the plumage of the Blackpoll Warblers. In the spring, these birds are neatly striped black-and-white with a solid black cap. In the fall, the black cap has gone. The birds are olive-green above and yellowish below, with darker streaks on their backs and the sides of their breasts. Except for the back striping, they are like fall Pine Warblers which I assumed them to be until Mrs. Andrews pointed out my error.

Coming back on the ferry from Nantucket to Woods Hole, for almost half of the two-and-a-half hour trip, we were being passed by a large, strung-out flock of Blackpolls. They were apparently cutting across from Monomoy Point on Cape Cod to the Massachusetts and Rhode Island mainland.

The fall shorebirds on Nantucket can also be very exciting. Several years ago near The Mothball, I saw my first Ruff, but this year the birding at that spot was disappointingly poor. Another easily accessible place for shorebirds is the Cut at Smith's Point at the southwest tip of the island. While we were there, a Pigeon Hawk, diving after a Sanderling, missed coming into our Jeep window by inches as the Sanderling veered off.

No birder should miss Great Point or Eel Point even though they can be reached only by a four-wheel drive vehicle equipped with beach tires. Great Point is the long sand arm that stretches to the north-northwest from the eastern end of the island. The drive out over its six miles of beach can of itself be quite an experience. We went out one day when there was a very high tide and a strong wind blowing from the east. There was room for the Jeep only high up on the beach. Even then, we were sometimes running through swiftly breaking waves.

Around the tip of the point and back on its western somewhat protected side, there is a tidal lagoon which is a favorite place for shorebirds. I think this year we caught just the tag end of the migration, but there were still large flocks of Sanderlings. I counted ninety-nine standing shoulder-to-shoulder facing into the wind as we went along the edge of the lagoon. We were constantly putting pipits into the air. We came back in late afternoon across the Gauls, an extensive area of flat beach between the dunes at the end of the point and those that come out from the main part of the island. There were between two and three hundred Black-bellied Plovers nestled down for the night in the short vegetation covering the sand.

Their heads popped up everywhere to watch us as we drove by. I believe that it is out here that the Piping Plover nests in the summer.

Great Point is also the nesting place for all three of our Atlantic Coast terns – Roseate, Arctic and Common. In the fall, however, the terns are more inclined to be at Eel Point, the northwest tip of the island. Here, as they sat on the beach within a few feet of the Jeep, we were able to pick out each of these hard to distinguish birds.

Sanderlings

The Roseate has long tails sticking out behind their folded wings, the Arctic has much shorter legs, and all the rest are the Commons.

There were also Dowitchers, Semipalmated Sandpipers, Yellowlegs and Black-bellied Plovers out there. Everywhere we were surprised with the high proportion of Great Black-backed Gulls. They seem to constitute about twenty-five percent of the gull population other than the Herrings.[31]

October 29, 1969: As fascinating as the Nantucket shoreline and its birds are, the moors and the heath hills are equally enchanting. To me, they have a certain eerie quality at all times, but especially in the early morning before the mist and fog have dissipated. On the south shore, the gently rolling moors are predominantly covered with hawk nests and savanna grasses. Out there, Short-eared Owls and Marsh Sparrows fly ahead of you before veering off to pop back into the grass.

In the lower areas where there is some protection from the ever-present salt spray, woody shrubs grow in dense patches. Here and there are Rufous-sided Towhees and catbirds. You can startle deer in there, too. In the three freshwater ponds that run back from the south shore – Long, Hummock and Miacomet – Mute Swans have moved in to nest. A few Canada Geese and Black and Wood Ducks can almost always be found. Green-winged

Rufous-sided Towhee

Teals are probable breeders in the marshes. Of course, many species of ducks winter there or just off-shore, particularly eiders and scoters. Sharp-tailed Grouse were introduced about three years ago and appear to be doing quite well. We put up several as we drove across the extensive moors.

The heath hills in the central eastern part of Nantucket, in the area known as Saul's Hills, are certainly unique in New England and

132

Nantucket's autumn moors

maybe so in the entire United States. I know of no other area even closely approximating them. A walk through this part of the island will show circular colonies of one kind of heath plant or another – Hudsonia, Cladonia, Bearberry and Bayberry. They may be ankle-high or waist-high, each started from as little as one seedling. Then, they grow to a round cluster, a foot across. As the circle enlarges, it will almost always be composed of many plants. Low blueberries and huckleberries are often found in the large circular colonies.

In the fall, each plant seems to turn a different color so that the hillsides are covered with separate circles, large and small, of deep red, yellow, orange and purple with much bright green in between. Some circles show a mixture of color. From any vantage point the effect is startling and, to me, quite beautiful. This is especially true of the view from Altar Rock, one of the high points on the island. It alone makes the trip to Nantucket a great success.

One of the dirt roads into Saul's Hills goes through an area known as the Hidden Forest, a maple swamp containing more different vegetation than any other place on the island with totally different colors in the fall. Surrounding much of the heath hills is a dense scrub

133

oak forest. None of the trees are very tall because of the constant wind. These woods were alive with Rufous-sided Towhees, migrating flickers and warblers which we couldn't identify. Just to the south of the hills is an extensive cranberry bog.

It is hard to realize that so much interesting terrain is crowded into such a small area. Exploring Nantucket in the fall is a most enjoyable experience.[32]

Cranberry bog

BERMUDA

June 18, 1969: Bermuda Island consists of lanes bordered with pink and white oleander, formal gardens lined with trimmed hibiscus hedges and flower gardens crammed with pink and white petunias. Coral pink houses with white roofs are guttered to catch the rain water. Sparkling white sand beaches tuck in under the limestone cliffs. It is also motorbikes, White-tailed Tropic Birds, which Bermudians call Longtails, European Goldfinches and Bermuda Petrels or Cahows. Whistling frogs call "gleep, gleep, gleep" all night. Glass-bottomed boat trips are available to see some of the hundreds of ship wrecks lying on the offshore reefs.

It is an island fast approaching population saturation. There is a total lack of land for expansion purposes and a consequent scarcity of wild areas. Serious talk of filling in some of the reefs to make more land has begun. This makes for the potential of a weird and fascinating ecological problem if all the land is used up.

Nevertheless, there are a few wild areas, and there are birds. In the middle of the island is the Paget Marsh Nature Reserve. Twenty-five acres have been set aside to remain forever wild as they always have been. Here, one can still see the cedars, palmettos and the different marsh and mangrove plant communities which covered the island in prehistoric times and which have survived virtually undisturbed.

A walk through the reserve was fascinating and would be much more so to a botanist. The greater part is dominated by the Bermuda palmetto. Under this high forest cover, and totally dependent on the special ecological conditions which it provides, are the only small

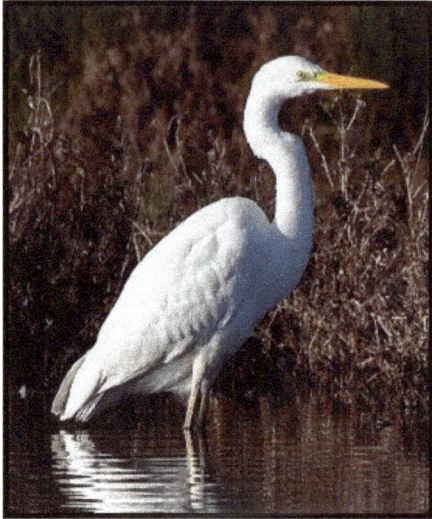
Common Egret

remaining colonies of Bermuda sedge and various types of grasses, ferns and mosses. Paget Marsh also is unique in containing a complete sample of all the stages of Bermuda marsh flora and a sizable mangrove swamp together with a considerable stand of almost the last surviving Bermuda cedars.

The Bermuda Audubon Society has acquired and maintains a sixty-acre sanctuary, known as Spittal Pond on the south shore to the east of the island's center. This area generally supports more water birds than all the other marsh areas combined. During stormy weather, sea water flows into the pond. The water level may rise several feet, and the pond becomes a bay. This disturbance apparently is the secret of the pond's unusually rich store of wildlife food.

The fall migration brings many more birds to Bermuda than in the spring but, in late May, Spittal Pond had a lingering Snow Goose, a young Great Blue Heron, just changing from immature white to adult blue plumage, a Common Egret, a Greater Yellowlegs, a male Ruff coming into breeding plumage and a Semipalmated Plover.

The most exciting natural history project is the proposed creation of a "living museum" on Nonsuch Island which lies in the mouth of Castle Harbour at the island's east end. This fourteen acre island has no safe harbor and is difficult to reach. Consequently, it has had little human habitation. Originally, it was privately owned and used for grazing livestock. Acquired by the colonial government in 1860, it was used as a yellow fever quarantine station and hospital. The mortuary and cemetery, so necessary then, can still be seen. After yellow fever was eliminated, the buildings were maintained by the government, but were uninhabited until they were loaned to the New York Zoological Society in 1928. It was here that William Beebe ran a marine laboratory and organized the famous bathysphere

136

descent. For fourteen years starting in 1934, the buildings were used as a school for delinquent boys. In 1948, this closed, and the buildings were abandoned. In 1961, David Wingate, warden of all of the Castle Harbour islands which were made a sanctuary by the government, took up residence there.

David Wingate conceived the idea of the living museum. He had found that the islands, being isolated, had remained comparatively untouched by all of the exotic introductions into Bermuda proper. This meant that an almost totally accurate representation of the prehistoric, native environment could be re-created by reintroducing the original plants and animals and by keeping the exotics from gaining a foothold.

This project now has been underway for about five years. Already some of the palmettos he has planted are more than four feet high. Non-native trees, such as casuarinas, have been planted as windbreaks but will be removed when they have served their purpose of protecting the seedlings of native flora. This obviously is a long range program. But if it is successful, its results should be most intriguing.[33]

Bermuda's shoreline

European Goldfinch

June 25, 1969: From a birding standpoint, Bermuda is interesting mainly for its transient and accidental visitors. There are only twenty-two resident or breeding species, but this is typical of small, isolated islands. Originally, hundreds of thousands of many species of seabirds nested on Bermuda. Being vulnerable to persecution by man, they all but disappeared three hundred years ago.

Only three species still breed there: the lovely White-tailed Tropicbird with its long salmon-on-pink streamer tail, a small colony of Bermuda Petrels, or Cahows, and a pair or two of Audubon's Shearwaters. Of the song birds, after the English Sparrows and Starlings which are common, the most numerous seemed to us to be European Goldfinches, with their red face patches and bright yellow wing stripes, along with Kiskadee Flycatchers, Cardinals, Eastern Bluebirds, Mourning and Ground Doves and catbirds.

Crows are scarce, probably less than one hundred on the island, and we saw only two Herring Gulls and three Common Terns. With the transients, however, the picture is different. More than three hundred have been recorded and about 125 are listed as "regular," the commonest being fall warblers and shorebirds.

In three sharply defined examples, Bermuda illustrates the results of man's interference with nature. Two of these are disheartening, but the third is a bright spot, even though its telling must end on a somewhat discouraging note.

The first example is the Bermuda cedar. Until the early 1940s, this was the dominant tree on the island. In 1943 or 1944, a local resident for reasons unknown, imported a batch of cedars from California. With them, by accident, came a scale insect. The native trees had no defenses against nor resistance to the scale. By 1952, the native cedar forest had almost

138

been destroyed. Only in a few isolated areas, such as the Paget Marsh, do living cedars exist. The skeleton forest of dead trees is the most prominent thing that meets the eye when flying in. It looks like a deciduous forest in winter.

The second example is even more disturbing because it was done consciously and not by accident. Around 1905, a small lizard – chocolate brown with a bright blue tail – was introduced into Bermuda to help control flies. It multiplied and to a great extent accomplished its purposes. Around 1945, a larger lizard of the same family was introduced, probably accidentally. About 1955, there was a demand on the part of some outspoken people to do something about the lizards, not because there were too many nor because they were harmful, but because apparently some people just didn't like lizards. Over the protests of many naturalists, the government brought in about two hundred Kiskadee Flycatchers from Trinidad. The kiskadee is a big, powerful bird – handsome, with a bright rufous back and wings, striking black-and-white head and bright yellow underparts. Almost the size of our Ringed Kingfisher, it will eat almost anything, including three and four inch fish. It has thrived and multiplied enormously on Bermuda. The lizard population is down, but it is not alone. Bermuda has been proud of its Eastern Bluebirds. They seem extra-special blue there, but their numbers are dwindling. The kiskadee sticks his big beak right into bluebird houses and plucks out and eats the chicks when they hatch. To stop this, people are building baffles into the houses so that the bluebirds have to go through a second partition to reach the nesting area. This works, but the kiskadees have been seen to pick off the young birds when they first come out of their houses.

Kiskadee Flycatcher

The Bermuda race of the White-eyed Vireo is disappearing. It builds its nest near the end of tree limbs. The eggs and young are ready-made food for kiskadees. The same is true of the Wild Canary which has been a Bermuda specialty for years. It is now difficult to find even in its favorite haunts. Kiskadees Flycatchers are exciting, noisy, spectacular birds in their proper environment, but it is a shame to see them wreaking havoc on Bermuda's song birds without any seeming possibility of control.[34]

July 2, 1969: My third example has a lot of romance. It is the story of the Bermuda Petrel or Cahow. Originally nesting by the hundreds of thousands on Bermuda, these birds are larger than Wilson's or Leach's Petrels which are known for their habit of following ships. When the first settlers arrived around 1600, it is estimated that more than 100,000 Cahows nested on Nonsuch Island alone. Their principal nesting place had been on the main island of Bermuda. But by about 1610, pigs released by Spanish sailors had destroyed almost all of these petrels on the main island.

Between 1614 and 1620, a plague of rats destroyed substantially all of the food on the island. The starving settlers ate all the remaining petrels and their eggs. After that, for more than three hundred years, the Cahow was regarded as extinct. In the early part of the twentieth century, however, occasional reports of these birds began to crop up. A skeleton was found washed up on a beach. The indications were that possibly a few birds still existed.

In 1951, an expedition led by Dr. Robert Cushman Murphy and Louis Mowbray relocated the breeding grounds on a few of the very small islands in Castle Harbour. David Wingate, then a very young man, and the late Fred Hall of Buffalo were also members of the

David Wingate and a Cahow - early 2000s

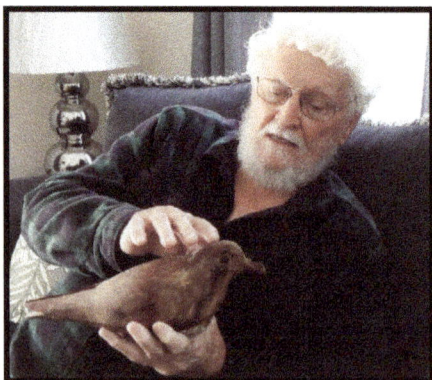

expedition. Since that time, David has been the patron saint and guardian of the birds. Fortunately, the outer islands are very difficult to land on. Consequently, even before they were officially established as sanctuaries about eight years ago, there was little interference with the birds.

When they are near land, the Cahows are completely night-flying and will not even come ashore to feed their chicks if there is a bright

140

moon. Also, they dig very long, deep burrows for their nests. These burrows are six or seven feet long with the nest hollow at least two feet below the surface. As part of his program to save the birds, David Wingate has built burrows himself with removable tops so that he can observe the birds and the chicks. The nesting season runs from March to early June. He tries to get out to each nest and make observations at least twice a day. Only very rarely does the weather stop him, even though waves may be practically breaking over the islands.

Cahows

When Dr. Murphy found the birds, there were less than ten nesting pairs. This year, twenty-two pairs raised young. One chick per pair is all they ever have. David Wingate estimates that there are now somewhere between only seventy and one hundred birds.

One serious problem has just arisen with which he cannot cope. Last year and this year, a few eggs proved to be infertile. On examination, it was found that the egg shells were soft. This had been the case with Ospreys and Peregrine Falcons in North America when these birds first began to feel the effect of DDT. An analysis of the embryos confirmed that they contained very high concentrations of this pesticide. The Cahow spends all of its life at sea coming ashore only to breed. All of its food comes from the ocean. Does the presence of DDT in the Cahow eggs mean that even our oceans are contaminated? If so, the Cahow is certainly doomed, along with many, if not all, of our sea birds. Hopefully, this is the wrong conclusion.

Only the future can tell. Happily, as many chicks were raised successfully this year as last, so at least for the moment the Cahow is holding its own.[35]

THE GALAPAGOS

M ay 21, 1969: Take five-and-twenty heaps of cinders dumped here and there in an outsized city lot, imagine some magnified into mountains, and the vacant lot the sea and you will have a rough picture of the Encantadas or Enchanted Isles. They are a group of extinct volcanoes rather than isles, looking much as the world might after a final conflagration.

"It is doubtful whether any spot on earth can, in desolateness, furnish a parallel to this group..." So wrote Herman Melville about the Galapagos Islands. I am sitting on the afterdeck of the S. S. Romantica as we sail from Wreck Bay on Chatham Island in the southeast corner of the Galapagos archipelago to Guayaquil on the Ecuador mainland. Reflecting on the very exciting last eight days, I couldn't disagree more. To me these islands are enchanting, rather than enchanted and, as so-called desert islands, unique.

Basically, the Galapagos Islands are all summits of volcanoes, rising as much as 10,000 feet from the floor of the Pacific Ocean. They are 600 miles off the coast of Ecuador and lie directly on the equator. There are five comparatively large islands, eleven smaller ones and over fifty rocks or islets. In geological terms, they are of recent origin. The oldest, those three lying to the southwest, are only a little over a million years old. Fernandina, the westernmost, still is active and has erupted twice since 1964. In land area, they cover about 3,000 square miles, over half of which is Isabela Island, the largest.

Entering the Galapagos Islands

The great Humboldt Current, which originates in the Antarctic, flows north along the western coast of Chile and Peru. It then turns west through the Galapagos, resulting in a considerably cooler climate than one would expect on the equator. We have not been uncomfortably hot except when walking through some of the coastal jungle areas.

These islands played a significant role in the development of Charles Darwin's theory of evolution. It was to a great extent the small finches on the island which brought him to the conclusions which were first published in *The Origin of Species by Natural Selection*. There are thirteen species of finches which have apparently evolved from one pair of birds which somehow reached the Galapagos centuries ago. Basically they are all the same, small black birds with short tails. But each species has a different shaped bill adapted to feeding on different plants or insects, thereby enabling each species to fill a different niche in the islands' ecology.

For example, there are ground finches with heavy bills for seed eating, cactus finches with sharp beaks for eating opuntia cactus, finches with beaks adapted for catching insects and the Woodpecker Finch which breaks off a twig or spine off a cactus and uses it to pry bugs out of small holes in the trees. Luckily, we have identified twelve of the thirteen species.

Magnificent Frigate, breeding male

Nesting female and her young

We landed first across the bay at Philips Landing, so called because Prince Philip landed there several years ago. We had to pull ourselves up a cleft in the cliff hand-over-hand on a rope fastened at the top. After this, I was more discriminating about the camera equipment I carried!

Tower Island is the nesting place of the Red-footed Booby. In this location, this bird is in its brown phase, a soft tan all over with bright red feet. In almost all other places where it nests, it is white with black wing tips. Tower is also the principal nesting place in the Galapagos for the Man-O'-War or Magnificent Frigate bird. This great black pirate with its seven-foot wing spread preys on the Boobies, forcing them to drop their food and catching it before it hits the water. On Hood Island, we saw one snatch the food from the mouth of a young Blue-footed Booby just as it was fed by its parent.

The male frigate in its courtship display is unbelievable. It sits on a low bush, blows up its blood-red gular, or throat sac, until it is over a foot across. It quivers its great outstretched wings, swings its head back and forth, and utters a curious moaning, winnowing sound, hoping to attract a female flying overhead. Most of the Galapagos birds are extraordinarily tame and to watch this display from a couple of feet away is amazing. Red-billed Tropicbirds, gull-like birds with two to three foot streamer-tails and bright red bills, also nest on the eastern end of the island. To stand in the midst of these hundreds and hundreds of frigates and hundreds and hundreds of boobies and to hear all their curious calls is a never-to-be-forgotten experience.[36]

May 28, 1969: Behind the beach and the small mangrove swamp which borders it, lies a strange twisted world of lava caves and craters of all sizes in reds, browns and grays. The ground is covered with plate lava which, as it cooled and solidified compressed into ridges that twist one way and another in series of parallel undulations. The last eruption here was less than one hundred years ago so very little vegetation, other than an occasional prickly pear or opuntia cactus, has gained a foothold. Although thin in spots, the plate lava makes walking relatively easy. Still, it can break beneath your weight and tumble you into a hole. Obviously the scene is bare but, rather than being one of desolation, it holds a strange, weird charm.

At James Bay on the western side, we spent a morning walking the rough lava shoreline watching the fur seals and the shorebirds – purplish-gray Lava Gulls, Brown Pelicans, Brown

Enjoying the Galapagos adventure -1969

Flightless Cormorant

Noddies, the little Lava Heron like our Little Green but darker, American Oystercatchers which are resident here, Wandering Tattlers and Semipalmated Plovers, late migrants on their way to Alaska to breed.

Inland, the scene is what the African veldt should be – flat, with mountains rising in the background, tall grass, acacia and other small trees and very easy walking. In a lagoon at the end of James Bay, there should have been flamingoes, but this is a wet year, and they have scattered. There were, however, White-cheeked Pintails, and here we got our first look at the Galapagos Hawk, a buteo about the size of our Red-tail, the only hawk in the islands. The Large-billed Flycatcher of the Myiarchus family is the only flycatcher here other than the Vermilion which occurs only at high elevations on a few of the islands.

Farther inland, there are great fields of raw, rough, jagged, sharp, cruel clinkers, twelve and fifteen feet high and virtually impassable without risk of falling and serious injury. But even this area is not without charm. We walked back in, looking unsuccessfully for the nest of the Galapagos Hawk in this wild jumble and came across a small tidal pool with little mangroves struggling to gain an existence. We were hot and the water was remarkably cool so, clothes and all, we went swimming.

What we had come to Espinosa to see were the Flightless Cormorants. They must have come to the Galapagos thousands of years ago as flying birds and became so adapted to aquatic life that they lost the use of their wings for flying. Like the Galapagos Penguins, they have changed characteristics because of their dependence on a particular environment. Their wings have atrophied and become much shorter. Still, as with all cormorants, when they emerge from the sea, they hold their tiny wings out to dry. In this pose, they look like bedraggled, moth-eaten birds in the moulting stage. The gaps between the few remaining feathers in their wings do nothing to enhance their appearance.

Swallowtail Gull

Fur Seal

Hooded Boobies

Sally Lightfoot Crab

Waved Albatrosses

Blue-footed Boobies

147

Galapagos Penguins

Between Fernandina, the easternmost, and Isabela, the largest, lies a long narrow strait. We landed at Espinosa Point on Fernandina, an outpouring of dark, black lava which juts out into the strait. If any of the islands conveys Melville's foreboding, this one does. Everywhere there are congealed forms of lava. Some is coiled and twisted like ropes. In other places, it looks like gnarled tree trunks. Walking on it produces a metallic sound as if we were walking on iron plates.

Also unique to the Galapagos are the marine iguanas. These large black lizards, some as long as four feet, have a heavy mane down their neck and back, long claws and a long tail. They are fearsome looking, like small dragons, but are actually quite harmless. They lie basking in the sun blending into the black lava rocks. All of a sudden you can be in their midst without knowing it. Their principle food is algae growing on the rocks at the low tide line. They are excellent swimmers, using their long tails to good effect.

Across the strait is Tortugas Point on Isabela. This is one of the principal breeding places for the Galapagos Penguin. One does not ordinarily think of penguins as living on the equator. This smallest of all the penguins came north long ago on the Humboldt Current and now lives in small numbers on most of the islands. They are very tame and a joy to watch as they hop from rock to rock. Swimming in open seas, they will "porpoise" in and out of the water like small dolphins.[37]

Marine Iguana

148

EAST AFRICA

May 13, 1970: East Africa's Serengeti Plains are incomparable. The national park occupies 5,600 square miles in Tanzania, stretching over a hundred miles south from the border and the Mara Masai Reserve. It is a vast, flat area, broken by rocky outcroppings covered with shrubs and trees. Standing at any point is like being in a boat in the middle of a vast, flat ocean. You can see to the distant horizon in every direction.

Many animals live in the Serengeti or migrate through it from Ngorongoro Crater on the east to the vicinity of Lake Victoria on the west. When we were there in early April, there were about 500,000 wildebeests and 100,000 zebras on the move. In another six weeks, there would be ten times that, with added numbers of gazelles and other plains animals.

Standing on a slight rise, you can see vast dark areas where there seems to be low-growing vegetation. On closer examination, however, these areas are herds of grazing animals. This great movement attracts its following of predators. We saw many jackals and scores of spotted hyenas. They dig shallow round pits to lie in during the day. Lions, leopards and cheetahs live in the rocks. We saw at least twenty lions that day including three beautifully maned old males. Our driver spotted a cheetah lying flat to the ground in a patch of low-growing ground cover with only its ears showing. It ran as we neared. We tried racing it, but it easily outdistanced the car.

Lappet-faced Vulture

All the carnivores were not mammals. We saw many of the huge Lappet-faced Vultures that day, feeding on the remains of kills and White-backed and Egyptian Vultures which I think are quite handsome with their black-and-white wings, long white wedge-shaped tails and slender yellow beaks. The real scavengers, however, are the Marabou Storks.

In a small marshy area, we found three more of the widowbird family – the Black-winged and the Red Bishop, both black birds with brilliant red heads, throats and backs, and the latter with red wings in addition. With them were Fan-tailed Widowbirds which look like our Red-winged Blackbirds. They fly the same way, hovering on thrust-forward wings with bright, shining red epaulets. Driving along the Seranera River at dusk, we saw the Verreaux's Eagle Owl, staring at us from its perch a few feet above the road.[38]

May 20, 1970: East Africa's Serengeti with its great hordes of animals and vast space is unsurpassable, but Ngorongoro Crater, lying about eighty miles to the east is almost as spectacular.

One of the world's biggest craters, or more properly called calderas, as it was caused by an implosion rather than an explosion, Ngorongoro is steep-sided, about twelve miles across one way and ten the other. The rim at its lowest point on the west side rises about 2,500 feet above the crater floor and is even much higher on the east.

To get some concept of its immensity, if the Adirondack's Whiteface Mountain were put in the crater, its 3,000' peak would come above the walls in only a few places. The descent

Ngorongoro Crater

road, although negotiable by only four-wheel drive vehicles, is fairly easy, but the exit road is something else. For about the first third of its length, it is a series of hairpin-turn switchbacks up the steep face. Then, it follows the general contour sometimes out over the wall and, at others, way back in deep canyons.

Verreaux's Eagle Owl

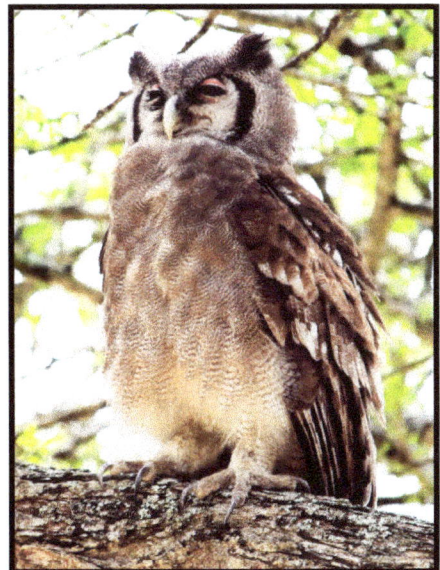

The floor of the crater is grassy plains with several brackish and fresh water lakes. The largest one was rimmed with an estimated 60,000 Lesser Flamingos in their bright pink plumage. In a small slough nearby were many species of ducks. I appreciated the Red-billed and the Yellow-billed most because they are so correctly named. There was one Pintail, a reminder of home and the Oak Orchard swamp. The rare bird of Ngorongoro, however, is the Rufous-tailed Weaver, an undistinguished bird, being mainly speckled brownish-yellow. It is a hard bird to see since it nests only here and in a limited area of the Serengeti.

151

Lesser Flamingos

Game animals are abundant in the crater, particularly in the winter months before many of them leave on a migration across the Serengeti. We saw lions, rhinoceros, buffalos, zebras, Grant's and Thomson's gazelles and elands. Driving across a very swampy area, using all four wheels, we found a great bull elephant who apparently wanted to use the same road to go the other way. We couldn't back up so we waited with the animal about twenty feet away, flapping his ears and trumpeting. Finally, after what seemed a really long time, he decided to go around us. It is a wonderful memory, even though a scary one.[39]

April 29, 1970: The Samburu-Isiolo Game Reserves are about 200 miles north of Nairobi off the northeast slope of 17,000 foot Mt. Kenya. Samburu Lodge, located on the Uaso Ntiro River, which bisects the area, is a delightful place, adequate without being fancy.

Before an afternoon game drive, mid-afternoon tea at the lodge's long porch overlooking the river is enlivened by the vervet monkeys trying to snatch the scones from your plate.

152

Egyptian Vulture

Red-billed Hornbill

White Pelicans

Goliath Heron

Kenyan Rock Agama

Sacred Ibises

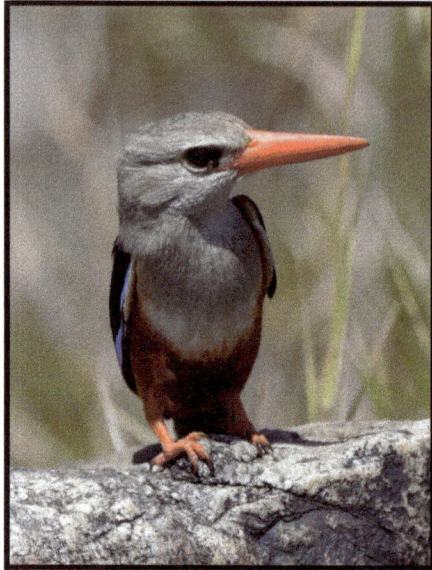
Gray-headed Kingfisher

In the trees, Gray-headed Kingfishers with their red bills and bright blue backs must be among the most photographed birds in the world. This is a wild and little visited area where traveling is rough. Except for a few widely scattered little villages, the nomadic tribes here have changed little over the centuries. One morning, we came upon a Samburu elder, wearing only the traditional robe. He had three-inch rings in his open-lobed ears and carried a long spear as he checked his cattle.

The country is almost as dry here as Tsavo, south of Nairobi. But at Tsavo, the general aspect of the land is flat. The thornbush, scrub and acacia vegetation is about the same. Here, however, the landscape is rugged splendor. A few miles to the north, a sheer cliff rises 6,500 feet above the savannah. Somewhat smaller, not quite so spectacular, mostly square mountains ring the area in all directions.

Our first day at Samburu, I was sitting on the porch of our cabin when I became aware of movement on the ground nearby. Looking over the railing, I saw a big flock of bright red, tiny Red-billed Firefinches feeding on the ground. They stayed a while and then were off in a flash of color against the green background. They were soon replaced by a pair of pretty fearless Red-billed Hornbills, scruffing up the ground for grubs.

On the game drive that afternoon, we got our first look at one of the African warblers, a Buff-bellied. This is an entirely different family of birds than the North American highly colored wood warblers. They are in the family Sylvidae, whereas ours are Dendroica, and are related to the flycatchers and thrushes. In the technical order of birds, they come between the flycatchers and the swallows. They not only are called Warblers, but also Apalis, Crombec, Eremomela, Camaroptera and Cisticola. Almost all of them are pale brown birds with puffy under parts and no distinctive markings. We looked at them in the

154

fine collection of birds in the Nairobi Museum. Even there, practically in the hand, they are very difficult to tell apart. One of their two distinguishing features is their tail length. The Crombec, for example, has substantially none. They are best identified by their voices, behavior, habitat and distribution, and this takes a lot of learning.

There were bright colored birds in the field that day, too. The Purple Grenadier – what a great name! – has a rich cinnamon-red head and bill, a black tail and in between is a brilliant cobalt-blue rump. The Black-backed Puffback is a member of the shrike family, with a downy patch of feathers on its rump which rustles in the breeze. The Secretary Bird is, I think, unique in that it is the only bird in its family. It is almost four-feet tall, with long legs. It stalks about in the open country looking for snakes and rodents. Its name comes from its long crest feathers which resemble quill pens stuck over its ears. We saw one on its flimsy nest atop of flat top acacia. Nearby, a white-breasted bird perched on top of a thornbush. As we got closer, we determined it was a Pygmy Falcon. This tiny falcon, only about half the size of a sparrow hawk, is not very common. It uses the nests of the Black Buffalo Weavers for breeding.[40]

Pygmy Falcon

Secretary Bird

Purple Grenadier

TRINIDAD

June 4, 1972: Trinidad is a big island, roughly rectangular in shape, about fifty-five miles from north to south and a little over thirty miles east to west. It lies near the delta of Venezuela's Orinoco River, just ten miles off the South American coast, and was at one time, ages past, part of the continent.

If I remember correctly, the only thing we were taught about Trinidad in school was that it was a big island in the southern Caribbean with the world's only natural asphalt lake. When we were there in March, we visited Pitch Lake. More than a hundred acres of dirty black tar with little patches of scrubby vegetation, it is singularly unattractive.

We stayed for two weeks at the Asa Wright Nature Center. Certainly the principal ornithological feature of the center itself is the Guacharo, or oil bird, colony. As Don Eckelberry, the noted bird artist and one of the center's trustees, writes, "If you can imagine a hawk's beak on an earless owl's head attached to a large rusty goatsucker's body, you have a Guacharo."

A half-mile walk down a steep, slippery ravine, through lush, green jungle brings you to the deep pitch-black cave where these birds roost during the day. The last short stretch of the walk is along a nearly horizontal, thirty-foot ladder over a chest-deep stream. This would be a real circus trick if it were not for the narrow passage between perpendicular walls, close enough to reach out and balance yourself. The Guacharos are completely nocturnal and fly out only at night to search for palm fruit which is their main food. The

156

young are very fat and used to be collected by the natives and rendered into oil, hence their English name.

When a flashlight is shone on the birds in their daytime cave, they flap their three-foot wings, their eyes reflecting bright red, and utter loud, ear-piercing screeches which echo weirdly about the cave walls. There are very few of these colonies left.[41]

June 11, 1972: Asa Wright Nature Center is more than a cave full of oil birds. Surrounding our house are brilliant hibiscus and bougainvillea bushes. In the quarter of a mile or so of open area below the main buildings, there are banana, grapefruit, tangerine trees and cocoa and white-blossom coffee bushes. Mango trees, with their broad, pinnate leaves, and matchwood trees rise a hundred feet on branchless trunks.

Birds are everywhere. Rarely can you look up without seeing Turkey and Black Vultures soaring on the thermals created by the clearing and, above them, a Black Hawk or two, the white bands across their tails plainly visible against the cerulean blue of the sky.

Below them, above the tops of the tall trees, Yellow-tails, or cornbirds, fly back and forth. They are crow-sized birds of the Oriole family, all black except for bright yellow beaks and brilliant yellow tails. They build their hanging nest high in the uppermost branches of the tallest trees. Their odd, squealing "hee-hawing" goes on all day long. Sometimes you see their courtship antics. They spread their wings and bend way forward on their perches so that their heads are below the level of the branches where they are sitting and their bright tails flash above them.

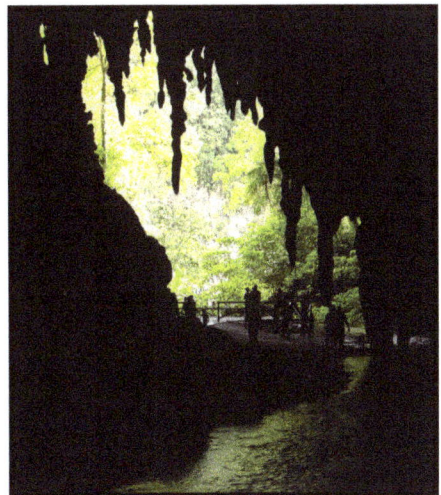
Guacharo Cave Entrance

Another all-day caller, surprisingly enough, is the little Pygmy Owl. Their easily imitated

Pygmy Owl

"whoo-whoo-whoo" notes are most handy in calling in many other birds which fly in to mob their enemy. Kiskadees are everywhere and, once in awhile, a Boat-billed Flycatcher joins the throng. The Boat-bills grating "kriss-kriss-kriss" is very different from the constant screeching of the kiskadees. Just above the lower treetops, little Spine-tailed Swifts whiz by, having no trouble in finding their insect prey.

There are tanagers in the tops of the smaller trees. The lovely Blue-gray has bright azure wings fading into overall blue-gray coloring. The Silver-bill is velvety red with a brilliant silver beak. The Gray-green has blackish wings and a most un-tanager like squeak for a song, and the Palm nests under the eaves like a House Sparrow. The Parson male is all black except for white inner wing coverts which flash when it flies. The female, always nearby, is a rich chestnut brown.

While sitting quietly in the shade of the big mango trees, I can see and hear a variety of birds. Smooth-billed Anis, the same birds that are around Lake Okeechobee in Florida,

Blue-gray Tanager

work their way through the grapefruit trees, their long tails flopping loosely and seemingly about to become disconnected from their bodies. Cocoa Thrushes come by. They get their name both from their coloring and because they prefer the cocoa trees. Their dawn song, in which they are joined by the Bare-eyed Thrushes, sounds almost exactly like our dawn chorus of robins.

Yellow-breasted Peppershrikes sing even in the heat of the day from deep within the smaller

158

trees. Their clear warbled song always seems to confuse us. The little vireo-related Hylophila flits about singing its distinctly vireo-like song. Off in the far distance, the slow, descending notes of the Ochreous-bellied Woodhewer provide a constantly pleasant background.

Up the steep bank behind the house is a large bed of spiked, purple-flowered vervain. This is hummingbird heaven. Tiny Tufted Coquettes, two and a half inches long, compared to our Ruby-throats at four inches, buzz from flower to

Bare-eyed Thrush

flower like big beetles. They are generally bronzy-green with a white band across their lower backs. The male has a high chestnut crest and white-tipped green tops on the sides of its neck.

Common Emerald Hummingbirds, bright iridescent emerald green with white leg feathers, are there with reasonable regularity throughout the day. In comes a Ruby Topaz, with a brilliant scarlet crest, an equally brilliant golden throat – an extraordinarily vivid bird. Once in awhile, a big Black-throated Mango flashes by, bronze-green above and blue-black below, with a long, slightly decurved bill. Even less frequently, there is a Green-throated Mango, very similar except that it has a green throat. In the early morning, a Hairy Hermit, with very long, very decurved bill comes in to feed. Once or twice, there is a Brown Violet-ear, plain brown except when the sun catches its shiny, purple ear patch.[42]

June 18, 1972: We hiked down the "trace," which is what the natives in Trinidad call a path, below the Asa Wright Nature Center across the citrus-planted clearing near the house. Suddenly, we were in a totally different world – the tropical jungle. Not a rainforest, but a vast expanse of forest just below the level of semi-constant moisture.

The foliage is very dense and, except for rare clearings, there is little light. The human eye does not recognize this readily because it has the ability to compensate for it by dilating

159

Bearded Bellbird

the pupil. But the difference is immediately seen on a camera light meter. All of a sudden we were taking pictures at five or six stops less than was the case only a few feet away.

In a jungle such as this, there are two distinct levels, or stories, of foliage. The upper story consists of branchless trees between 100 and 150 feet tall. I do not pretend to know the names of many of them, but there are sipps, fine-grained and excellent for woodworking, cecropias, also called trumpetwood because of their hollow stems, mahoganies and the tall immortelle.

Traces lead in many directions through this jungle. Some of them are very narrow and overgrown, while others are wide and almost roads, obviously the remnants of old paths to now-abandoned cocoa and coffee plantations.

One of the most interesting and elusive birds which inhabits this tropical jungle is the Bearded Bellbird. Robin-sized, it is grayish white with black wings, a coffee-colored head and a black throat. From its throat hang numerous string-like waddles which are up to an inch or more long, giving the appearance of a very scraggly beard. Its voice is the real fascination. I find it close to impossible for me to put it into words. It is supposed to sound like an anvil being pounded with a hammer and has somewhat the resonant, carrying quality which that would produce. But there the similarity stops. The best I can do is to say it sounds like a series of very loud "tung-fung-tung" notes, followed by a crashing noise which I can only describe as "graaaack."

We first heard the bellbird late one afternoon, and I followed the sound for a long way into the jungle, seemingly getting closer to the source. Having come to the conclusion that it was not a bird at all, but some giant tropical frog, I gave up. A few days later, we saw the

Chachalaca or Cocrico

Laughing Gulls

Owl Butterfly

Motmot

Red-crowned Woodpecker

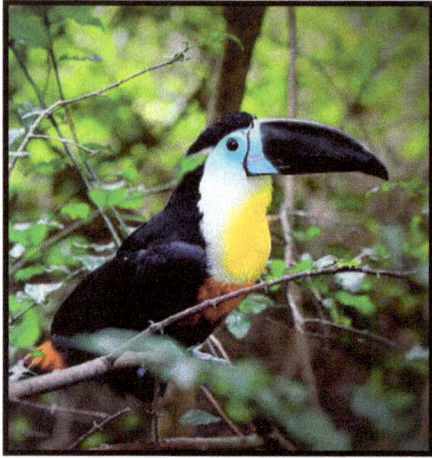

Channel-billed Toucan

bird, several in fact, in the next valley to the east of Arima where the center is located.

Several times we saw Channel-billed Toucans flying over the jungle. These crow-sized birds seemed almost prehistoric as they fly by, with very long, deep black bills. Once, one perched in the open, and we could get a better look at that monstrous beak. The bird's coloring is remarkable – black above with a bright crimson rump and a yellow and orange breast. In spite of its initial grotesqueness, it is definitely a handsome bird.[43]

Trinidad shoreline

OBSERVATIONS AND OPINIONS

April 23, 1969: A little more than a year ago, the wildlife sanctuary at Hawk Mountain in Pennsylvania was sprayed with pesticides, dylox and sevin, in an effort to control gypsy moths. The effect was devastating. For days after, there was no insect life. For the entire summer, the bird population was almost non-existent. And the gypsy moth continued its spread beyond the sanctuary.

The spraying had been done by the state, over the vigorous protests of Hawk Mountain officers and members and evoked a flood of letters to the Pennsylvania legislature. As a result, a Pennsylvania Senate special committee was constituted to investigate the matter. The committee held hearings last summer and fall and published its findings early this year. It recommended the establishment of an advisory ecological board of review whose primary function would be to make studies and reviews of all the major environment changing activities occurring in the state. A few weeks ago Hawk Mountain was advised that no further gypsy moth spraying was planned for this year. This fight may be on its way to being won.

In a somewhat similar situation, a major confrontation is under way in Wisconsin. Groups of conservationists have petitioned the Department of Natural Resources to ban the use of DDT in the state. This hearing has been under way for some time with the chemical companies which manufacture the pesticides about to present their case. The decision here could have far-reaching effects. While there is no way to tell what the ultimate ruling may be, some indication may be gathered from a technical bulletin put out last year by the

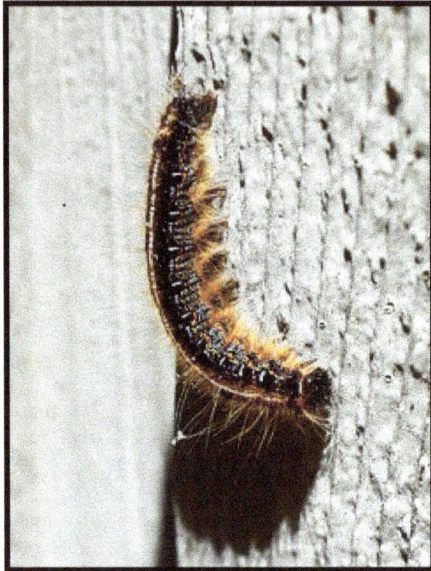
Gypsy moth caterpillar

Department of Natural Resources which stated in part, "The use of any persistent pesticide which includes DDT remains a calculated risk. Science has already shown chlorinated hydrocarbon pesticides, the family to which DDT belongs, to interfere with fish reproduction, behavior and hereditary factors. Further, these residues may be harming animal life in many subtle ways, which will only become apparent through intensive research. To continue the use of DDT in the face of the present level of contamination would seem to be an invitation to disaster."

These two instances, and other similar ones, certainly indicate a growing awareness of what may be happening to our natural world and a willingness to go to bat to stem the increasing pollution of our environment.

In the same vein is the desire to save wild lands from the inroads of our civilization. Along these lines, one of the very finest conservation programs which has been undertaken in this area is the acquisition of property at El Dorado Shores by the Nature Conservancy. This property, which comprises two hundred fifty acres and about 3,600 feet of shoreline, lies at the eastern end of Lake Ontario, a few miles south of Henderson Harbor. This rocky, seaweed covered shore is one of our more important shorebird stop-offs on the fall migration route.[44]

July 23, 1969: A news release out of Texas indicated that the Army Corps of Engineers, with the advice of the U. S. Department of Agriculture, planned to sterilize 2,300 acres of Texas grasslands by using thirty pounds of 10% dieldrin an acre – a total of 69,000 pounds. Dieldren is one of the most vicious of the chlorinated hydrocarbon pesticides. The acreage to be poisoned was near San Antonio on the San Antonio River, only one-hundred-fifty miles from the Gulf of Mexico, and even closer to the Rio Grande and a very definite part of the Gulf watershed.

The stated reason for the poisoning was to control the fire ant. The fire ant, an import into the United States from Argentina, is admittedly an unwanted insect. It builds large mounds on farmland, occasionally kills young birds and has a vicious sting. But experience has shown that it can be easily controlled by individually treating mounds with poison. Broadcasting the poison doesn't even work.

Several years ago, tens of thousands of acres in the southeastern states were sprayed with DDT and dieldrin for the same purpose. In many areas, 73% of all wildlife was eradicated. There were stories of poisoned cats, dogs, and even calves. Children had to be kept indoors. And the fire ant lived happily on. The states involved finally refused all permission for more spraying.

The news release started a storm of protest. Late in June, this release was followed by a second which named the acres to be treated and gave a totally different reason. The area is Kelly Air Force Base and the purpose is to kill all living animals (except, hopefully, man) in the area to prevent possible importation of insects by planes coming in from foreign countries, particularly Vietnam.

1973

This is at best an equally foolish reason for the poisoning. Planes from foreign countries are landing all over the United States every day. Many government officials fly to Vietnam and back from airports other than Kelly. An insect escaping from a plane landing at Kelly may not conveniently alight there. It can easily fly or be blown to some other area. 2,300 acres is

165

not all that big. And planes have been coming in from Vietnam for the past six or more years. Certainly, this would be locking the barn door after the horse is stolen.

Nevertheless, with a lethal poison, we propose to sterilize 2,300 acres of Texas. It could be argued that, for a good reason, we can afford to lose this land if that's all there was to it, but it isn't. Apparently, no thought has been given to the probable effect of the release of this huge quantity of vicious poison on the rest of the country and the world. It is certain that it won't all stay in that 2,300 acres. Some of it will become airborne on dust particles. Not so long ago a fallout of dust on Cincinnati was found to contain chlorinated hydrocarbon pesticide sprayed in Texas. Much of it will eventually work its way into the rivers, to the Gulf of Mexico and into the oceans of the world.

Already DDT has been found in seals and penguins in the Antarctic, in Cahow Petrels in Bermuda, in marine fishes far out at sea and in salmon in Labrador. How many tons of fine edible fish protein will this new dose poison and for how long? Crustaceans are particularly susceptible to chlorinated hydrocarbons. What will happen to the great Gulf jumbo shrimp beds?

Most importantly, what will be the effect on us? We need oxygen to breathe and live. Oxygen, however, doesn't just exist. It isn't something that just happens to be floating around in the atmosphere in limitless supply waiting for us to breathe it. It has to be produced. It is created by the photosynthetic process in which green, chlorophyll-containing plants remove carbon dioxide from the atmosphere and return oxygen. These green plants are not only the trees, flowers and grasses we see around us, but also of major importance the marine diatoms in the ocean.

Over half of the oxygen necessary for life on earth comes from these ocean organisms. No one knows what the effect of long exposure to increasing amounts of persistent chlorinated hydrocarbons will be. Already there is evidence that the present concentrations of DDT in the ocean are interfering with photosynthesis in diatoms. Will it injure their oxygen release capabilities? The future of man's existence on this earth may hang on the answer to this question. It's time we stopped taking chances with it! [45]

August 20, 1969: Amchitka is an island in the Aleutian chain about 250 miles east of Attu. Acanthaster planci, also known as the Crown of Thorns, is a starfish living in the South Pacific. These two have a terribly frustrating and frightening connection which goes far beyond either of them.

Amchitka is a sizable island, forty-two miles long and four and a half mile wide. It is the

Crown of Thorns starfish

nesting place of seabirds – murres, murrlets and auklets, gulls and eider ducks. There is also a small colony of the almost extinct Aleutian Canada Goose and a small population of Peregrine Falcons. Once in a while, Sea Eagles, Whooper Swans and other Asiatic bird species wander over there. It is also one of the principal breeding places of the sea otter which is making a real comeback from almost certain extinction.

The Fish and Wildlife Service has done a lot of work on Amchitka in recent years, mainly in eradicating the introduced blue fox. It has mounted an effort to remove the effects of the World War II depredations of the U. S. military forces and restore the island to its former status as a major bird breeding ground.

Amchitka is also the site of the Atomic Energy Commission's upcoming underground nuclear explosions. These will be the most powerful this country will have ever made. A blast of one megaton yield, the largest ever set off in the Nevada desert, is scheduled for October of 1969 to see if the island can withstand the shock. Much larger, probably double or more, detonations are planned for 1970 and 1971, if Amchitka is still there. Although the possibility is denied by the Atomic Energy Commission, many responsible people feel that the explosions could trigger a series of earthquakes not only in Alaska where Anchorage was badly hit in 1964, but also as far south as southern California.

These tests can no longer be conducted in Nevada because of danger to buildings in cities, remote as they may be. Because of the possibility of "venting" – the release of radioactive gas and debris into the atmosphere – which happened once in the Nevada tests, there is

167

an even greater danger of some kind of subterranean venting where radioactive debris can get directly into Pacific waters. Either way, the real possibility of further nuclear contamination exists.

The Crown of Thorns starfish has always been a member of South Pacific marine communities. It devours live coral by a process of ingestion through the walls of its stomach. Wherever the starfish have grazed, the coral surface is bleached white and lifeless and breaks into rubble under the action of the sea.

Until a few years ago, its still unknown natural enemies kept its numbers under control. Then in 1966, it underwent a major population explosion. With the killing of the coral which forms protective reefs, the low-lying sandy Pacific islands are exposed to the battering of storm-driven waves. In time, they will disappear as livable places.

Already the starfish have destroyed ninety percent of the coral reef which provides wave protection and the source of fish along the northeastern shore of Guam. Even the Great Barrier Reef protecting Australia is threatened. It is difficult to imagine the disappearance of the beautiful Pacific atolls but, unless controls are found soon, it could happen.

Nuclear weapons testing is the foremost suggested cause for the present overwhelming numbers of the Crown of Thorns. The delicate balance of nature which kept them under control is upset by excessive atomic radiation.

So, there you have it. We are changing further radioactive poisoning of the oceans by setting off underground nuclear bombs in Alaska. At the same time, we are trying to save the Pacific islands from the possible after effects of earlier blasts. Is it impossible to think these things out ahead of time? Must we try to run in all directions at once? Should we take care of our present problems before we chance creating new ones? If the earth survives for a future historian, he may well look back on today as a time when we were all mad. I think he could well be right.[46]

August 26, 1970: One of the most interesting and encouraging aspects of the Environmental Conservation Department's hearing on the proposed ban on the use of certain pesticides was that almost no one said the ban is wrong. There were questions about specific pesticides. There was concern that the licensing system might be too cumbersome. It was pointed out that we might have to put up with occasional wormy apples. The general consensus seemed to be that we do have a pesticide problem, and that it is real and serious.

It was, therefore, a distinct shock to find a most extraordinary document in the mail – a copy of an article by Donald A. Spencer. The general theme was that overall environmental benefits come from our present use of pesticides. He claims that many segments of our environment are better today than they were forty years ago. I find this quite incredible. Maybe Dr. Spencer hasn't looked out his window on "clear" nights to notice that our Milky Way is disappearing from view. I think that's scary.

I have met Dr. Spencer. At the time of the hearings in Harrisburg, Pennsylvania, on the use of pesticides at Hawk Mountain and vicinity, Dr. Spencer appeared as an independent consultant, along with representatives of chemical and agricultural interests. He opposed any letup in aerial spraying. His article is divided into four parts. On three of them, I do not have sufficient knowledge to comment, although I have some ideas. On the fourth, however, I have some definite thoughts. Dr. Spencer states that there has been no "Silent Spring." In support, he points out that the U. S. Fish and Wildlife Breeding Bird Surveys recorded nearly a million birds in 1968. What he ignores is that we are concerned with the quality, not just the quantity, of our bird life.

It would no doubt be possible to record a million birds by just counting blackbirds, but this fails to recognize that the numbers of many of our songbirds – warblers, for instance – are way down. The start of this decline coincided with the first uses of DDT.

Dr. Spencer cites increases in some game bird populations as evidence that pesticides do no harm, completely overlooking that, in most instances, continued restocking is necessary to maintain the numbers. He points out that the Endangered Species list mentions pesticides as a contributing factor in the decline of only four species, the California

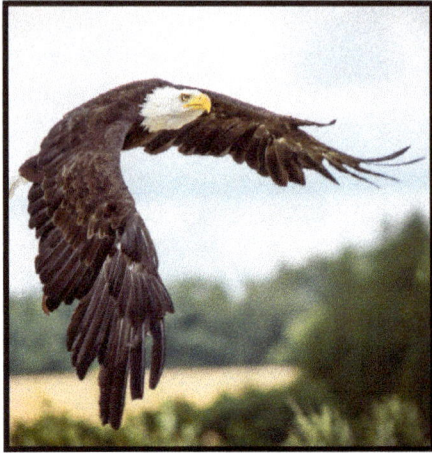
Bald Eagle

Condor, Bald Eagle, Peregrine Falcon and Osprey. He then flatly states that these birds had been declining for a long time before organic pesticides came on the scene. This is just plain false. The Ospreys had no problems at all before DDT, and the other three birds suffered only from the inroads of our civilization and then only slightly compared with the post-DDT catastrophies.

Lastly, he uses the Hawk Mountain records as evidence that hawks and eagles are increasing. In fact, Hawk Mountain Sanctuary publications have pointed out that this apparent rise is due to increased hours of observation and not more hawks. Dr. Spencer, being a Hawk Mountain member, must have read this and has simply chosen to ignore the truth. If the balance of his article is as inaccurate as the chapter on birds, and I suspect it is, then the whole thing may be consigned to that limbo where this type of reporting belongs – alone and forgotten.[47]

December 3, 1978: For the past three years, in cooperation with the Laboratory of Ornithology at Cornell, eight-week-old young eagles, not yet ready to fly, have been put "out to hack." The hacking procedure is an old method developed by falconers to enable young hawks to learn to fly and hunt on their own while still remaining basically wild. The birds are placed in an open box atop a pole or tall stump. Food is raised to them on a long stick and dropped over the side of the box. They cannot see their human provider and thus do not lose their instinctive fear of man but continue wild. When the birds begin to fly, they venture into the nearby countryside where they instinctively attempt to hunt. This is difficult for them without the example of their parents to follow. They can return to their box at night. Gradually, as they develop their flying and hunting skills to the point where they can be on their own, the box roost is taken away.

170

Under the Cornell program, two eagles were put to hack in 1976. Both learned to fly and hunt. One returned in the summer of 1977, and again this year. In 1978, five more were put out. All learned to fly and fend for themselves, and one of these came back this year. Four were hacked out this year, and all of them are now on their own. They have left the refuge, presumably having gone south. With the Finger Lakes and Montezuma programs now having consistent and apparently effective hacking, we hope we will again have the great Bald Eagle breeding successfully in western New York.

Several weeks ago, I reported on the record flight of Broad-winged Hawks at Hawk Mountain Sanctuary in Pennsylvania. Now I have figures for all species through November, almost the end of the southward flight. It was truly a memorable fall. The flight of close to 22,000 Broad-wings in September will never be forgotten. The curator of the mountain counted 8,000 in forty minutes at mid-day.

The thirty Bald Eagles flying south were better than in the past several years, and maybe one of the immatures was a Montezuma bird.[48]

Peregrine Falcon

Osprey

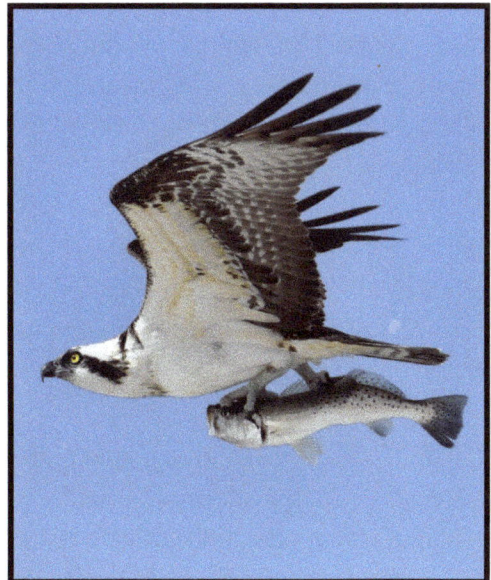

171

November 11, 1979: Among birdwatchers there is a growing interest in bird behavior: Why do birds do what they do when they do it? As with all animals, we have studied the behavior of birds and gained knowledge, yet there are still vast areas of mystery which may never be fully explained.

One set of questions concerns migration, a facet of bird behavior which still is considerably shrouded in mystery. Why do birds go south every fall and return every spring? How do they navigate so precisely?

Possible answer to "why" may go back before the Ice Age. Then, the Arctic and northern climates were warm and birds lived there year round. Later, the ice came and forced the birds south. When it finally melted, birds followed the retreating glaciers back to their ancestral nesting sites. Thus today, birds go through this ritual annually, instinctively reminded of the ancient cold by the chill of our present northern winters. But there is still no explanation concerning how they return to the general area which they had left six or seven months before, much less to the exact spot.

What about the hummingbird which returns to the feeder you hung out last year, whether the feeder has been hung out yet or not? We know now that there are several means by which birds find their way, including celestial navigation and the magnetism of the magnetic poles, but certainly much of the accuracy must be just plain memory of visual landmarks.

Why, for instance, do birds sing? About half of the world's roughly 9,000 birds are classed as songbirds. If you examine your bird guides, from flycatchers to sparrows to longspurs, you will learn that all of them have songs of sorts. The other half of the birds can croak, chuck, grunt or hoot, but cannot sing.

Generally, only the males sing, and they do so mainly to define and defend their nesting territories. A battle of songs takes the place of a physical combat. Because almost all songbird species differ in their food and nesting requirements, birds' territories are defended only against others of the same species. Many species co-exist within any given area.

172

Male birds also sing as part of their courtship rituals to woo their mates. Once the pair bond is established, singing probably serves to strengthen it and to improve reproductive success. Also – and this will be a delight to those who just enjoy birds as they are, without wondering how or why – birds apparently sing, too, just for the joy of it. That mockingbird singing from the television antenna in the moonlight keeping the whole house awake as his song reverberates down the chimney is just enjoying himself!

Birds apparently are not born with the ability to sing. They can make noises, but they must learn the songs from their parents. Experiments have shown that young birds taken from the nest and raised in isolation can make only rudiments of their song. Birds kept isolated will stimulate one another and come up with songs which have little or no resemblance to those of their wild counterparts. On the other hand, young birds isolated after their formative months, when they have listened to adults sing, know the proper songs.[49]

November 25, 1973: An article in a recent issue of *The Explorer,* published by the Cleveland Museum of Natural History, points out the problems of many endangered species of birds and mammals, particularly relating to the destruction of their natural habitats. When the first explorers from Europe landed on this continent, whether they were the Norsemen under Eric the Red or the pilgrims at Plymouth Rock, stretching before them they found more than three million square miles of majestic wilderness, wilderness literally alive with wildlife.

Today, almost all of that vast wilderness is gone, fallen before the onslaught of the descendants of those first settlers. Only about one-and-a-half percent remains. Very little of that is in its pristine state. At the present rate of destruction, what does remain may be gone before the end of this century. Yet, in spite of this almost incredible destruction of habitat, the largest part of the original wildlife has survived and survived in good numbers. From the standpoint of the birds, at least before the widespread use of DDT in the early 1950s, I think it is safe to say the populations of most bird species have suffered very little.

173

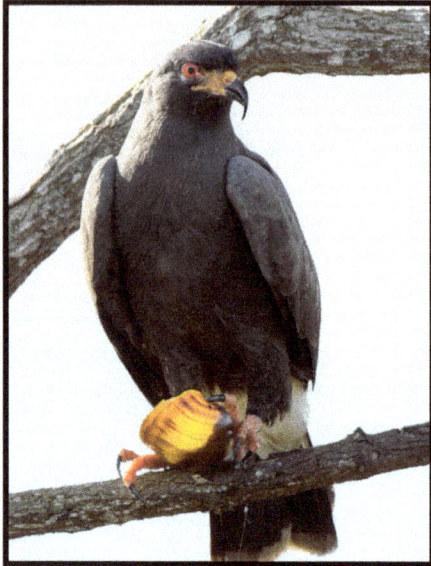
Everglade Kite

About thirty years ago, it was reliably estimated that in the United States alone, the summer, pre-breeding number of birds was between five and six billion. To a considerable extent, these species had maintained close to their original numbers because they had not lost their adaptability to changes in the environment. They had not become specialized.

Long term natural selection – the survival of the fittest – does not favor specialization, and those species which do become specialized are flirting with extinction, especially when this specialization is combined with less habitat. Our list of endangered bird species contains many examples of specialization of one kind or another. Consider, for instance, the Everglade Kite which has become so specialized in its feeding habits that it eats only one species of snail found in a few locations in the Florida marshes. If these marshes are drained, the snail will disappear – and so will the kites. Or take the Whooping Crane which needs the particular features of the south Texas coast for its wintering grounds and is confined to the very small Aransas Refuge. Already the crane population is beginning to be limited by the confines of the refuge.

Kirkland's warbler breeds only in the jack pine country of northern Michigan and there only when the trees are the right height. With the rapidly increasing inroads of civilization and modern fire fighting methods which prevent forest fires and thus the explosion of the pine cones necessary to spread seeds, their territory is disappearing all too fast.

What can be done about all this? We cannot, of course, reverse the effects of specialization. But it may not be too late to set aside as yet relatively untouched areas for these birds. The case of the Dusky Seaside Sparrow is an excellent example. For many years, it was believed that these birds bred only on Merritt Island, halfway down the Florida coast. Then

174

came the Florida land boom, compounded by the Space Center at Cape Kennedy at the tip of the island. With the marshes drained, the duskies population went from 2,000 to less than 35 pairs – almost a total wipe-out. Then a colony of about 1,000 Duskies was found north on the St. Johns River. Immediately, the Federal Bureau of Sport Fisheries and Wildlife moved to acquire this area. When it ran out of money, a private conservation organization stepped in to retain the balance and hold it until the bureau had the funds to take over again.

So the special habitat can be saved if we have the willingness to save it. We must save all we can.[50]

Writing the "Bird Report" - 1979

175

Attu, Aleutian Islands, Alaska - 1972

176

RETURN TO ALASKA
June 1972 and May 1978

Seeking to augment his formidable life list, in 1972 Joe returned to Alaska – this time to the far reaches of Adak and Attu Islands in the Aleutian chain. He birded there alone for two weeks and was remarkably successful. Attu became such a popular birding spot in the following decades that, in 2010 when the Coast Guard Station closed, access of the island to birders was greatly restricted.

After leaving the Aleutians, my brother Joe and his wife Pam joined him for two more weeks. They took their search for new species to the familiar territory of the western Alaskan mainland.

Scott Weidensaul's interview for *Bird Watcher's Digest* examined his trip to the Aleutian Islands: "Joe Taylor knows the difficulties – and the joys – of personal discovery firsthand. In 1972, he spent several weeks on Attu at the end of the Aleutian chain, a flyspeck of land in the Bering Sea. Attu is famous among birders for the Asian migrants that pass through each spring but, when Taylor arrived, it was *terra incognita*. Only one other birder had spent any time on the island, and that was in the fall.

"'In all, I think Attu was my best birding experience, because it was totally new. I didn't know what birds I was going to see, there were no guides. It was great,' he says. His first stop was Adak, about four-hundred-fifty miles to the east where he found Whiskered

Gray-spotted Flycatcher

Auklets, as well as Spotted Redshanks and a Bean Goose, both Asian species. 'Then I went out to Attu and got my 700th North American species, a Gray-spotted Flycatcher,' Taylor says, smiling at the memory. 'I got a couple of Smews, Common Sandpipers, a Greenshank, and Wood Sandpipers.' These Eurasian birds were like gold to a lister.

"'It was as close to wilderness as there was in this world,' he recalled. 'There was the Loran station with thirty-eight guys and one dog, and that was it. Most of the guys never left the building unless they absolutely had to. I was totally on my own. You look at Attu on a map, and it's a pinpoint, but when you get there, it's forty miles long and thirty wide, all mountains and cliffs.' There was lots of ground to cover, lots of birds to find. Each morning at 5:00, Taylor made himself breakfast in the station's kitchen, slipped a sandwich into his coat pocket and headed out, averaging ten miles a day on foot.

"But explorers, almost by definition, pave the way for others. Six years later, Taylor returned to Attu. This time with his wife Helen. They found three organized birding tours on the island, and people everywhere. 'It was nowhere near as much fun, even though I did see more birds,' he grouched." [58]

Bean Goose

178

As usual, Joe kept journals of these trips:

May 26, 1972: The plane was about four hours late leaving Anchorage, so I arrived at the Adak Naval Station late. Flying in, I was surprised at how much snow there was as we flew over the lower part of the Kuskokwin Delta. Until very near the coast, most of the ponds and little lakes on the delta appeared to be covered with ice. We saw none of the Aleutian peaks partly because we were too far north and because, I expect, they were cloud-covered, as Adak was when I arrived. I was brought over to the Bachelor Officer Quarters where I have a nice room.

May 27: It is a beautiful clear morning. I've seen several Bald Eagles from my room, gliding by against the snow-covered mountains. Hank Haggard, my host, picked me up about 10:00, and I was with him all day. We went first to Havens Pond, a small marshy pond not very far north of the naval station. Then on to Clam Lagoon which is a very large lagoon with shallow water, mud flats and deep water. We found Pelagic Cormorants, a European Wigeon and various ducks, gulls and terns. Out beyond the lagoon is the island dump. Literally, there were Bald Eagles by the dozens. We counted fifty-four. I had twenty in the field of my binoculars at once. Most of them are young birds, the ratio of young to old being better than ten to one.

Immature Bald Eagles

We visited Finger Bay, south of the naval station which is very long and very narrow. During World War II, it was the only submarine base in the Aleutians. The water is deep enough so submarines and other deep-draft ships were able to dock. We finished the day at Lake Andrews, an artificially-made lake, where I saw two Wood Sandpipers. They were scaly, with unstreaked backs and crowns, rusty, spotty breasts and longish yellow-green legs. During the war, the Navy built a sea wall across the wide lake entrance to keep the water relatively

179

Great Sitkin Volcano

level and to reduce the action of the tides so that it could be used as a seaplane base. A problem today is that you cannot walk out from the road across the sea wall toward the beach because it was heavily mined. The mines have never been removed. This can be true anywhere on this island.

May 28: I was on my own and did some walking. For close to three hours in the morning, I walked out toward Finger Bay. In the afternoon, I walked along the wharves built out into Kuluk Bay where the birds were in close to shore rather than out in the middle of the bay. I saw one Bean Goose – number 694 – on the water and flying near the underpilings of the wharf. It is smaller than the Canada, dark brown on top of its head, a paler brown face, a bill with some orange and a little white in its tail when it flew. Also, there was a Horned Puffin and two Whiskered Auklets – number 695 – both of which are not common on this side of Adak. From there, I walked out to Bayfront where there is a nice, sand beach, but there were literally no birds. I was a little weary after four hours of walking when I returned to my BOQ about 5:00.

Both yesterday and today were cloudless. Great Sitkin, the almost 11,000 foot high volcano about twenty-five miles to the northeast, has been beautifully clear. It is an active volcano so there is always steam coming out of the crater near the top. It rises out of the mist around its base and is quite spectacular.

May 29: A misty morning rain cleared around noon. I again walked out to Finger Bay, but there were not many different birds. Along the way were seemingly endless Lapland

180

Longspurs and many immature eagles soaring overhead. In a little cove off Kuluk Bay, I found a Kittlitz's Murrelet – number 696 – still in winter plumage which makes it much easier to identify.

After lunch, I walked out to the wharves again. Out at the end of the stone jetty, there was a sea otter. It was difficult to see because of the fog, but I could hear it crunching clam shells. Once in a while, I could see it lying on its back and eating them. After seven and a half hours of walking, I was tired.

May 30: Another clear, cloudless day. I spent the day at Clam Lagoon. Every time I glanced around, there was Sitkin off in the distance. Low tide was about noon so, in the early afternoon, I could walk all the way across the lagoon flats. Certainly, the bird of the day, and maybe the bird of the trip, was the Spotted Redshank – number 697 – generally dark purplish, its back spotted with white, a white-barred tail, white rump and eye-ring, a very thin bill and dark red legs. I really hadn't expected to see anything along the main road out to Comsta because there was a noisy, dusty grader working on the road. Then I heard a strange shorebird call and the redshank flew and landed about fifty feet in front of me where I could get the telescope on him. He was very cooperative. Later in the afternoon, I was walking the shore and looked up to see what looked like a great swarm of vultures circling above. It was twelve Bald Eagles!

Spotted Redshank

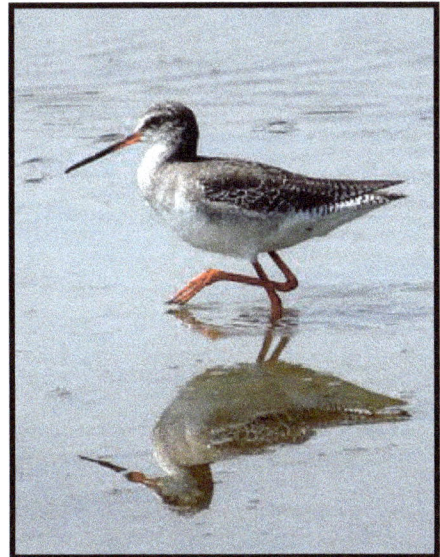

May 31: It was a very foggy morning. I walked from Havens Pond over the hill past Lake Andrews to the Comsta boathouse on the far side, about seven-and-a-half miles. The fog didn't clear so I didn't see very many birds.

June 1: The fog cleared, but it was very windy. I was driven out to Heart Lake on the high tundra about four miles to the west of Navsta,

181

Smew

the Navy Station, only about a mile from Shagak Bay on the far side of the island. I had hoped to walk over to the bay, but the gale winds blowing directly from that direction made it just about impossible. There were no birds on Heart Lake, so I walked over to Lake De Marie which is a lovely lake down in the hills. It provides part of the water supply for the Navy Station. If there were any birds on this high tundra, I didn't see them because of the wind. I walked downhill with the wind on the way back to town but, when walking uphill, it was very difficult. I had to lean backward to keep from being blown on my face.

June 2: I flew from Adak to Attu and arrived in the late afternoon. It was a lovely afternoon with temperatures up in the sixties. I stayed at the Coast Guard Loran Station with a room of my own, small, but totally adequate. Following an early supper, I walked out to the beach. The first thing I saw were two Common Sandpipers – number 698. Their call is completely different from Spotteds – a somewhat quiet "whit, whit, whit," their legs are greenish yellow and, of course, they do not have spots.

June 3: I walked the rocky beach out all the way to Murder Point, a good five miles. Formed by the point on the east is Casco Bay. Off its point is a small island with Tufted Puffins, Red-faced Cormorants and two Smews. In the early evening, I wandered up the Peaceful River which empties into Massacre Bay about half a mile from the station and found a White Wagtail near some abandoned buildings.

June 4: I was driven about three miles down the beach and then inland to the Henderson Valley at the lower edge of the snow fields. I found several Rock Sandpipers – number 699. Not uniform in coloration, they are quite reddish on their backs with only small black centers and their legs are pinkish-brown. Some have breast spots, and others do not.

June 5: A very foggy, misty day, apparently typical of Attu. Walking along the beach again, I was soaked even though it wasn't raining. So, I went back to my room to wait for it to clear.

June 6: It still didn't clear. It rained until noon and was very windy. Because of the weather, this was a lost day so far as birding goes. The birds couldn't possibly get about in the fog and wind. I wandered around the tundra for a while, seeing nothing but a Snowy Owl and Snow Buntings. It is remarkable how they do not seem to mind the wind at all, but everything else is tight to the ground.

June 7: The morning, as usual, was cold, foggy, misty, rainy and windy. There was a bit of sunshine in the afternoon. I was sensible today and wore my raincoat, but below the bottom of it, I was soaked within five minutes. I walked around Casco Point again. I saw a Gray-spotted Flycatcher – number 700! It was flying back and forth catching insects below a high bank where there was shelter from the wind. It is a small bird, brownish-gray above, white below with very noticeable dark streaks on the sides of its breast, on its flanks and across the upper part of its breast to the base of its bill.

At the back end of Casco Cove where there were always more birds than anywhere else, a Red Phalarope female flew out from the kelp and landed on the water about twenty feet away. At the very end of the cove, I had just begun to watch a Rock Sandpiper when a Peale's Falcon appeared overhead and made a dive for it. It dove twice, nailing it both times.

Breeding female Snow Buntings

June 8: A little spitting rain early, but mostly a lovely, partly cloudy, warm day. I was driven to Point Alexei, but only reached part of the way because the road had washed out. Walking along the beach, I saw another Gray-spotted Flycatcher, a little paler than the first. It was working about in the tall grasses back from the

183

the beach. This time, it was singing or calling – a thin, kinglet-like call, but longer, "seeeeeep."

This is a lovely part of the island with only a narrow flat between the high cliffs and the beach. Except for a couple of large buoys which had washed in, there was no man-made junk. On my walk, I found three Common Sandpipers, two Winter Wrens and large flocks of Harlequin Ducks.

When I went out again after dinner, I found a Greenshank – number 701 – a large shorebird. Only thirty feet away, I could see it had green, not yellow legs. Compared to a Yellowlegs, it was a very gray bird with a long, very slightly upturned bill and a smudge across its breast. When it flew, I could see its white rump and back.

June 9: Cloudy, rainy and foggy again. I walked out around Casco Point and cove for the last time and found nothing unusual. The afternoon was the worst weather during the week I was on Attu. The plane came in late for me. We flew off for Shemya where I was put up for the night at the Airforce BOQ.

June 10-12: I got in to Achorage on the 10th after a routine flight from Shemya. It was a little exciting landing in Amchitka with the ceiling at absolutely zero. On the 11th, I picked

Casco Bay

184

up a rental car, did some personal chores like greasing up my leaky boots, and went to the airport to pick up my son Joe and his wife Pam. On the 12th, we picked up our camping equipment and drove down to see Portage Glacier and the Kenai Peninsula almost as far as Kenai Lake.

June 13: We are at Cape Krusenstern on the Chukchi Sea coast about halfway between Kotzebue and Kivilina. We flew with Nelson Walker, an excellent bush pilot, who told us

Dunlin

there was an old, abandoned airstrip here where he could land. There was nobody within miles, and there should be birds. It looked absolutely wonderful. He was right. I don't think I have ever seen so many Long-tailed Jaegers concentrated in one place. Looking out at the tundra at supper time, we could see six at once. There are not as many shorebirds as there were five years ago at Hooper Bay because it's a dryer tundra, but there are many Dunlins and Semipalmated Sandpipers.

We camped on a long strip of tundra between a long lagoon on the east and the ocean on the west. There is ice on both sides of us. The ocean ice pack extends as far out as you can see. It is just beginning to break up. In the lagoon, the ice appears to be solid, except for a narrow open strip along the shore. So, we are surrounded by ice, but the tundra ponds are pretty much ice-free.

June 14: It was an absolutely beautiful day, cloudless. We are using melted snow for water. The wind off the ice keeps the temperature down. The ground here is very level. We are camped on a slight rise built up by wave action on an easy slope down to the lagoon.

I am surprised to see both Hudsonian and Bar-tailed Godwits. There are many Long-tailed Jaegers hovering in the air like Sparrow Hawks or coursing low over the spring tundra. The ducks are principally Oldsquaws. They have a most peculiar call, like a little doll being

185

punched – "ung, ung, unguuh, uuh, uuh" – all sorts of odd squeaks.

Much of the tundra here is very dry, making for easy walking, with some very swampy wet spots, but relatively few birds. It is a very pleasant place to be, absolutely quiet, but it would be a little better if it wasn't so cold.

June 15: The weather wasn't too bad in the early morning, but then it began to rain, quite hard at times. We stayed in Joe and Pam's tent until it stopped, and it became quite warm. When we went out, I almost stepped on a Long-billed Dowitcher which got off its nest right under my feet. We had a good look at Parasitic Jaegers doing a broken wing act and, by chance, found their nest – two eggs in a small depression in the tundra. I followed a very small bird for quite some time this afternoon along a row of stunted scrub willows. I turned out to be a Blackpoll Warbler. It was odd to see it way out here beyond the tree line, but they do breed south of here along the Kobuk River.

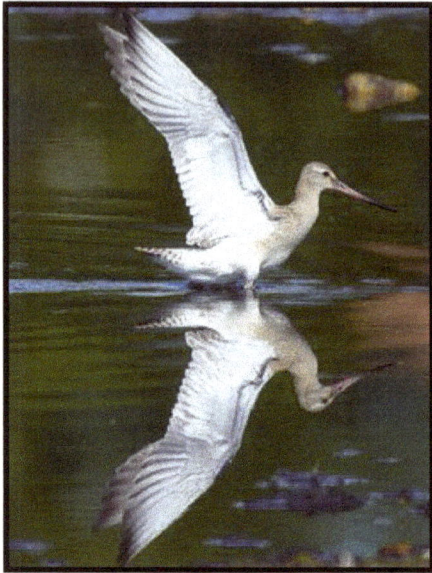

Bar-tailed Godwit

It is amazing how much the ice has moved out from the shore in just a couple of days. The tundra ponds are now completely clear. There is a wide open space between the shore and the ice and many leads in the ice pack, but the lagoon is still frozen.

June 16: When I got up this morning, the fog was so thick you couldn't see a hundred yards in any direction. It cleared some during the day and then fogged over again.

We walked about the marshes and sloughs for the better part of the afternoon, despite the fog. The bird noises were fascinating. The cries of the Glaucous Gulls we could hear all the time. They are typical gull calls. At least every fifteen minutes, cranes flew over. They do not have the "krop" call of migration. Rather, it is a high-pitched gabble. The quacking of the Red-throated Loons, like Mallards, is pretty consistent. In the distance, we could hear the almost whistled calls of the Arctic Loons and the trilling of the Dunlins and the Semipalmated Sandpipers. Mixed in is the high-pitched "yip" of the Long-tailed Jaegers. Along with all the rest are the "zee zee" half songs of the Savannah Sparrows and the tinkling, lark-like songs of the Lapland Longspurs, mostly sung on the wing.

June 17: Nelson Walker came back to pick us up in his plane. There was a strong wind blowing at right angles to the little runway. There was a real question whether he would be able to get in, landing crosswise. He landed very slowly and only went about ten feet on the ground. He was concerned about taking off with the weight of all three of us and our equipment. So, he decided to do it in two trips. Joe and Pam and their bags went first and then, about fifty minutes later, he came back for me, and we got off easily.

Wales was fogged in so we spent the day in Kotzebue where Joe made us a reservation at the Drift Inn, next to the airstrip. It was very nice and quite modern. We spent the afternoon wandering around town and did a little shopping at the Kobuk Valley Jade Company store.

June 18: The weather had cleared at Wales. We flew off about eight with Nelson's pilot Warren and landed on one of those old mesh airstrips. He was able to taxi down a little dirt road to the beach so we didn't have to carry our stuff too far. So, we are now camped in the sand dunes about half a mile from the runway.

After setting up camp, we walked several miles on the tundra side of the dunes. Essentially, we were looking for the Mongolian Plover because that would be a good place to find it, but we had no luck. The area was alive with Red Phalaropes and a few Northern Phalaropes. I watched the Northerns do two things I had never seen before: one was spinning around on land, absolutely dry land, just as if it was in the water and the other was flying up like a flycatcher to catch insects out of the air.

I came back to camp before Joe and Pam. When they returned, they said they had seen a plover on a slightly different route. I went out to look at it and, sure enough, it was a Little

Little-ringed Plover

Ringed Plover – number 702. I could easily see the white stripe all around its crown, and very pale pinkish legs. When it flew, it had no wing bars.

June 19: I awoke to very thick fog. It was a very, very cold damp morning, so I put on all the clothes I had. We obviously couldn't go up the mountain, so we decided to walk into town. We had an absolutely delightful time. The Eskimos were very friendly. They all seem to speak English which they didn't do five years ago when I was first here.

When we got back to our camp, we dug a pit, got some driftwood and built a fire. Why we haven't done this before, I don't know. We were reasonably warm with the fire. It also served to dry out our boots and socks which had been soaked walking on the soggy tundra.

June 20: Today, we climbed Wales Mountain. Looking at the contour map when we got back, we found we were up over 1,400 feet. We found several Rock Sandpipers and, as we climbed higher, more Westerns than Semipalms. There were at least six Red-throated Pipits.

Even the weather cooperated. We were up on the mountain for a good five hours. With the climbing and moving around, we were quite warm for the first time. At night, we were cold again, but we had a good fire going because there was less wind.

June 21: It began to rain again in the early morning. Not hard, but enough to get everything really wet. We decided to try the east half of Wales Mountain which lies on the other side of Village Creek. The creek flows down between the two halves of the mountain. This terrain was very open, barren of plant life, dry and gravelly – a series of stone benches made for pretty easy going.

About two hundred feet from the summit, I climbed around up to the north and put up a pair of shorebirds. They flew off with a whistled call, turned high overhead and then came back toward me. I followed one with binoculars, and it came in very close. It was a Great Knot – number 703 – overall gray. I could see its white rump, a very spotted breast and a stocky bill. It came within forty feet of me and then flew around the mountain to the west.

There was really very little life of any kind up there. I did, however, see one Horned Lark and, farther down, a pair of Rock Sandpipers. Weather-wise, it was a very pleasant day. Being sheltered from the wind on the east side of the mountain made all the difference in keeping us warm.

June 23: In the morning, Nelson picked us up. We flew to Kotzebue because Nome was fogged in. The fog cleared after lunch, and we took an Alaska Airlines plane to Nome. We talked with birding friends about the Dotterel which had been seen in the mountains north of Nome and made a plan to try to find it the next day.

June 24: We went after the Dotterel on the mountain – no luck. But I was sure that it was there. We camped right below the mountain on the Nome River. We tentatively planned to try again the next day, although it was a long way up through very soggy tundra and a massive tangle of willows.

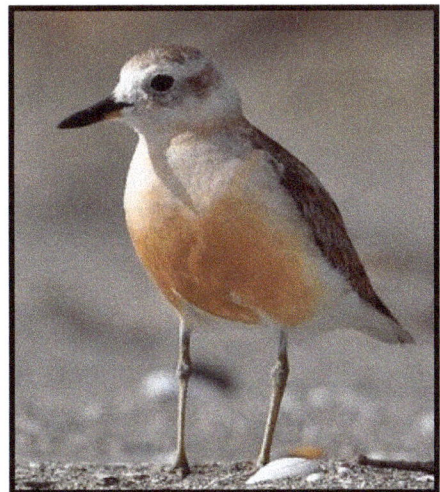
Dotterel

The singing chorus of birds near our campsite was lovely. In the willows at the base of the mountain, we heard Arctic Warblers, Gray-cheeked Thrushes, Fox and Tree Sparrows. White-crowned and Golden-crowned Sparrows, a few Northern Waterthrushes and Lapland Longspurs flew along the river. Overhead, we watched Arctic Terns and Glaucous-winged Gulls.

June 25: Today, we found the Dotterel. By chance, Pam and I were walking the wet tundra

Arctic Tern

way up, and the bird flew out from under Pam's feet. I hadn't thought to bring the big camera, but I was able to get within eight feet of it to get some fair photos. We were at about 1,400 feet, and it was a long way back.

After lunch, we broke camp and went back into Nome. Then we drove out toward Council, past Safety Lagoon, only to find that the ferry across the outlet was not yet operating. So, we turned around and drove west and camped about thirty miles west of Nome on the Sinuk River. It was a very pleasant evening even though it did rain again while we were cooking.

June 26: We spent most of the day in airports in order to fly to Fairbanks where we rented a large, pretty uncomfortable truck. We got the truck because the Hertz people had already rented all of their cars big enough to handle all of our gear. Leaving Fairbanks, we drove to the Savage River at Denali Park where we camped.

June 27: We got up early this morning, about 5:30, to catch the bus to take us through the park. Unlike five years ago when we were here, the procedure to Wonder Lake had changed from personal cars to buses. The first bus was full to capacity, so we walked a

couple of miles to a check point beyond which you cannot drive. There, we were told that when the buses are full, it is possible to use your own car.

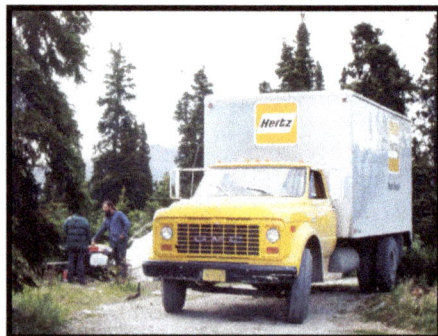
Our truck at the Savage River campsite

We didn't want to try driving the truck through the park, but a man whom we met while we were walking went back and got his car and drove us as far as the Toklat River. We walked a couple of miles farther and then caught a second bus which was also jammed, so we stood up for the twelve miles to the Eielson Visitor Center. We stayed there for a couple of hours.

On the way back to our camp, I found a seat on the last bus, but Joe and Pam had to sit on the spare tires on the floor in the rear. To make matters totally bad, Mt. Denali was completely clouded over. It was a full three-hour drive back. In addition to being crowded, the buses were old uncomfortable school buses with very dirty windows, so you couldn't see out. Tonight, while Joe was beating me at Russian Bank, a cow moose and her calf came wandering by – the best thing of the day.

June 28: It rained very hard in the night, and the tents leaked quite badly. It was still raining this morning, so we moved inside the back of the truck, cooked and ate breakfast there. Then we packed up and, after some trouble with the spare gas tank which luckily happened right at the park's gas station, we were off around noon to the south. At about a hundred miles south of the park, the road was still being worked on and, especially in the truck, it was a rough ride. After that, we had clear sailing. We camped at an area about seventy-five miles north of Anchorage. Fortunately, it was almost free of mosquitoes which had become very thick in the woods.

June 29: We were into Anchorage about noon, and shipped off our camping equipment and went to the Holiday Inn, got cleaned up, had dinner, went to the airport and found our plane was canceled because of a pilot's strike. We caught the last flight to Seattle just before the bewitching hour. It was jam-packed. We spent Friday, the 30th, there and flew home on Saturday.

––––––––––––––––––––––––––––––––––––

Alaska is addictive. If you love it, as we all did, it was difficult to stay away. Joe's fascination with Attu focused largely on two things: its pristine wilderness and its propensity to lure straying Asian birds. Six years after his solo journey there, he returned with Helen and several close birding friends. The trip was rough, but certainly rewarding. Joe's journal records the details.

July 16, 1978: The bullfinch which was seen on Attu at the far tip of Alaska's Aleutian Islands when we were there in late May completely eluded us. We went to look for it the first day. We had to walk about six miles each way from where we were staying. Slightly misunderstanding the directions about where to find it, we missed it by a couple of hundred yards. The next day, it was gone. I wondered where these wind-blown vagrants go. They seem to rest for anywhere from a few minutes to a few days and then disappear. Do they go somewhere else on the island? Do they head again out to sea and never make it? Or do they somehow actually get back to the Asian mainland where they should have been all along? It was a shame that we didn't see this bird for it is both very handsome and very rare. This was only the second time it had been seen in North America, but I guess you have to plan on missing some of the rare ones. We did not, however, miss the White-tailed Sea Eagle.

When Helen and I were on Attu, we stayed at the old Loran Station which sounds rather grand, but certainly wasn't. About a three-mile walk around Casco Cove from where the plane stops was a shed labeled "Attu International Airport," an old, square, concrete structure, unused since about 1960. Its windows were all broken out. The insides were full of junk, broken furniture and furnishings. Dripping stalactites formed from the lime in the concrete ceilings. There was, of course, no heat, electricity or running water. Fortunately for us, our birding friends who had arrived a week earlier had swept and cleaned the debris out of two small rooms and nailed heavy, translucent plastic over the windows. Thus, we had a floor for our air mattresses and sleeping bags without the wind howling through. They had mostly cleaned the one big room so we had a place to cook and sit in broken-down, tottery chairs. The only problem with the cooking was the dripping ceiling. Water and lime were either nearly in the food or on the cook's head. Helen, as chief cook, wore a hat while cooking, very attractive. In spite of the constant seeping cold and wind, it was really quite comfortable.

But back to that eagle. Our second day was, weather wise, the worst of all with a cold, hard rain driven almost horizontal by a strong northeast wind. We all staggered back home in mid-afternoon, pretty drenched and discouraged after missing another good bird, a Dusky Thrush. Then someone had the bright idea of starting a fire in the open, two-stall, doorless garage. There was plenty of old lumber around, and soon a roaring fire was burning.

I was standing with my back to the fire looking out the open side when, out of the corner of my eye, I caught a movement outside the side window. Then right in front of us, not more than a hundred feet away and no more than twenty feet off the ground, was the White-tailed Sea Eagle. It swooped in and turned sideways as it started to swing around the end of the building. We could see its great wingspread – ten percent wider than a Bald Eagle – and its long, white, wedge-shaped tail. We all dashed out, screaming, "Eagle, eagle, eagle" just in time to see it snatch a Pelagic Cormorant out of the air and carry it down to the beach. Then all our commotion scared it off its prey. It flew off, releasing the very frightened but apparently unharmed cormorant. We watched until it disappeared over the mountain behind us. What a magnificent bird!

This apparently broke our spell of bad luck and missed birds. The next day a Smew, the little Siberian member of the merganser family, showed up on one of the ponds behind our "ice palace" on Murder Point. It was in almost exactly the same spot where I had seen it six years before. Later, the following afternoon came the news that a Rustic Bunting had shown up near the old gym. Tired as we were, the adrenaline started to flow. We made the five-mile walk over and back to see it. A couple of afternoons later, as we were dragging ourselves "home" around Casco Cove, a bird flew past and landed on a nearby post. The Hawfinch was a truly fantastic coincidence as it was only the fourth United States' record of this bird.

Hawfinch

Two days before leaving was a wonderful, clear, cloudless 55 degree day. As I was lying on the thick, soft tundra at the top of Murder Point bluff, I watched a Laysan Albatross soar by just a bit offshore. That evening, we again made the long walk around Casco Cove. This time we saw an Eye-browed Thrush.

Already we are talking about when we can get back onto Attu – remote, rough, rugged, wonderful, romantic, wild and full of exciting exotic birds.[51]

193

1978

LIFE LISTING

Lists document success in birding, serving as résumés of a sort. They are the seductive summons to birding. Why the fascination? It is not so much the list, but listing as a process. It is a birding game. The rules are delineated clearly, and the high-scoring participants are all friends. In fact, they assist one another by joining a hotline which announces each rare bird. Joe had the will, the means, the knowledge and the determination to follow those leads.

Beginning in the late 1950s, Joe began listing North American bird species, according to the American Ornithologists' Union checklist. He and Helen traveled to a myriad of wildlife habitats. The exploration and appreciation of our vast wilderness refuges complemented his birding quest. Initially, his listing goal was to reach 600 individual species. Then, when completed, the target morphed to 700 which he achieved and surpassed.

The American Ornithologists' Union Checklist of North American Birds was first published in 1886. Through seven editions, it has served as the official authority on classification and names of all bird species on this continent. In 1982, the AOU checklist was again amended to exclude Greenland and to include Hawaii, Mexico, Central America and the West Indies. Later in 1984, the American Birding Association's checklist area was defined as being just North America north of Mexico and adjacent waters to a distance of 200 miles from land.

Joe Taylor began life listing with the AOU checklist. He revised his list according to their rules, regardless of how it affected his total count.

Carving of an Eskimo Curlew [52]

In 1974, John W. Brown, a columnist for the *Times-Union*, wrote: "A widely-known veteran Rochester birder has qualified for membership in the '600 Club,' a small group of professional and amateur ornithologists who, in their lifetimes, have identified 600 or more species of birds inside or in the coastal waters of the continental United States and Canada.

"Joe Taylor and his wife Helen just returned from a trip which took them 7,200 miles in less than three weeks. On it, they added fourteen species of birds to their life lists which gave Joe exactly 600, making him one of the eighteen living Americans known to have seen that many. And one of those fourteen new birds on his life list may well be the rarest bird on the continent, the Eskimo Curlew, long thought to be extinct.

"The Taylors' fabulous journey really started in Texas. He says their fantastic success in finding rare birds was the result of almost unbelievable good fortune, but it was not all luck. He had spent hours on scores of telephone calls, lining up aid from local experts in all sectors of the Southwest and South. For an outstanding example, he consulted Roger Peterson about who to contact on the possible whereabouts of the Eskimo Curlew. Peterson referred him to Jerry Strickland of Houston, Texas who gave him precise directions on how to reach the most likely beach on Galveston Island where the only known surviving Eskimo Curlew must have been sighted. There were apparently only two or three left of the millions and millions of these tame and trusting shorebirds slaughtered by hunters to the brink of extinction between 1870 and 1890.

"The Taylors scarcely dared hope to catch a glimpse of one, but they had hardly reached the appointed beach when a flock of shore birds – plovers, Yellow-legs and a Whimbrel wheeled in. In the flock, one smaller bird with cinnamon underwings stood out. It was the bird which, alone, would have made their trip worthwhile. It landed with the other birds. The Taylors watched it through binoculars at close range for several minutes and then through their Balscope as it wandered away through the grass. The odds against their seeing this bird had been astronomical. They were so shaken, they gave up birding for the balance of the afternoon.

"They had good luck elsewhere, too. At Bentson State Park in the Rio Grande Valley, they were directed to a certain telephone pole with a hole in the side. If they watched it, they were told, a tiny Elf Owl would look out. They did, and it did. At Santa Ana Refuge, a few miles away, they were directed to an area where a Mexican Jacana, an odd marsh bird, had been wintering. They found it within minutes. Other new birds added in Texas included the Black-capped Vireo, the Black-headed Oriole and, within the city limits of Houston, the Greater Prairie Chicken.

Driving east to Florida, they hoped to get out to the Dry Tortugas for the Noddy, Sooty and Bridled Terns, but the weather was too rough. They did take the boat to Bimini, and everyone was seasick except Helen. It was worth it to add Audubon's Shearwater to the list. A sailfishing cruise added Blue-faced Booby, Long-tailed Jaeger and Wilson's Petrel, and they found the Spot-breasted Oriole in Miami. They were directed to a place where they easily found the rare Cape Sable Seaside Sparrow, and on their way home they found Joe's 600th bird, the Swainson's Warbler in Pocomoke Swamp in southeastern Maryland. They had given up and were about to leave when they found it singing a few feet from their station wagon." [53]

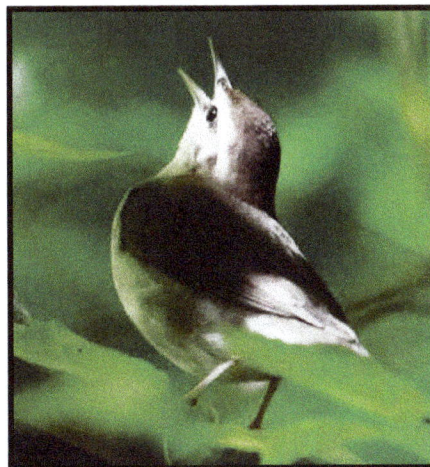

Swainson's Warbler

After becoming a founder of the American Birding Association in 1969, Joe had seen 678 bird species. In 1970, writing for the ABA newsletter, he considered the possibility of identifying 700: "Nearly two years ago, I was asked to present an article for publication in *Birding* giving what I thought the possibilities were of seeing 700 species in the territory covered by the AOU checklist. At the time, I would probably have said, 'I doubt it.' Now, six or seven birds later, I can see it as a real possibility. But to do it will take luck, being in the right place at the right time, lots of travel, 'hotlines' around the country plus the ability to follow them up, and something else which we really do not enjoy that much – listing for the sake of listing.

"How would we get to 700? To tell it is quite simple, but the doing would be something else again! There are five species we haven't seen which breed regularly in the checklist area – the Black Rail on either coast, Kittlitz's Murrelet in Glacier Bay, the Whiskered Auklet and the Ancient Murrelet in the Aleutians and the Craveri's Murrelet in the Gulf of California. In addition, there are two more regular breeders that would be tough – both in southern Baja California – the San Lucas Robin and Baird's Junco. Then there are seven more birds that we know of which may or may not breed, but at least are showing up with fair regularity – the Yellow-green Vireo, the Mexican Crow and the Ringed Kingfisher in the Rio Grande Valley, Wagler's Oriole in the Big Bend, the Rufous-backed Robin in southern Arizona, the Ivory Gull off Boston and Cape Ann and the Curlew Sandpiper in the Brigantine Refuge. Lastly of those that occur with some regularity, it should be possible to get the Pale-footed and New Zealand Shearwaters on pelagic trips off California, if one is sufficiently persistent.

"This is sixteen species and would bring us up to 694. For the rest, we would have to rely on strays and newcomers. Unfortunately, most of the strays occur in Alaska where at least a dozen species of Asiatic shorebirds have shown up. I personally feel quite certain that some of these wanderers may be more regular than is recognized because much of Alaska's northwest coast has been covered very little. We may do a little exploring there next year.

"As I said it would take a lot of luck, but it is quite possible.

"Now I would like to take the opportunity to add a word to those who are decrying 'listing.' If they mean listing solely for the sake of listing, then I couldn't agree with them more. But, if they have never used birding as an excuse to see some more of the beautiful and remote parts of this country, then they don't know what they have missed. I think I first began to realize this in the early 1950s bumping along that very bad, dusty, forty-mile road from Homestead down to the hurricane-swept, deserted Seminole Village of Flamingo at the southern tip of the Everglades. The Park Service had not yet turned it into a blacktopped, noisy tourist attraction. It was wild, remote and exciting. I have no recollection of whether or not we saw any new birds there, but I well recall the Peregrine Falcon, in a jet dive, which picked off and carried away a Louisiana Heron and the Black Vultures which perched around our campsite eating the throw away pancakes which had somehow gotten mixed up with the coffee grounds.

Black Vulture

"Without birds as an excuse, I doubt we would have worked our way out that rocky, rugged peninsula of Newfoundland, or gotten lost in the lovely, lush green valley of the Margaree in Nova Scotia, or walked that rushing stream down Spearfish Canyon in the Black Hills, or gotten seasick in a small boat off the tip of the Olympic Peninsula, or dumped in the Pacific trying to get ashore in rough seas on the Santa Barbara Islands, or found Guadalupe Canyon in Arizona with the cottonwoods just starting to turn green with the first bloom of spring, or camped at Hooper Bay on the Bering Sea in the midst of all those shorebirds, geese and eiders, or leaned far out over the great cliffs of St. Paul Island to watch the sea birds nesting below us. These are memories which come when I look back on the past twenty years of pretty concentrated birding. These and many more like them. Offhand, I can recall only very few birds we 'listed' in any of those places, but with birds as an excuse to get there, we've seen a lot of the majesty and wonder and excitement of this country.

"So, if just plain birdwatching needs an apology, let this be it. If it is just a game, so be it. It is a wonderful one, and one we hope to continue playing for a long time."[54]

"Writing for *National Wildlife* in 1975, Marjorie Valentine Adams reported: "Nature seminars, nature camps, bird identification classes and resorts which cater to birding, and nature buffs are increasing. Guided birding tours now visit nearly every spot on earth. It is estimated that the famous Whooping Cranes bring at least one million tourist dollars to Texas annually. In some localities, special telephones give recorded information on the latest local bird finds, and bird lists are included with tourist information from many Chambers of Commerce.

"Along with this interest has come a game officially called 'birding,' with a membership that is estimated to have multiplied 100-fold in the last ten years. The game started in the United States, but has spread to a score of other countries on five continents.

"The goal of life listing birds is to find and identify different species of birds in order to tally them as a score. There are, for example, about 700 species of wild birds in America. The first to identify that number in this territory was Joseph W. Taylor. He trudged, cold and wet, an average of ten miles a day over the inhospitable tundra and glacial rocks of Attu Island in Alaska to complete his record. Asian and Pacific birds sometimes stray to this westernmost point of North America, and Taylor's 700th bird was just such an occasional wanderer, a Gray-spotted Flycatcher, the only member of its family ever to be seen on this continent.

"To count in a birder's score, a new bird must be wild, unrestrained and alive, must be correctly identified by the player himself, and must be seen in a 'designated territory.' A designated territory includes whatever area the individual player chooses. But whether it's an invalid's backyard or a continent, once it has been decided upon, its boundaries must be strictly adhered to. When a birder positively identifies a bird species for the first time within this territory, he gets to add one point to his list for that territory. A list of all the species a birder has identified anywhere in the world is his life list.

"Such scores listed for states or provinces, nations, continents, or the world are in direct competition with the scores of other birders scouting the same territories. The American Birding Association is, at this time, the official recorder of all such scores."[55]

In 1972, Joe was interviewed by Stuart Keith, then president of the American Birding Association.

Stuart Keith: Well, Joe, you finally did it! On behalf of the American Birding Association, I want to congratulate you on a magnificent achievement. You are the first and only member of the '700 Club,' and are likely to be so for a long time to come. How do you feel about it?

Joe Taylor: Thanks very much, Stuart. How do I feel about 700? Well, naturally I'm pleased, but I must add that getting there is really half the fun. I miss that carrot dangling out there. This does not mean, however, that we are going to stop chasing after rare birds, so I hope our 'hotline' friends will keep this in mind. Without them 700 would still be somewhere off in the distance.

Keith: What was your 700th bird and where did you see it?

Taylor: The 700th bird was a Gray-spotted Flycatcher, a rather undistinguished looking little bird. I found it on the west shore of Casco Cove on Attu Island in Alaska. It is a small flycatcher – smaller than a Least, grayish–brown above and dirty white below with pronounced breast and flank streakings. It is a member of the Muscipapidae family and, I believe, the only member of the family to have been seen in North America. It was first recorded in 1956 on Amchitka Island where one was collected by Karl Kenyon. It breeds regularly on Kamchatka, about 400 miles to the west. I saw two more of them several days later about eight miles away.

Keith: Back in 1970 you wrote an article in *Birding* entitled "Is 700 Possible?" You have now answered your own question, and it didn't take too long, either. I am sure everyone wants to hear a blow-by-blow description of how you got the last twenty or so birds that put you over the top. Please give us the exciting story.

Taylor: I am afraid this might be more than mildly boring, so I'll make it as brief as possible. By coincidence, all of the last twenty birds were seen after January, 1971. We arrived at the Santa Ana Refuge in early February 1971 to learn from Wayne Shifflet, the refuge

Ruddy Ground Doves

manager, that a Ruddy Ground Dove had been around for the past couple of days but had, momentarily at least, disappeared. So Helen and I were back out there early the next morning, and very shortly she spotted it perched in a fairly open thicket – 680. The next day we drove down below Falcon Darn, as we had done twice before in previous years, but this time we didn't even get the motor turned off before the Ringed Kingfisher flew in and lit at the end of a. nearby branch – 681. Craveri's Murrelet nests on the rocky islands off the east coast of Baja. Passing Ceralvo Island off La Paz on the ferry from Mazatlan, two of them were swimming off the bow – 682. We found the San Lucas Robin while driving through the back country near Santiago in southern Baja. Normally, this bird is found high in the mountains, but some winters it does wander down to lower elevations. We were lucky – 683. Back in the United States in early March, after driving up Baja, the Rufous-backed Robin on the western outskirts of Tucson was too easy, thanks to the excellent directions we got through Bill Harrison – 684.

And then in mid-May, an exciting two months began. For the previous three years, we had gone to Elliott Island in the Chesapeake to try to get the Black Rail. We had heard it, taped its call, but never saw it. So, of course, we were trying again. On the way we stopped at Tuckerton and the Brigantine Refuge. At Tuckerton, I was walking across the short marsh grass hoping for a Curlew Sandpiper when a Black Rail went up from right under my feet. It's easy if you're finally in the right place at the right time. Later, we saw another at Elliott Island – 685. There were no Curlew Sandpipers at Tuckerton, but the next day at Brigantine we saw two, one in beautiful breeding plumage – 686. Back home on June 9th, Bill Harrison

Rufous-backed Robin

202

told us about a Yellow Grosbeak. We were in Tucson by noon the next day and saw the bird that afternoon – 687. A week later, word came of a Black-tailed Godwit at the Brigantine Refuge, so back to New Jersey for – 688.

On the way back from Bathurst Inlet in Northwest Territories where we did a little birding for about ten days in early July, I checked with Bill Jamson and found that there was a Berylline Hummingbird at Cave Creek in the Chiricahuas. So, we came back from the Canadian Arctic by way of southern Arizona. Again, I think we were lucky as I understand the bird was not seen very often after we left – 689. That was it for 1971.

Yellow Grosbeak

In January of 1972, we again drove Baja California, this time from north to south. Among other things, I really wanted to see a Baird's Junco, the only endemic that had eluded us. I was ready to get horses for a pack tnp into the high mountains near the tip to see it. Late one afternoon, at the end of a little road which wound back into the foothills, we came on one of those fabulous pockets of birds with about twenty species flying about together. All of a sudden, out popped a Baird's Junco which perched on the end of a branch where we couldn't miss it – 690. A week or so later, back in Phoenix, I checked in with Jim Tucker and learned about the Loggerhead Kingbird and the Stripe-headed Tanager in the Florida Keys. I was in Islamorada that night, found the tanager after several hours, and the kingbird in a few minutes and was back in Phoenix for dinner – 691 and 692. This was too simple. But I guess the simplest was the Ancient Murrelet. We just hadn't looked for them before. Off Monterey Bay in California in early February, from a party fishmg boat, we saw several. They winter there – 693.

And then came Alaska. It was a pretty rough, wet and cold trip. I was without wheels, so I walked on the average of about nine miles a day. You sure see many more birds on foot.

Ancient Murrelet

On Adak Island over Memorial Day weekend when the traffic along the Sweeper's Cove wharves was very light, many birds were in close, I saw a Bean Goose and two Whiskered Auklets. Seeing the auklets there saved me a long climb over the high tundra to the other side of the island where they nest – 694 and 695.

A few days later in an inlet on the other side of the Cove, I found a Kittlitz's Murrelet, still somewhat in winter plumage, making it easier to identify – 696. Then I found one of the best birds of the trip. While walking along the rocky shore of Clam Lagoon, the big tidal lagoon where so many wanderers have been found on Adak, I heard a shorebird call that I knew 1 had never heard before. Suddenly, coming around a point ahead of me, there it was – big, like a Greater Yellowlegs, and very dark. Something said Spotted Redshank, and this it was – dark purple all over, with white spots on its back, red legs and a long, incredibly thin bill – 697.

I arrived at the Loran Station on Attu. With thirty-eight men, it is the only human habitation on this 368 square mile island. After an early dinner, I wandered down to the beach. Within minutes, two Common Sandpipers came workng their way through the kelp. They are the Eurasian version of our Spotted Sandpiper, and I saw several more on Attu – 698. The next morning six miles out off Murder Point, two Smews were playing in the surf. They eventually took off and disappeared around a headland – 699. And this brings us to the Gray-spotted Flycatcher. I should add that it was a lousy, cold, misty, rainy morning morning. In spite of my raincoat and all, I was soaked to the skin. Only a real nut would have been out on a day like that.

Keith: Those were certainly the sort of thrilling experiences all birders hope for, Joe. What is your score now? Have you added any more? Is there anything left that you might still reasonably expect to see in North America, outside of the real accidentals?

Common Greenshank

Taylor: After the flycatcher, I picked up four more birds in Alaska – a Common Greenshank on Attu at the edge of a small pond; a Little Ringed Plover along a beach pond at Cape Prince of Wales; a Great Knot 1,400 feet up on a gravelly part of Wales Mountain and a Dotterel in the soggy tundra 1,700 feet up a mountain north of Nome.

As to what is left, the list is short, of course, but there are a few. Forgetting Alaska where almost anything can show up, there are Bridled Terns off Florida in the summer, always a possible Yellow-green Vireo in the Lower Valley in Texas, maybe Pale-footed and New Zealand Shearwaters and Laysan Albatrosses off California in the fall. But there will be the accidentals to keep the pot really boiling.

Keith: Well, I guess most of us have thought of 700 as the Impossible Dream, but you have shown it to be a reality. Great work, Joe! You are truly assured of a place in the Birding Hall of Fame! [56]

————————————————————————

In 1972, John W. Brown, columnist for the *Times Union* continued to follow Joe's exploits: "Only a relatively few American birdwatchers have seen and identified enough different species in North America to qualify for the exclusive '600 Club.' Of these, only

205

Bridled Tern

one has cracked the 700 barrier, once considered a virtually unattainable. goal. And, impossible as it may seem, the man has done it not just once, but twice.

"This super birdwatcher is Joe Taylor of Parrish Road, Honeoye Falls, a retired Bausch & Lomb executive who has been known to fly 4,600 miles round-trip in a single day to get a look at one rare bird.

"Joe listed his original 700th species on an expedition to Alaska and the Aleutians in 1972, and by the spring of last year his total had grown to 707. Then a year ago last April, the Classification and Nomenclature Committee of the American Ornithologists' Union, which has the last word on such matters, renamed and relegated several species to the status of subspecies. His list suffered a crushing net loss of 13 birds. He was back to 694.

"Undaunted, he went right on logging thousands of miles a month, tracking down reports from his network of informants of birds rare or new to the continent. On March 13 of this

White-tailed Sea Eagle

year, he hit the 700-mark for the second time by recording the Black-capped Gnatcatcher in Patagonia, Arizona. On May 12, he found a tropical hummingbird called the Bahama Woodstar at Homestead, Florida. That was 701 again. The next day he added the Bridled Tern off Marathon in the Florida keys.

"One Sunday night in June, the telephone rang in Honeoye Falls, and it was a Texas colleague on the line. A Rufous-capped Warbler had been

Rufous-capped Warbler

sighted in the Big Bend National Park in West Texas. The sun was barely up when Joe boarded a plane and headed for Austin. He was in Big Bend Park and had seen the bird by early evening. The following evening he was back in Honeoye Falls for dinner, and a new No. 703 was on the list.

"A summer trip to Greenland, considered then part of North America, paid off on August 22 when he saw his first White-tailed Sea Eagle. That made anew No. 704. Under the old, pre-revision checklist, it would have been No. 717.

"Earlier in the year, on his way to the new 700, Joe had found the Bahama Duck, a close relative of our Pintail at Flamingo in Florida and the Caribbean Coot at Fort Lauderdale the day before. His 1973 additions included the Elegant Quail at Bisbee, Arizona, the New Zealand Shearwater off Monterey, California, and a Blue Tit, a little, blue-capped cousin of our chickadee that had somehow wandered from Britain or Europe to Gravenhurst, Ontario, where it was also seen by other serious birders.

"There aren't very many birds that appear regularly in North America that Joe Taylor hasn't seen, maybe only one or two. One of them is Ross's Gull which wanders into Alaska from Siberia every year, but Joe is not about to go up there and wait for it. Meantime, other new wanderers from abroad may show up.

"Joe's wife Helen is a member of the '600 Club,' ranking fourth behind her husband with 677 which makes her the top ranking woman in the club."[57]

207

In 1974, Mark Starr of the *Wall Street Journal* wrote: "Zealous pursuit of winged creatures isn't unusual for Joseph William Taylor. He has flown 4,600 miles round-trip in a single day just for a glimpse of a rare bird. That dedication has made him the country's No. 1 birdwatcher, according to the rankings of the American Birding Association. He is believed to be the only person to have seen more than 700 species of birds in North America. His nearest rivals trail by more than thirty species.

"Whatever birding's appeal, it's growing. Spurred by increased interest in conservation and ecology, birdwatching now claims at least several million participants in the United States. The National Audubon Society has grown to about 325,000 members from only 50,000 in 1965.

"Birdwatching has two basic elements – seeing the bird and identifying it. Experts like Mr. Taylor identify birds through a combination of characteristics such as appearance, sound, flying pattern and perching technique. It's a skill he finds difficult to teach.

"'1 remember when I first started watching with Joe,' says his wife Helen, 'A bird would fly by as fast as you could blink, and he'd say, "There goes a goldfinch." 'I'd ask him, 'How do you know it's a goldfinch?,' and he'd say, "because it flies like one." 'He just couldn't explain more than that.'

"Mr. Taylor is the first to admit he's a lousy teacher. But he's convinced that anyone can become a proficient birder, and cheaply too. Though he spends thousands of dollars on his sport, Mr. Taylor says all you really need is a good bird guide book, a top pair of binoculars and a willingness to get up early in the morning. But don't ask Mr. Taylor along on any birding trip without an abundance of corned beef hash, peanut butter and jelly sandwiches and good whiskey!

"Birding experts estimate there are only about 645 species that breed regularly in North America (including Baja California, Bermuda, Greenland and the Arctic to the North Pole), another 50 that visit regularly and about 100 which are freakish occurrences.

"Mr. Taylor, a large man with full silver-gray hair and prominent white mutton chop sideburns, says only one regularly occurring bird has eluded him. That's the Ross's gull, a

Siberian bird which wanders in the Canadian Arctic. Not that he's too lazy to make the effort. Mr. Taylor has traveled throughout the world in pursuit of birds. And while some birdwatching can even be done right from a car, fellow birders say they have watched him trek up mountains and trudge through high water to get his bird.

"Mr. Taylor's love of birding combines an appreciation of both aesthetics and competition. He says the species-number competition is friendly, and most usual sightings by any top birder are quickly spread by an informal telephone network to the country's other leading enthusiasts. He also insists that the competition is honest, though no verification of a sighting is required.

"Mr. Taylor has seen his share of rare birds such as the California Condor with its ten-foot wing span. Most thrilling, he says, was the Eskimo Curlew the Taylors saw in Texas in 1966. The bird had been believed extinct since the 1920s and is considered extinct again. Mr. Taylor believes they were the last to see it. 'I couldn't even breathe I was so excited,' he recalls.

"While bird watching is a quiet pursuit requiring great patience, Mr. Taylor has also had his share of excitement. He was grilled by the U. S. military in 1942 when he was found peering through a telescope at a spot on Seneca Lake in New York that, unbeknownst to him, was about to be named the site of a new naval base. In an other incident in Ecuador, an army officer pulled a gun on him, fearing that Mr. Taylor's birding equipment might contain hijacking weapons.

"Most frightening of all was a trip through Alaska with a semi-competent bush pilot who kept running out of gas and making forced landings on the tundra. Worse than that, the pilot was a teetotaler who remained true to his convictions by dumping the Taylor case of whiskey on the shore of the Bering Sea.

"'Do you know how to tell a crow from a raven?,' Mr. Taylor asks. Without waiting for an answer, he confides, 'The raven says 'Nevermore.'"[58]

From the top: Joe Taylor, Benton Basham, Steve Oresman, Jim Tucker

Photographs by Ed Kasper[59]

THE GREAT BIRD BASH

F ascinated by a unique birding event in 1979, Clive Gammon wrote an article titled "The Great Bird Bash" for *Sports Illustrated* magazine: "It is 2 a.m. on the salt marsh at Anahuac, Texas, a black-velvet night, warm, moist, entirely silent. A necklace of dim lights is visible across Galveston Bay. A sweet-rotten scent rises from the wetlands. Then, violently, the peace is shattered.

"Out of the darkness, blazing with light, splattering through the mud, an extraordinary vehicle comes on like something out of a James Bond movie. Basically it is a tractor, equipped with enormous balloon tires and festooned with spotlights. It tows a tumbrel with a generator aboard that puts up a continuous howl. It is Rolligon, a mechanical dragon. Its purpose is to expose, then intimidate, the quarry that its crew of men, clinging on precariously, is hunting down.

"Suddenly it comes to a jolting stop.

"More lights, hand-held strobes flash on. And from the men comes a yell of triurnph, 'Yay!', they shout, 'Woo hoo!' Pinned in the cross beams is the quarry in the marsh grass. It is five inches long, black and sandy markings with a tiny yellow beak. Somebody shouts, '"We got us a Yellow Rail!' The little bird comes to its senses and wings off into the night. For the birdwatchers on board the Rolligon, the big day has started triumphantly.

211

"Birdwatchers? Too passive, too tame a word, as they will tell you themselves. Birdwatchers no doubt still exist, crouching stealthily, studying a favorite species for hours on end. The men on the Rolligon are birders. They go, and they check 'em out, man. And the more they check, the happier they are.

"The record for bird species observed in a single twenty-four-hour period is 288. That figure was achieved in Zambia, East Africa in 1975. The North American record was set in California last year: 231 species. Last Wednesday, starting on that Texas marsh, five men set out to beat both of those figures. They felt that 300 was a distinct possibility. Given the sophistication of their plan, it seemed that their optimism was justified.

"The birders gathered at Houston last Tuesday at the airport restaurant. There was Steve Oresman, a 46-year-old New Yorker, a Park Avenue management consultant who started his birding at age ten in Central Park 'A great spot. The birds haven't got anywhere else to go.' There was Benton Basham, an anesthetist from Chattanooga, and Jim Tucker of Austin, Texas, executive director of the American Birding Association, a psychologist and the acknowledged Texas expert. There was young Jon Dunn from Encino, California, one of the group that had set the national record.

"And there was the chairman of the board, Joe Taylor of Rochester, New York, president of the ABA. Uncle Joe, 65, a rubicund, white-whiskered man, started the final planning session with a large tequila on the rocks. 'I'm in training,' he pointed out, 'but not in the strictest training.'

"The plan, in fact, was pretty well cut and dried already. The Big Day – the birders' own term for a record attempt – would begin in the Anahuac salt marsh at 2:00 a.m. By dawn the assault group would be close to Houston again, working the mixed hardwood and pine forest fifteen miles east of the city. Next they would drive to Galveston and Galveston Island. And then they would play their trump card.

"At Galveston Municipal Airport, a Lear jet would be waiting. The birders would be whisked down the coast to Rockport, where they would clamber into a rented station wagon and check out the ducks of Copano Bay and the shorebirds of Mustang Island and Oso Bay.

That would bring them close to the Corpus Christi airport where they would rendezvous with the Lear again and hurtle on to McAllen, to the Mexican border and the birds of the Rio Grande.

"Then the big jump, to the green canyons of the Huachuca Mountains in Arizona. Plenty of hummingbirds there, they figured, and maybe a Golden Eagle. Traveling westward through the day, they would lose some hours in flying, but they would gain light through two time zones. By 3:00 p.m. Pacific time, they would be in San Diego where the great talents of Jon Dunn would come into play. All the richness of west coast birdlife would be added to the list, and the last act, in the darkness, would be to drive out to Mount Palomar. The owls, naturally, would respond to the taped hootings the team had prepared.

"It was a finely organized scheme. But already, at the planning lunch, there were forebodings. Five days earlier a front had come through from the north which, Jim Tucker explained, had forced thousands of migrating land birds heading from Central America to Canada onto the Texas coast. That was fine except that since then there had been warm weather and a gentle breeze from the south, giving the exhausted migrants time to recover and head north again. 'The big wave may have gone through,' Jim said.

1979

"Joe Taylor ordered another tequila to see him through the bad news, then added some news of his own. The fragile ecology of the Arizona canyons, green oases in a desert of sand, had been hit hard by the phenomenally cold winter. 'A lot of the oak trees are dead,' he said. 'I don't think we'll see any quail.' But the Lear might compensate for all that. California alone would make up the deficiencies. The doubts were shaken off. This, after all, was one of the most ambitious birding expeditions ever planned. No time to sit over lunch harboring gloomy thoughts.

213

Back: Benton Basham, Jon Dunn, Joe Taylor
Front: Steve Oresman and Jim Tucker

"In all probability, none of the late crowd at the Rice Lands Motel 24-hour restaurant at Winnie, Texas was aware that history brushed them on the shoulder on the eve of the big count. Indeed, they seemed more interested in listening to country music on the jukebox than to Uncle Joe's team, which had just risen from a two-hour rest, the last it would get until it returned into Texas very early on Thursday morning. Unacknowledged, the team furtively moved out into the humid night.

"Long before 2:00 a.m., the official start time, the team was in position and had seen its first bird, which did not, of course, count. A Black-crowned Night Heron flapped slowly over the car. 'Can't we put it in escrow?' pleaded Oresman. He couldn't, he learned. Like the rest of the team, he had to wait until it was legal time to set off in the Rolligon, the terror of the marshes.

"Laymen might well imagine that birding involves, well, a lot of creeping through the woods. Not so. Creeping is too slow. You have to go get 'em. In a salt marsh, a $30,000 Rolligon is about the only way. Rails, tiny, plump, desperately shy little birds, the team's main objective at Anahuac, have to be hunted down, exposed. There are six North American species. In less than an hour, Uncle Joe's boys had checked off five. The mechanical dragon flushed other species, too. The total was up to ten by the time they headed back to the car. Not a high rate of scoring, but these were bonus birds collected in the dark. The big rush would come at dawn. 'We have 99% of what we wanted,' declared Tucker, 'We missed the Black Rail, but that Le Conte's sparrow was an extra!'

"Now it was a mad scramble for the car and the big rush back to Houston. The woods were silhouetted against the sky, but the yellow light was not the dawn, only the glow of the city. The objective at this stage was to gather in a few owls, maybe a Chuck-Will's-Widow which sings before dawn. The team drove along with windows down, listening for calls.

214

When the road went through heavy timber, Tucker, the Texas expert, called for a stop and whistled plaintively at the trees, but no Chuck-Will's-Widow responded. When the headlamps picked out the golden eyes of an owl on a stump, it flapped slowly away before it could be identified. No need to sweat about that. There'd be owls aplenty when they got to Mount Palomar.

"Now, slowly, an undramatic dawn, misty with the promise of sun, began to cast a true light on the woods. And suddenly every bird in Texas seemed to be singing. It was still too early to check species visually, but under the American Birding Association rules a properly identified song is enough. 'We should get a Swainson's Warbler around here,' Tucker said. Magically, as if the bird had been listening, the five clear notes of the little warbler rang out. 'Everybody recognize it?' Tucker asked. The ABA rule is somewhat difficult to interpret on this matter. Most birders take it to mean that 95% of the species recorded must be identified by every member of the group. This was the way Uncle Joe's crew understood it. Everybody recognized the warbler's song.

"At first light, birds came thick and fast: the group was scoring at a rate of 1.6 species a minute, and an overall rate of one every three minutes during actual birding time in daylight was all that was needed to crack the world record. The Houston woodlands yielded 45 in all. Time to head for Galveston, picking up whatever chance species the drive yielded.

Le Conte's Sparrow

"At the planning meeting Tucker had said, 'There'll be, uh, some creative driving this trip.' He was entirely right about that. To the imminent peril of other cars on Route 146 and later on Interstate 10, he slammed the car to a halt whenever something of interest turned up along the road. Once it was a hawk on a telephone pole, difficult to identify, even through binoculars, because it was hunched with its head down. If you are a birder you know what to do about this.

215

Swainson's Hawk

"Like a grenade man detached from his squad to take out a sniper, Jon Dunn rolled out of the car, sidled across the road and moved up on the hawk, using available cover. Stooping, he picked up a piece of pipe and hurled it at the hawk. The bird flapped away, showing all its markings – Swainson's Hawk.

"The Houston Ship Channel docks yielded a Red-breasted Merganser, apparently unmindful that it was swimming on the surface of one of the most heavily polluted bodies of water in the United States.

"The team hurtled through Bay Town and Texas City. Amid the shipping in Galveston, it found a glorious Roseate Spoonbill. And then the station wagon was screaming to a halt at Kempner Park in the city, alongside an old mansion almost submerged in greenery, a crumbling pile that looked like a Fellini film set. This was the place for migrant warblers. Three days earlier, when Tucker checked it out, it yielded 19 species of warblers.

"But now came the first piece of really bad luck. The warblers had left for the north. The birders checked off only four species. And when they moved off again, to run along the beaches of Galveston Island, Tucker was downcast. 'The world record has probably slipped away,' he said, 'We've lost at least 20 species here.'

"The North American record, though, still appeared to be within their grasp. And the Lear was ready and waiting at the airport. As the jet climbed almost vertically, Tucker was muttering over the checklist. 'One hundred fifteen,' he announced finally. 'I'd aimed at 130 by the time we boarded the plane.' By now it was past 9:30 a.m. The team was half an hour behind schedule. The next stop at Rockport, they fell even farther behind the clock.

"That was, Tucker confessed later, because they enjoyed themselves too much, because the birding was so magnificent. The total they achieved was outstanding: 42 species, some of

216

them what birders laconically call 'good.' Meaning rare. A Grasshopper Sparrow for example, a Buff-breasted Sandpiper and an Upland Sandpiper. And a Purple Gallinule, an imperially hued member of the coot family. Oso Bay, the last stop before the rendezvous with the jet at Corpus Christi, was particularly rich. Almost the whole family of plovers, from Semipalmated to Wilson's, turned up. But by the time the team was in the Lear again, they were ninety minutes behind schedule.

"On board, a hasty conference. The national record was still a strong possibility, but the schedule would have to be amended. At the next stop, the Rio Grande, only fifteen minutes birding would be possible. And the time in Arizona would be cut to one hour.

"They figured without the Lear and its crew. They had been told the flying time to McAllen would be twenty minutes. It took thirty-five. Instead of keeping to a low altitude for the short hop, the jet took time to climb to 30,000 feet and to descend again.

"And the birding at Santa Ana, on the Rio Grande, was disappointing. Because they were so late arriving, they had hit the dead time of the day. This was the warm, humid noontime when the birds just shut down for their siesta. Santa Ana yielded only seven species.

Purple Gallinule

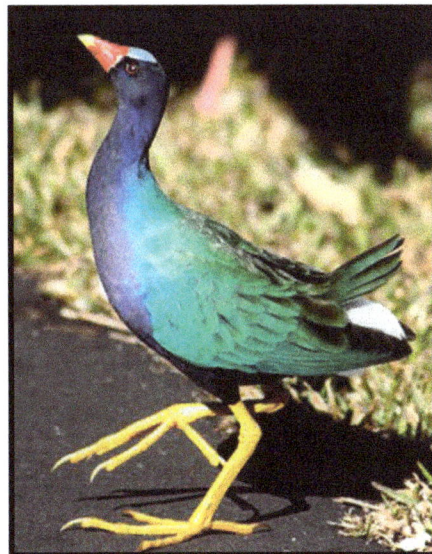

"But the really bad news came once the team was airborne again, on its way to Ramsay Canyon in the Huachuca Mountains. Steve Oresman spoke to the pilot, then came back and broke it. 'A head wind of 150 knots,' he said. 'It's going to be three hours to Fort Huachuca, not two.'

"The mountains around Huachuca were magnificent, redolent of history, of Cochise's last stand for the Apaches, but by now Uncle Joe's team was a little too sick at heart to

217

Anna's Hummingbird

appreciate them. The birders, too, seemed to be heading for certain defeat. On the ground, locals who had volunteered to drive the team up into Ramsay Canyon had been patiently waiting for hours. As soon as the jet pulled up, they had the team aboard. The chance of even the national record now was slim, but it was still there, barely.

"It flickered to life a little more when it became plain that the birders had hit a good hummingbird day. Of the twenty species on the North American list, eight were identified. And a hen Golden Eagle sat on her aerie on the high cliffs. In all, 18 species were added. Now the list was up to 182 and in an hour the team was back in the jet again. Dunn, a young professional birding guide, second only in California to the great Guy McCaskie, had maybe an hour only to show his skills when the team got to San Diego, but there might be something to be squeezed from the dark hours as well. The twenty-four hours would not be up until midnight, Pacific time.

"On this leg, though, the Lear did not seem to gain height as swiftly as it had done before. Indeed, within minutes it was descending again. With despair, the birders realized that they were heading straight into Tucson, only forty miles away. Had to pick up gas, the pilot explained airily. None at Fort Huachuca.

"It was the last bitter blow. The birders managed to swallow the explanation that the plane hadn't been flown to Tucson for gas while they were in the canyon because it would have been too heavily laden to land again at Huachuca. But why hadn't arrangements been made ahead for a fuel supply at the Arizona field? Well, uh, said the company later, we were playing it by ear, we had to check as we went.

"The birders were hardly mollified.

"They had made the schedule months before and had confirmed it days ahead. They had gone over it once from the hotel in Houston the previous day. Now the chance of even the national record was gone. It would be dark long before they got to San Diego. No point in going to California at all.

"Birders, however, are made of stern stuff. Even while the crew of the Lear was looking for fuel at Tucson, even while it was discovering that the base operator there had run dry, even after it had found some at the plane manufacturer's own establishment, even after their plane had to be pushed around manually because it had been parked the wrong way, even after someone had departed with the pilot's credit card to check that it was okay to let him have fuel – even after all this, Uncle Joe's team kept at it, scanning the darkening airfield with binoculars.

"And scoring. When Taylor said he thought he heard a quail call, Jim Tucker let out a cry of triumph, 'Hey! On that sandpile! Gambel's Quail!' Game to the end, the others gathered around and confirmed the sighting – 183. A gleam came into Tucker's eye. 'The owls,' he said. 'The Mount Palomar owls. We could still get those. We could turn a searchlight on the surf, maybe get some Scoter Ducks.' Like one of Cochise's braves, he was ready to charge single-handed, go out fighting. 'Get those birds!' he said like a man in a trance. 'Check 'em off!'

"Uncle Joe talked him out of it. There would be other Big Days. They had learned a lot, not least about air travel. And Steve Oresman had a contribution. 'The Concorde,' he mused aloud. 'You could do Southeast England. Then Long Island...'" [60]

219

Joe summarized the trip in his weekly newspaper bird report:

May 17, 1979: Over the years on our "big-day" spring censuses, my friend, Steve Oresman, and I have pondered about how many more birds we could see in that twenty-four hour period if we had a helicopter. It would move us from area to area instead of our having to depend on a slow, traffic-burdened automobile. As a corollary to this, we have wondered how many species we could see in a twenty-four-hour period of transcontinental birding, speeding from place to place in a small jet.

We have never tried the helicopter locally. But, in late April of 1979, five of us – Jim Tucker of Texas, Benton Basham of Tennessee, Jon Dunn of California, Steve, who now lives in New York City and I tried a version of the transcontinental trip.

A very large portion of the bird species that summer in the Northeast migrate north from Mexico along the Texas coast before spreading out across the whole East. Therefore, we decided to start our day in eastern Texas. We planned to bird down the Texas coast, hopping over unproductive areas by jet, then to Santa Ana Refuge in the lower Rio Grande Valley for Mexican species, next to Sierra Vista in Arizona principally for the hummingbirds in Ramsey Canyon and finally to San Diego for California birds.

We would start at 2:00 a.m. at the Anahuac Refuge near the Texas-Louisiana border to try for rails, and end twenty-four hours later at midnight, because of the two hour time difference, at Mt. Palomar east of San Diego, looking for owls.

It was a great plan. Even though it didn't work, it might have. But that's putting the end before the beginning.

In retrospect, one of the highlights of the trip occurred not during the "big day" itself but late in the afternoon before. We all drove to Anahuac to make arrangements with the refuge manager to go out at 2:00 a.m. in his rail buggy – a tractor equipped with three-foot-wide tires which enable it to haul a box-like cart through the soggy marshes so we could flush out the rails. We were amazed at the huge numbers of shorebirds in the plowed fields there.

There were Black-bellied, Golden and Semi-palmated Plovers, Killdeers, Stilt Sandpipers, Black-necked Stilts where there was casual water, big Marbled Godwits and Long-billed Curlews, Yellow-legged, Least, White-rumped, Pectoral and Solitary Sandpipers. Above all, Buff-breasted Sandpipers abounded, more Buff-breasteds than I had ever thought existed. We must have caught the great bulk of the population because they were everywhere, particularly overhead, where huge flocks wheeled and flew past, all of them calling at

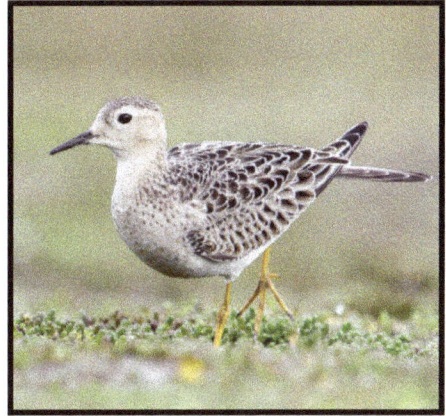

Buff-breasted Sandpiper

once – a low, trilled "pre-e-e-e-t," a wonderful chorus. With their solid, yellow-buff undersides, they are lovely birds to see at any time, and especially in the thousands.

The next morning, our "big day" was off to a bang-up start. During the first half hour in the rail buggy, we had four of the five North American fresh-water marsh rails – King, Virginia, Sora and the very rare Yellow. We were missing only the Black. Before we left Anahuac at 3:00 a.m., we had the only salt-water marsh rail, the Clapper.

Pre-dawn light found us in a sizable swampy woods northeast of Houston. With us were a whole chorus of different species singing, among them Hooded and Swainson's Warblers, the latter much more easily recognized here than in the East, probably because there is nothing else here that sings like it.

Then we were off for Galveston and our first big disappointment of the day. Two days earlier, Jim and Jon had found nineteen species of warblers at Kempner Park in the middle of the city, but this day all but one – a Blackpoll – had gone north.

Our first hop in the Lear jet from Galveston down to Rockport was a real thrill. It is really more rocket than plane with the stubby wings acting, I think, to a large extent as stabilizers. It takes off like a scared rabbit and goes almost straight up. Seatbelts don't do a thing, because you couldn't move out of your seat if you tried.

221

From Rockport, we drove down the coast to Corpus Christi where the plane met us. Along the way, we picked up many duck species in small ponds. There were Upland Sandpipers in open fields and several shorebirds at Oso Bay near Corpus Christi, including the day's lone Buff-breasted Sandpiper, a far cry from the thousands of the evening before.

Then a relatively quick hop took us to McAllen and the Santa Ana Refuge, and the unbelievably low score of only seven species, although the Green Jays and Altamira Orioles are always a joy to see.

Then came the real, heart-breaking frustration of the day. When we were up at a cruising altitude of 46,000 feet out of McAllen, the pilot informed us that we bad headwinds of up to 150 miles per hour. The time to Arizona would be at least three hours instead of the little less than two hours for which we had made our plans.

So far as getting any truly good total, we knew we were licked.

Carroll Peabody of Mile Hi Lodge met us when we finally did land at Sierra Vista at the base of Arizona's Huachuca Mountains and drove us on a quick trip to Ramsey Canyon. We gained seven hummingbirds, including the rare White-eared, and a dozen other species, almost what we had planned on at Ramsey.

Gambel's Quail

Then we were back into the plane and off to San Diego, we thought. But, no. The headwinds had used up far more than a normal amount of fuel. We had to set down in Tucson for refueling. And there the official "day" ended.

In Tucson, we taxied about the airport trying to find someone who had fuel, and then had to have the pilot's credit charge checked. It was dark. And there was our last bird of the day – Gambel's Quail – calling from atop a pile of dirt alongside the runway.

222

It was our 183rd bird, not a very good total when you consider that we have had 181 in one day in Monroe County and vicinity. But it was indeed an exciting day. We learned a lot about how to do such a trip, and maybe next time we'll do better.[61]

Disappointed, but undaunted.

223

Geese in flight

GOOSING AT OAK ORCHARD

Rising before dawn on a near-freezing March morning, Joe and Helen annually led a caravan of friends and fellow birders to Oak Orchard Refuge, a wetland near Tonawanda, New York west of Rochester. Assembling on a steep bank overlooking a small pond with telescopes and binoculars, we huddled in warm parkas, sipping hot, sherry-laced consommé, and waited for the geese to arrive at sunrise. On the distant horizon behind us, dots appeared like swarms of bees. As they grew closer, we marveled at hundreds, if not thousands, of migrating Canada Geese careening toward the pond. Their honking cacophony was loud and clear. We were no longer conscious of the cold as we witnessed one of nature's wonders.

Birding friend, Steve Oresman, remembered, "One of the largest social events that the Taylors' organized was an annual trip to Oak Orchard to see the large flocks of northbound migrating Canada Geese. For simplicities sake, the trip was always referred to as 'goosing' and was always held on the same weekend in March.

"Oak Orchard Creek runs into Lake Ontario about halfway between Rochester and Buffalo. The surrounding area is marshland and farmland including the Iroquois National Wildlife Refuge. In the spring, tens of thousands of geese rest at the refuge during their migration and feed in the corn stubble on the local farm fields.

Canada geese

"The geese at Oak Orchard in those days were an unusual and wonderful sight with large numbers flying in and then setting their wings, tumbling and honking to the pond. The refuge also attracted a number of different species of ducks and a special pair of nesting Bald Eagles.

"In the 1970s, the lower forty-eight's population of Bald Eagles had not recovered from DDT poisoning so seeing eagles was exciting, particularly for non-birdwatchers. All this made the trip attractive to Rochesterians who were by then pretty tired of winter. The trip included drinks and lunch in a large gravel pit nearby, well sheltered from the wind and attracted a large, varied and substantially non-birding crowd. A good time was had by all. A nice drive, some fresh air, libations and lunch and home before dark."[62]

Joe wrote about Oak Orchard in 1972: Out of the skies they come, tumbling and gliding down to land on the water of the big pond until the surface is black with them. These are the Canada Geese at Oak Orchard, north of Batavia. No matter how often one sees this annual early springtime morning flight, the wonder of it never ceases.

What we refer to as "Oak Orchard" is an area along Oak Orchard Creek, just northwest of the village of Oakfield and running west for some fifteen miles. The creek varies in width from nothing to somewhat over five miles. It is under the control of the Oak Orchard and Tonawanda game management areas and the Iroquois National Wildlife Refuge.

Here, in late March and April, thousands of Canada Geese pause and rest for a week or so on their way from where they have wintered in the south to their breeding grounds in northern Ontario and farther north. In the pre-dawn, many of these birds leave the ponds and water impoundment of the area and fly out to neighboring fields where they feed on last year's corn and other grain. Then, between 7:30 and 8:00, if it is a bright day they return to the refuges.

And it is this return flight that is so always thrilling and spectacular. Standing at the overlook above Stafford Pond, you can see them come, babbling and honking, sometimes as singles or in twos and threes, but more often in their typical long "V"s and, once in awhile, in monstrous flocks – long skeins upon skeins stretching across the horizon.

With an estimated 70,000 Canada Geese, it would seem almost impossible to pick out other goose species, but sharp eyes can do it. In the two trips we made this year, I saw four Snow Geese, pure white with black wingtips and stubby beaks and four Blue Geese, white-headed with blue gray bodies. Rare here in the East was one White-Throated Goose with a dark body, a white face patch and a pink beak. Amazingly, I also saw the purest albino Canada that I have ever seen, all over creamy white without a trace of black markings and with pale, if not truly pink, eyes.

Northern Shoveler

With the geese are hundreds of ducks – great pale flocks of pintails, winging by on long, pointed, swept-back wings, colorful Wood Ducks, Mallards, Blacks, beautiful Canvasbacks, Scaup, Ring-necks, Buffleheads, Ruddys, Goldenheads, Goldeneyes, Oldsquaws, Northern Shovelers and both Common and Hooded Mergansers. One should never miss this truly great spectacle in the spring.[63]

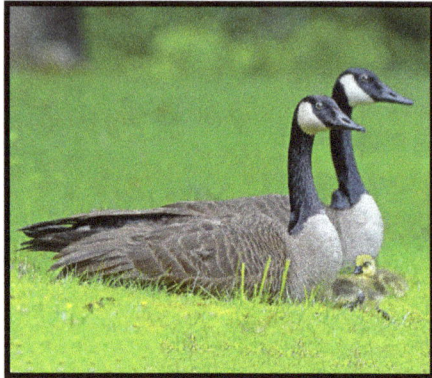
Canada Geese with their gosling

As he entered the second decade of his "Bird Report" for the Democrat and Chronicle, *Joe's interest and articles turned more and more to bird behavior and conservation issues rather than simply bird identification and birding travels. In 1979, he mused:*

Why do birds such as geese mate for life? It is probably to eliminate a lengthy courtship year after year, when they can't really spare the time. Researchers now believe that because geese nest in the high Arctic, where the arrival time of spring is uncertain and the summers are short, it helps if they already have a mate by the time they arrive. Experts reason that if geese waited until they got to these northern nesting grounds to pick a mate, go through courtship, breeding and egg-laying, they would have little time left for the normal events which follow. Those include waiting for the chicks to hatch which takes almost a month, waiting for the babies to develop flight feathers and start to fly, another six weeks, and then leaving for the south before early September when the Arctic winter sets in, in earnest.

So, to avoid wasting precious time, pair bonds are formed for life. It eliminates the need for extensive courtship every year. It makes it possible, instead, for the birds to breed on the way north. The female would also be ready to lay her eggs as soon as they get to their nesting grounds.

Other birds nesting in the Arctic do not have the same problems. For most songbirds, the incubation time is less than fourteen days, and the young fledge no later than fifteen days after they hatch.

For shorebirds which are the most abundant tundra-nesters, the incubation is about three weeks. The chicks are precocial. They are open-eyed and ready to run as soon as their down is dry, and they can fly in less than three weeks. In addition, the shorebird young have learned to go south by themselves, an instinct the geese have never acquired.

228

It seems to me there may be another reason why geese mate for life, along with the hawks and almost all other big birds. Is it not possible that they do so because once they have reached breeding maturity, their mortality rate is relatively low and their potential life span relatively long, ten to fifteen years or more. They can, therefore, "afford" the luxury of a lifetime bond. This, on the other hand, would be unworkable with smaller birds because their mortality is always high, and their life spans are short. Additionally, they can become so easily separated and scattered by storms and the other hazards of migration, which is not anywhere near so likely with the larger birds.

As with migration, maybe there is no single answer. Incubation behavior also is not the same among all bird species. As an article in *International Wildlife* pointed out, while most birds sit on their eggs in the traditional way to keep them warm, a few have evolved other means of incubation. Perhaps the ones we know best, the non-sitters are the ones we regard as brood parasites. In North America, that includes the cowbirds and, in Europe, the cuckoos. They have evolved the technique of laying their eggs in other birds' nests and forcing foster parenthood on them. We all know how very successful these methods can be, and how detrimental it is to the foster parents' own young.

And then there is the group of a dozen or so megapod species of Australia, New Guinea and nearby islands, which make mounds of leaves and sandy soil, or dig pits and fill them with similar materials. They lay their eggs in them letting the heat of the sun do the incubating. They are real users of solar energy.[64]

Brown-headed Cowbird

1964

AMERICAN BIRDING ASSOCIATION

Founded in 1969 by Joe and a few other serious birders, the American Birding Association is now an internationally-recognized, non-profit organization dedicated to recreational birding. The organization has members from every state in America, the Canadian provinces and more than forty other countries. The early ABA concentrated on finding, listing, and identifying rare birds and sought to connect avid birders with each other and establish rules for listing. Interest in birding has expanded the ABA, providing members with publications, conferences, workshops and tours. ABA's educational programs promote birding skills, ornithological knowledge and the development of a conservation ethic, encouraging birders to apply their skills to enjoy and protect wild birds and their habitats.

Scott Weidensaul wrote: "Joe Taylor says, 'You can't stand still. You've got to keep moving ahead with new ideas.' Taylor was deeply involved in Hawk Mountain Sanctuary when he got a call from Stuart Keith at the American Museum of Natural History. Keith, with a number of other prominent birders, including Joe, was starting something called the American Birding Association. Would Joe serve as treasurer? He would.

"'It was obvious even then that National Audubon was, to some extent, getting out of the bird business. We felt that birders needed an organization and some kind of journal to keep them up to date with what was going on in the country. Five of us got together for

231

meetings once or twice a year and began to put the magazine *Birding* out – it was pretty lousy at first,' he says. 'I guess it was Stuart who came up with the idea for an ABA convention in 1973.'

"For the meeting they settled on Kenmare, a little North Dakota prairie town between Minot and the Canadian border, in the middle of rich birding country. 'My God, nothing like this had ever even been conceived of in Kenmare. The whole town was decorated with red, white, and blue and big "Welcome ABA" signs,' Taylor said. The conference center was the local high school. The women of the town did the cooking. Instead of the fifty people they'd expected, two-hundred-fifty showed up. The gathering was so successful, in fact, that the National Audubon Society which was running its own conference in the same year complained about the competition. To avoid stepping on toes, the ABA switched its biannual conferences to even years.

"The ABA's growth has been terrific. A later convention in Mobile, Alabama attracted nearly six hundred birders, and Taylor says the hardest part now is limiting the number of people attending. *Birding* has evolved into a slick, informative magazine, and the addition of a monthly newsletter makes the ABA as essential for many birders as their binoculars.

"There have been problems along the way, however, some of them serious. In the mid-1980s the board was stunned to discover that the organization was nearly a quarter-million dollars in debt, much of it from unpaid bills to the National Geographic Society for copies of its new field guide, for which the ABA was primary distributor.

"'The ABA was broke,' Taylor says. 'I mean, by any definition of insolvency we were insolvent.' With Taylor taking over as acting executive director and Larry Balch as the new president, a number of past and then current board members put up $80,000 of their own money to keep the organization alive. 'We said we'd pay it back by the end of 1989, but most people thought they'd never get their money back,' Taylor says. 'But we pulled the thing off, and the last of those director loans was repaid last year.' The ABA is back on solid footing now with more than eight thousand members on the rolls.

"The growth of the ABA is indicative of the incredible boom in birding's popularity in the past twenty years. While some observers think the potential for further growth is unlimited, Taylor thinks birding may be reaching a peak. 'I don't think it will go much beyond where it is today.' he says, musing. 'I think we're getting close to the saturation point. There's just too much competition with other things, too much to do – and birding isn't something you do in a hurry.' Birders, he believes, will continue to become more organized, more specialized, more skilled. This, too, is inevitable, as each generation builds on the legacy of the one before.

"Like the man said, you can't stand still." [65]

Lawrence Balch, past president of ABA, reported: "It is no exaggeration to say that there would be no American Birding Association today without Joe Taylor. I also am not exaggerating when I say that getting to know and work with Joe was one of the most rewarding consequences of my membership in the ABA. Acquaintances saw his modest, charming, and slightly gruff but affable exterior. Those who knew him better could not help but admire, respect and – he would be embarrassed to hear this – love him.

"I first met Joe in June 1972, when I was looking for a Curlew Sandpiper at Tuckerton, New Jersey. I returned from a fruitless search of the beaches to find a couple with binoculars around their necks relaxing in chairs set up by the open tailgate of their car. Joe and Helen Taylor were resting before starting a search for Black Rails. When we introduced ourselves to each other, I recognized immediately who Joe was – the man who had seen more species of birds in North America than anyone else. I had joined ABA about three years earlier and had seen his name often in *Birding*. Joe had been one of the founding members and was ABA's treasurer. He would serve as an officer for twenty years, including two terms as president.

Although I was a relatively inexperienced, untraveled birder, Joe and Helen treated me as though I were their birding equal. They spent an hour accommodating me by patiently

Whiskered Auklets

answering my many questions. Gracious, unassuming, and thoroughly charming, they never displayed the slightest impatience with this stranger who was taking up their time. I remember Joe telling me in response to a question that of all the places he had birded in North America, southeastern Arizona was his favorite. His next trip was coming up in a few weeks. He was going 'to the end of the Aleutians' to try to find Whiskered Auklets.

"I got to know Joe, the person, after I began to serve on the ABA board of directors that same year. Joe and Helen were always generous. They supported many individuals in the arts and helped friends in need in many ways. Their active support of the ABA was obvious to many members, but few knew the extent of their financial support. Neither did I, even as a director. I did learn, however, what kind of person Joe was. Caring, but realistic. Open to others, but decisive. Principled, honest and totally straightforward. After I succeeded Joe as president, I would learn of the considerable financial support he and Helen had given the ABA in its first sixteen years. While others might have used such support or their years of service as leverage to influence others, Joe never did. I will never forget one measure of his character. Once, he was the only officer to vote against an important policy matter I had presented to the board. He met me after the meeting and said that a president deserves the total support of his officers, and that if I wanted his resignation, he would offer it.

"In 1986, an unforeseen crisis struck this organization, and we found ourselves a quarter of a million dollars in debt. As president at the time, I had the most immediate responsibility for action. While the whole board of directors was of help, I depended most upon Joe. No one could have been more supportive, or of more help. What to do, how to do it, and where to find the resources occupied most of my time and, therefore, much of his. Finally, in March 1987, when we were without editor, director, staff, or money – only faith and ideas and plans – Joe met me for breakfast in Philadelphia. He made me the offer that would rescue the ABA: if I could get present and past directors to pledge a significant sum in interest-free loans, he would match it. They did, and he did, and it was enough to carry

234

our plans to get the ABA restarted, improve its operation, and eventually make it financially sound and self-supporting for the first time in its history. Its present healthy state and future promise are a testament to Joe's faith, vision, efforts and support.

"It was my sense that for all his efforts on behalf of organizations he believed in, Joe was happiest when he and Helen were in the out-of-doors, seeing and hearing birds, and – more importantly – the larger whole of which they are a part."[66]

_____

At its meeting in April of 1993, ABA's board of directors discussed the Joe Taylor Fund, a memorial endowment celebrating one of its early founders. Due to the outstanding response to its appeal for donations, ABA was able to spend up to $10,000 to launch the proposed program. The key elements for its initiation were scholarships to youth birding camps and workshops, half-price ABA memberships for all students, a Bird Study Merit Badge booth at the Boy Scout national jamboree and a pilot ABA newsletter for students. Joe Taylor's legacy lives on.

1976

236

LATER ON

After retiring from business in May of 1969, Joe fostered his ultimate passion. Already president of Hawk Mountain Sanctuary and a founder of the American Birding Association, he eschewed his traditional past and reveled in the pursuit of unencumbered birding and service to conservation causes.

After more than twenty years, he and Helen sold the family home. The era which ushered in a constant procession of family, friends and neighbors, countless dogs, celebrations and memories had come to an end. They built their new contemporary house, designed by their son-in-law Peter Wendt, on Parrish Road in Honeoye Falls, south of Rochester. On forty acres of field and woods, their new home would expand to more than a hundred acres when the opportunity arose. The setting was perfect for their love of nature. Walking paths were mowed through the fields. Wooden bridges were built over the rambling creek. A broad butterfly garden sloped down from the deck. Eventually, an extensive pond was dug to attract water fowl and accommodate fish. By day, countless birds were omnipresent. At night, foxes barked from their dens, and deer fearlessly strolled closeby. Although their new home never quite had the warmth of 590 Allen's Creek Road, it embraced many activities which the whole family enjoyed – birdwatching, identifying butterflies, bass fishing, hiking or simply absorbing the purity of nature. Joe and Helen were in their element. They had built an ecological Eden.

Shortly before moving to Parrish Road, Joe began writing a weekly bird report for the Rochester *Democrat and Chronicle*. In those early columns, many of his extensive observations originated from their new site, "It's a forty-acre piece of land, with a dip through which runs a tributary of Irondequoit Creek. There are a few dead elms scattered throughout. I've been fascinated by the bird life it supports.

"Walking down the rough driveway, a Horned Lark flutters off from the shoulder while her mate spirals high overhead singing his tinkling song. A Killdeer flies off the other way – no broken wing act so you know you're not near the nest. Two pairs of robins are moving around in the hedgerow along the road and a pair of neat, trim Cedar Waxwings perches on one of the small maple trees planted along the driveway..

"The commonest birds in the upland fields are Savannah Sparrows, with a couple of pairs of Vespers scattered among them. There are Eastern Meadowlarks, Bobolinks and Red-winged Blackbirds, losing a little of the early spring brilliance of their scarlet epaulets. I

20 Parrish Road in Honeoye Falls, New York

have a special fondness for Bobolinks with their sharply contrasting black and white. About three-quarters of a mile away on the main road, an Upland Plover has been sitting on the telephone wires. I would like to know how to entice him into our fields, but I doubt if there is much literature on how to entice Upland Plovers.

"Farther along the driveway where the grass is thicker, several Song Sparrows nest and a Grasshopper Sparrow lilts his thin insect-like song from the top of a tall weed. Off in the distance, a Ring-necked Pheasant crows and an American Crow caws. Overhead a Mallard wings his way along the creek, to be followed shortly by a Black-crowned Night Heron. I am surprised there are no Little Greens.

"On the hillsides bordering the creek are many thorn bushes and here the Yellow Warblers abound and, of course and unfortunately, so do the Brown-headed Cowbirds. The warblers nests must be the favorite place for hosting the cowbirds' parasitic eggs. Field Sparrows are here where the vegetation is thicker, along with a few more Song Sparrows. From the top of a big thorn bush an Alder Flycatcher sings 'fitz-bew.' Later on, sitting in the shade by the creek, I heard his low 'whit' call note consciously, I think, for the first time.

"Down among the willows bordering the creek are more Yellow Warblers and American Goldfinches, bounding from the trees to weeds and back. They are our latest nesting songbirds, not starting to nest until late June. A Spotted Sandpiper flies upstream on stiff, fluttering wings, and the rattling call of a Belted Kingfisher can be heard just ahead of him. There are many more tent caterpillars this year so it was not surprising to hear a Yellow-billed Cuckoo. These birds do a great job eating those infernal pests.

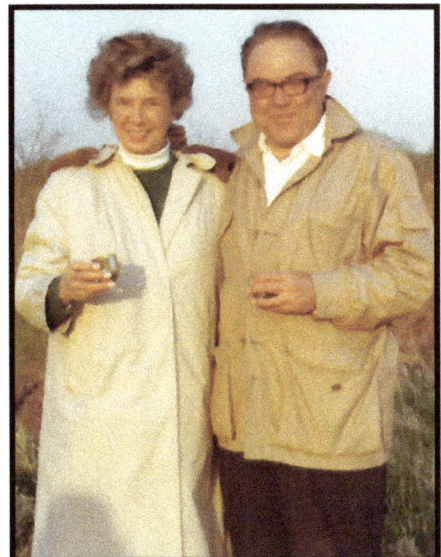

On their new land - 1968

"The little creek must have been high and strong in the spring because it has pushed

Red-headed Woodpecker

downsteam the two big beams we put across the creek as a footbridge. A pair of Eastern Phoebes is nesting under one of them, so we'll have to wait until later to move them back.

"The dead elms make fine perches for Eastern Kingbirds and homes for woodpeckers. There are a few Downys, and, most exciting, at least one pair of Red-headeds. These strikingly handsome birds really have become scarce. Starlings also perch on the tops of the elms, but there are surprisingly few of them. And there are no English Sparrows, but I expect this state of Utopia will not last when there is a house and bird feeders.

"Going up the hill on either side of the creek, a pair of Brown Thrashers bursts out of some shrubbery. I have not seen any Eastern Bluebirds, but there must be some nearby. The thrasher does a near perfect imitation of their soft song. For reasons I do not yet understand, there are fewer birds in the field on this side of the creek, but the fringe of woodland makes up for this. A Cardinal is singing there and a House Wren, and a catbird mews occasionally. A Crested Flycatcher and a Yellow-shafted Flicker can be heard calling. The Common Grackle skulking through the lower branches of the trees is probably nesting, but he's the only one I've seen. I know a pair of Red-tailed Hawks is nesting in the top of an old tree a few hundred yards into the woods. I'm going to like living here."[67]

Like living here? They loved it! Life in this bucolic setting was a dream come true, a new beginning. A certain amount of existential freedom accompanied these new surroundings – license to mold their landscape for birds and critters, freedom for themselves to roam. And for Joe, the unencumbered space to pursue his ornithological and conservation goals. Their children had married and moved away – Ann went to New York City, Joe and Mary to northern California. They still managed to visit Joe and Helen often at Parrish Road as they developed and nurtured families of their own.

240

With freedom from the responsibilities of his previous work, Joe also pursued his love of crafts and puzzles. He ignored conventional expectations by embracing needlepoint, traditionally stitched by women. This was unusual as well for someone considered to be an outdoorsman. In the seventies and eighties, he made dozens of practical items. Straps for binoculars and cameras, tennis racquet covers and large, impressive needlepointed rugs could be found in their home and on birding trips.

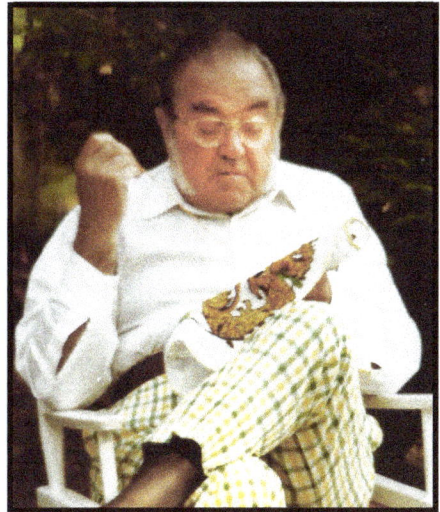

1974

Eleanor Jones of the *Honeoye Falls Times* found this fascinating. "Joe Taylor's birding has brought him fame as our nation's No. 1 birdwatcher. His latest pastime is stitching as well as designing needlepoint. One of Taylor's favorite pieces is a needlepoint vest, bargello-stitched in brilliant greens. He enjoys wearing it to his board meetings at the Hawk Mountain Sanctuary in Pennsylvania."[68]

Beginning in the 1950s, Joe became enamored with the double crostics created by Thomas Middleton for *The Saturday Review of Literature*. He was never without one. During casual gatherings, Joe could occasionally be found in profound reverie with his puzzles or needlepoint, only putting them aside when the conversation became too riveting to ignore.

1989

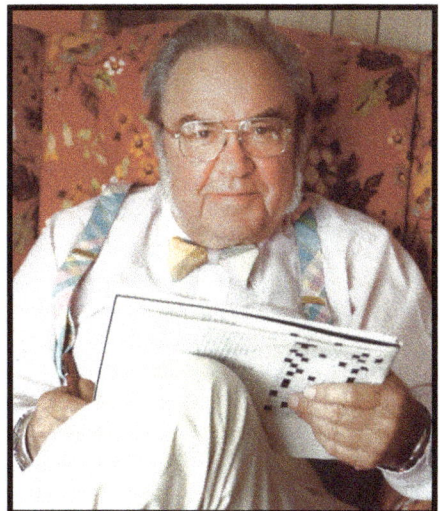

Away from the conservative nature of the family business, Joe was able to further explore his flamboyant sense of attire. In addition to sporting mutton chop sideburns, his signature looks included sport coats of rainbow hues,

241

1984

fancy patterned Lilly Pulitzer slacks, colorful western shirts, bow ties, unusual belts and distinctive suspenders. In the West, this mode featured bolos and Native American bracelets, which he often purchased directly from the artisans. These fanciful accents were well balanced with his rugged outdoorsman style, most often featuring khaki shirts and trousers, anoraks and lace-up waterproof boots.

The transformation of his life at age fifty-four allowed Joe time to increase his life list of birds, promote conservation, advocate for the preservation of bird species and travel globally. In the ensuing decades, Joe and Helen took many bird-oriented cruises and tours into the far reaching wilderness areas throughout the world.

A columnist for the *Times-Union*, wrote, "A roof over man's head is a necessity, so the Taylors did the next best thing. They built a rambling home and brought the outside indoors. The house steps back a half mile from the road and has a background of woodland and a jagged track from Irondequoit Creek. It's a beautiful setting that attracts many kinds of birds. The outdoor beauty can be seen from every room in the house. Each has large windows and many have sliding doors which lead to redwood terraces which adjoin every room."[69]

"There are birds all over the Taylor's spacious house in Honeoye Falls – stuffed birds, wooden birds and painted birds, metal, glass and stone birds. A pair of binoculars sits on Joe's desk, and his bookcases are full of bird books. He says that birding has been a good reason to see most of the United States. The Taylors are leaving Honeoye Falls on a meandering birding trip that will wind up at their home in Arizona."[70]

Starting in the mid-sixties, Joe and Helen visited Arizona in the winter months. They purchased a rambling adobe house in Sonoita. This town southeast of Tucson was the queen of the wide, open grasslands, southeast of Tucson and fulfilled Joe's love of the desert and its wild natural habitats. Furnished in their usual discerning style, this home was comfortable and inviting. Picture windows across the west side provided a stunning, panoramic view across the live oak, prickly pear and cliff rose studded hillsides to the beautiful Santa Rita Mountains. Their children visited often to birdwatch, fly kites, identify wildflowers and cactus, hike, tour the area, help with Joe's projects and enjoy time together.

"Tunnel Springs Ranch was for a number of years a cattle ranch, and then in the early 1970s, the owners tired of 'running cattle' and planned a residential development. The thousand acre property was divided into twenty-four lots, averaging about forty acres. Architectural restrictions required houses to remain loosely in the southeastern Arizona style, but the principal restriction, and the one which for us makes it so charming, is that no house can be built where it can be seen from or by any other house. Thus, this untamed countryside will remain pristine without the intrusion of viewing any other buildings. Someday, perhaps, this will be our principal residence."[71]

Tunnel Springs Ranch, Sonoita, Arizona

1991

Joe birded throughout Arizona, "Phoenix in February has certainly lived up to its reputation as the land of the sun – day after day of warm cloudlessness followed by cool nights. Where we are visiting there isn't much reason to go out of the yard to go birding. A big proportion of the bird species which winter in this part of Arizona are right here.

"Invariably, the first bird every morning is a Northern Mockingbird, singing one short melodious burst of song at just the first crack of dawn and then lapsing into silence until full daylight. A touch later, the Mourning Doves start to 'coo' and once in a while a Great-horned Owl gives his last "who-whoo, who, who-whoo" for the night, and then suddenly it is daylight.

"Behind this house are citrus trees, palms and flowering shrubs. The front is typical desert with saguaro and barrel cactus, cholla, and palo verdes. So far as the birds are concerned, never the twain shall meet. These two different plant associations have their own typical bird populations. The commonest birds in the backyard are the Western Robins. Around

244

flowers are Costa's Hummingbirds with ruby-red throats and foreheads. Gilded Flickers work on the palms. Audubon's Warblers and Verdins flit about in the citrus trees.

"Out front, there are different birds. Gila Woodpeckers spend the day pounding on the biggest of the saguaros. Inca Doves call incessantly throughout the day. Their two-note song was translated as 'no hope' by the old-time prospectors. Curve-billed Thrashers, with their loud 'whit whit' alarm notes, sometimes burst to a snatch of their springtime songs."[72]

From his home in Sonoita, Joe wrote, "In early April, we had our bird of the year if not the decade. For a long time, we have only seen Harlequin Quails as blurred bullets when they whizzed out from under our feet. Then today as I looked out, there was a chunky little Harlequin sunning himself on the patio wall, seemingly perfectly at home. He has a brightly marked black and white face, a wonderfully handsome bird. We were entranced. Then he hopped down and walked quietly away. Oh, what a terribly fine thing to happen to us!"[73]

Joe and Helen loved their home in Sonoita, although they maintained a full life with family and friends in the East. In the late eighties, the high altitude in Sonoita began to effect his breathing, making it difficult for him to sleep. Reluctantly, they decided to sell the house and move back East where Joe actively resumed his birding and conservation pursuits.

For more than two decades, Joe had remained president of Hawk Mountain Sanctuary and a member of the Hawk Migration Association of North America. He joined the administrative board of the Laboratory of Ornithology at Cornell University, became a trustee and Fellow of the Rochester Museum and Science Center and a Fellow of the Rochester Academy of Science. As a founder of the American Birding Association, he served as treasurer, president and secretary and remained on its board of directors. In addition to his twelve years writing a weekly column for the *Democrat and Chronicle*, he *was* editor of *The Kingbird,* the journal of the Federation of New

Harlequin Quail

245

York State Bird Clubs. And he was the first person to see over seven hundred bird species in North America, a remarkable feat.

In Rochester in the late eighties, Joe underwent abdominal surgery. At seventy-five, this was his first operation, miraculously his first stay in a hospital. Apparently, the surgeons botched the operation. During the next three years, he stoicly suffered great pain and often found it difficult to eat and digest. His heart went into atrial fibrillation. No medical assistance helped.

Joe's astute mind never faltered, but his body was beyond repair. Death did not daunt him, and he knew it was approaching. While alone at home on Friday evening, the 25th of September 1992, he unexpectedly died sitting in his favorite chair. His heart just stopped.

Joe's ties to the past were traditional and strong. But his heart was in the present and the future. His boldness was impressive; his vision unlimited. In the words of the great Welsh poet Dylan Thomas, he did "not go gentle into that good night." He "raged, raged against the dying of the light."

1983

Joseph William Taylor – the traditionally-educated scholar, the elder patriarch, the comprehensive thinker, the lauded ornithologist and seasoned naturalist, the husband and father – lives on in his legacy.

The Family - 1985

Back: Helen, Joe, Mary; Charles McIntyre, Mary's son; Sheila Menzies, Joe's wife; Joe; Amy Taylor, Joe's daughter; Alyssa Wendt, Ann's daughter; Paul Brown, Jr., Ann's husband and Ann
Front: Lee and Alistair Hamilton, Sheila's sons; and Lucas Taylor, Joe's son (Missing: Paul Brown III, Paul's son.)

1974

REFLECTIONS

Joe Taylor died quite suddenly on September 25, 1992. Stunned, our family gathered in Rochester. A memorial service replete with trumpets and bagpipes took place several days later at St. Paul's Episcopal Church for hundreds of those who knew him. Condolences flooded in.

In 1992, Winston Brockner wrote on behalf of the Federation of New York State Bird Clubs: "A dedicated friend of the Federation has left us. Very interested, even before we were organized, Joseph William Taylor, or Joe to just about everybody, was always ready to support the idea and freely gave wise advice when asked.

"I first met Joe in the 1930s at Oak Orchard Swamp south of Medina. In March and April, birders from Buffalo, Rochester and many other places scheduled trips to this wonderful area for the spring migration. Many times our paths would cross, and we would compare sightings. The spark plug of the Rochester contingent most times was Joe. I looked forward to seeing and conversing with him.

"Early meetings of the federation were held in Rochester. Joe and his charming wife Helen were generally in attendance. About the same time the federation was hatching, Joe became deeply engrossed with Hawk Mountain. He and Helen fell in love with it. He most certainly was the man for the time, the perfect individual to follow the great Rosalie Edge. He was the logical leader for the next steps to be taken by the Hawk Mountain Association.

249

"Along with Hawk Mountain was Joe's love of birding. In this field, too, he inspired and fired the birding world to new heights. First came the '600 Club.' Joe quickly wrested top position in this group, passed 600 and roared on to 700 species. In the middle of this activity, a new organization was born – the American Birding Association. Here again, Joe was in on the ground floor and became a moving force in the ABA.

"Threaded through all these activities was Joe's abiding interest in the federation. In some respects, Joe was a private man. Constantly at his side, was his understanding wife Helen. Some may have felt that he was a man hard to know. Far from it. In his quiet manner, Joe still would talk to anybody who wanted to talk with him.

"Birding in New York State and the Federation and, yes, the United States, has lost a giant and a dedicated friend. Many will never know the quiet, unpublicized things Joe did.

"Happy birding, Joe..."[74]

———

John Peterson, from the High Peaks Audubon Society in the Adrondacks wrote: "We note with sorrow the passing of Joseph W. Taylor, a longtime member and supporter of High Peaks Audubon. In 1972, Joe was the first birder to see 700 species of birds In North America. In fact, if memory serves, he had to accomplish the feat several times, due to changes in the AOU checklist which kept deleting species by 'lumping' them.

"On May 25, 1974, Joe – whose mother had a camp on Lake Placid – helped lead one of our first field trips to Cobble Hill in Elizabethtown. An exhuberant, side-burned man, who had just seen a Pechora Pipit on St. Lawrence Island, Alaska, he gently and patiently pointed out to beginners the difference between the 'zoo zee zoo zoo zee' song of a Black-throated Green Warbler on one side of the road with the 'zur, zur, zur, zreee' of a Black-throated Blue Warbler on the other. He glowed as he listened to a Blackburnian Warbler – a bird he had doubtless heard for many seasons – noting that he never heard this song in Rochester during migration, but only here on the Adirondack breeding grounds.

"Joe Taylor was a director of the Hawk Mountain Sanctuary beginning in 1948, and served as president since 1966. He was editor of *The Kingbird*, the journal of the Federation of New York State Bird Clubs, from 1969 to 1974. From its inception, Joe was also a great supporter of the American Birding Association, helping the organization to safe passage through financially troubled years.

"Lister, editor, philanthropist and friend, we are grateful for all Joe Taylor did to advance the cause of birding – and birds – in North America." [75]

Blackburnian Warbler

Laurie J. Goodrich, Director of Conservation Science at Hawk Mountain Sanctuary, remembered: "Joe Taylor was the president of the Hawk Mountain board when I was hired. He appeared larger than life to me and the other young staff. We would often see him arrive at midday on a Friday. With his arrival, the busy staff would just suspend their work with an unspoken break time signal. Joe would sit down at the lunch table, and we would cluster around giving him updates and answering his questions about recent bird sightings or just listen to his stories.

"In his presence, although he seemed intimidating, he was immediately appreciative and approachable even to a young naïve biologist like me. All of us were mesmerized by him and looked forward to the stories he could unwind of early days at Hawk Mountain. He laughed about the times when he and Roger Tory Peterson would whisper about birds at the board meeting and raise the wrath of Rosalie Edge. Our Friday chats were never rushed, it was as if Joe knew building bridges with the staff was important. Eventually, he would retire with the director or curator to talk business, and we would fade back to our desks.

251

Golden Eagle

"Joe and Helen were so generous with the staff over the years he served on the board. He would invite the entire staff out to dinner occasionally, and the restaurant selected was always one of the best in the area. Those dinners were full of good food and drink as well as stories and laughter. Joe Taylor was a leading birder at the time. He often talked about trips he and Helen had taken or the bird trips he took with other friends. His enthusiasm for birding was evident in the excitement of his voice.

"I recall him coming to the North Lookout in November in those early days, with Michael Harwood and other board members. Their goal was to see a Golden Eagle pass over Hawk Mountain. Joe's bird knowledge was evident and intimidating to me but, looking back, I know he would never have been one to critique others. Joe and Helen always conveyed deep kindness and respect to the staff and visitors and seemed to love people, especially birders. Indeed, our first conversation was always about the birds being seen at the sanctuary.

"I feel that both Joe and Helen truly enjoyed their visits to Hawk Mountain as much as we enjoyed them.

252

"The legacy of time given by Joe Taylor to Hawk Mountain is significant. His leadership took the sanctuary through a period of staff expansion and growth in the 1980s and 1990s and set a foundation for success which continues today."[76]

Writing for the *Reading Eagle* in Pennsylvania near Hawk Mountain Sanctuary, Carl W. Brown, Jr. reflected, "Joe Taylor was the mountain. And the mountain was Joe Taylor. "That's the way it was at Hawk Mountain for twenty-six years, when Taylor served as president of the mountain's sanctuary association. That's the way it was until September 25th, when Taylor died in his New York home. His passing came as a blow to many who admired and respected the seventy-eight-year-old conservationist.

"By the early 1970s, Pennsylvania had passed a law to protect all raptors from the senseless sport of shooting hawks. So the association was at a crossroads – should it preserve the status quo, or blaze a new trail into the realm of conservation? As board president, Joe was faced with differing opinions among directors. The older ones were satisfied with staying the course, while newer members were itching to try something different.

"Using his subtle style of persuasion, Joe was able to close the association's ranks and helped direct the association toward a new frontier. But, as was his style, he didn't take credit for what many consider the greatest accomplishment of his presidency – the creation of the Visitors Center.

"Joe's understated influence was just one of his admirable qualities, noted Jim Brett, the association's curator. 'He had a deep wisdom that everybody respected,' said Brett, who admitted his relationship with Joe was like that of father and son. Brett also credited him with having great vision and being a 'master builder of ideas.' One of those ideas was the creation of the Visitors Center. Although it took more than ten years to become a reality, the impressive facility now draws thousands of people through its doors.

"Joe's genuine interest in other people is a lasting memory for Jack Holcomb, a board director. 'I always appreciated him because he showed a deep concern for everyone,' Holcomb said. 'He wanted to know how you were doing, how's the family, things like that.' Holcomb conceded that Joe was a bit daunting when they first met, but that they developed a mutual respect over the years.

"And over the years, Jim Brett grew closer to the man who, he said, became the most influential person in his life. 'His passing is an incredible loss for me in one sense,' Brett said in an emotion-choked voice, 'His strength carried this mountain forward to the plane it is at today.'

"On September 25, 1992, Joe Taylor finally let go of the mountain. But the mountain will never let go of Joe Taylor."[77]

From Minturn Wright, a fellow birder and Joe Taylor's successor to lead Hawk Mountain: "I followed, Joe Taylor, as 'president' of Hawk Mountain when he retired in 1992 after twenty-six years on the board and most of them as president. I was an unwilling successor at first because, working full time as a senior lawyer at a large law firm in Philadelphia at the time, I knew I couldn't devote to Hawk Mountain the enormous amount of time Joe did. Since its founding, the Mountain had essentially been run by the president and the curator. Joe persuaded me that, with the recent advent of a third person as executive director, much of the administrative and day-to-day work the president had been doing had already been passed over to the director. To emphasize that I was unable to be the CEO which Joe had in effect been for so many years, I changed my title to 'chairman.' For ten years or more, the mountain had no one designated as president or CEO, although it was the chairman's desk where the buck stopped. We got by.

"During Joe's tenure, which included the first ten years of my service on the board, I was amazed at the amount of time he devoted to the mountain. He and Helen would typically drive every week the three hundred or so miles from Honeoye Falls to the mountain, spend a couple of days, and return home. He would spend time with every staff member. He knew what everyone was doing. He supervised the fund-raising and financing. And, of course, because he had been involved at Hawk Mountain for many decades, he knew its history, its strengths and its problems better than anyone else. His devotion was so strong that, so I was told, if at the end of the fiscal year the treasury was running short of funds, he would simply write a check for the needed amount. I recall one board meeting when Joe, noting that the mountain's income was once again running behind budget, urged all of us to pitch in and help with fund-raising, because this year he was determined not to be the only one to make up the difference. We pitched in, and spared him the role of solo angel. I think it was the first time that the board approved and ran a fund-raising effort from supporters, generally.

"I cannot claim to have known Joe well. We overlapped only briefly, and the overlap was, on my part, limited. But I got to know him well enough to admire him tremendously, not just for his devotion to the organization and its objectives and for his personal generosity, but because of his friendly and out-reaching manner with everyone with whom he dealt. He made a newcomer feel a part of the team from the start."[78]

From Frank Gill, fellow birder and Hawk Mountain board member: "This biography sparked a few memory pulses of good times with Joe Taylor. I would echo Minturn's recollections of our roles on the Hawk Mountain board. I was the kid scientist, and Joe was my second father. Hawk Mountain was his domain, the intrepid birder who led the evolution of birding in North America as a serious 'sport.' Crosslinks between Hawk Mountain and the American Birding Association fueled our deep friendship and precious times together in southeastern Arizona. Our friendship deepened over the years as we modernized the Hawk Mountain programs and facilities. Joe was generous financially and patient with his leadership.

Painted Redstart

"Joe also introduced me and many others to serious birding. Far corners of North America beckoned, especially if the target was an accidental waif from another land. Joe changed the way we thought about birding and travel. The formation and evolution of the thriving ABA is Joe's legacy. It was not easy, neither politically nor financially. But Joe prevailed.

"Southeast Arizona was one of his favorite wintering grounds. He and Helen invited me to stay with them and get to know that avifauna. I'll never forget our first morning there together. It was snowing, and a Painted Redstart hopped into spectacular view. Arizona became my favorite birding destination for decades, thanks to Joe.

"Last, but not least, was Joe's devotion to Helen. They radiated love and affection for each other. I remember one evening with them in Arizona when dinner plans were uncertain. Joe winked at Helen with their secret code for 'let's eat out.' Helen giggled like a kid who had just been invited to a dinner date. We had a great time together."[79]

Stanley Senner, the first executive director of Hawk Mountain Sanctuary recalled: "In summer 1981, I was living in Washington, D.C. and working for the United States House of Representatives Committee on Merchant Marine and Fisheries which handled much of the wildlife and environmental legislation in Congress. I wanted to get out of D.C. and get back to birds when I learned that Hawk Mountain Sanctuary was looking for its first executive director.

"Although I knew little about Hawk Mountain, this search caught my attention. My wife Pat and I made a quiet, unannounced visit on a hot-but-lovely day in August. As we drove up the mountain, yellow wildflowers were blooming along the road, and the forest was cool and inviting. We both thought this just might turn out to be a very interesting opportunity and, not incidentally, a great place to raise our anticipated child.

"Later that fall, we met with the progressive wing of the Hawk Mountain board and its president, Joe Taylor. They had a vision to update its operation as a nonprofit organization and extend its reach beyond the sanctuary boundaries to the growing national and international raptor movements and to the centers of political power in the environmental effort.

"I realized that this was an extraordinary opportunity for me. The men around the table – led by Joe – were far-sighted, exceptional, wonderful people. In November 1981, Joe and the committee offered me the job of executive director. I was only twenty-nine-years-old and had never managed an organization. The committee, however, opted for youth and change and was willing to take a chance.

"I started work at Hawk Mountain in July 1982. For the next eight years, Joe and I talked at least weekly and met in person many times at the mountain, in Honeoye Falls or their winter home in Sonoita, Arizona. Joe was my boss, but he also was my co-conspirator in moving Hawk Mountain forward.

"By the time I came on the scene, Joe had been associated with the sanctuary for nearly forty years and had as much love and appreciation for that special place as anyone alive. He also had a firm vision for where it needed to go. Although it was always my sense that Joe preferred to avoid direct confrontation, he had a steely resolve to do what was necessary to advance that vision.

"The sanctuary curator, Jim Brett, had wanted to be named executive director, which was a challenge for both of us. In many ways. Joe loved Jim like a son, nonetheless, he made clear to me that I was the executive director, and he had my back. Jim saw that our successes gave him new resources and opportunities for growth. We made our peace and became an effective team.

"The Hawk Mountain Sanctuary 50th anniversary celebration was a turning point. The events required the entire staff and our volunteers to work seamlessly together. More than 10,000 people visited the sanctuary over a three-day period. It was a great occasion both to honor the past and look to the future. Roger Tory Peterson commented, 'Hawk Mountain has certainly come a long way since the old days. Now the research, educational, and public relations values are paramount.'

"Joe was highly sensitive about the need to preserve the character of the sanctuary and the sense of family among staff, volunteers and long-time members. Characteristically, in his president's messages, he highlighted everything from the hiring of a new maintenance man or the purchase of our first computer to the deaths of important figures in the sanctuary's history.

"Under Joe's steady leadership, we made enormous progress in fulfilling our mission of the conservation of birds of prey and other wildlife and the creation of a better understanding of the natural environment. We doubled the size of the paid staff, vastly increased the volunteer corps, built solid support from businesses and foundations and added important acreage to the property. We implemented and endowed an international internship program and launched raptor research projects. And Hawk Mountain became a credible advocate for raptor conservation in the halls of Congress.

"On a more personal note, Joe was for me a warm, wise friend and mentor. Joe and Helen became surrogate grandparents for our young son, Nathan. They celebrated the birth of our second son, Paul. Our youngest son, Daniel Joseph Senner, was so named in honor of Joe. I regret they never had a chance to meet in person.

"When Joe and Helen let us know that they were coming to the sanctuary, it would set off a flurry of tidying up and other preparations. After arriving, they would circulate and talk with the staff and the members they recognized along the trails or at the North Lookout.

"Jim and Dotty Brett, with Pat and me and sometimes the whole staff, would typically join Joe and Helen for dinner in Pottsville or Orwigsburg. With ample food and alcohol, those dinners became occasions for stories about Rosalie Edge, her son Peter Edge, Roger Tory Peterson, the American Birding Association or the Appleton-Whittell Research Ranch in Arizona with which Joe was deeply involved. We heard many hilarious tales about their drives from Honeoye Falls to Hawk Mountain, complete with picnic baskets of food and adult beverages.

"One of my fondest memories was a visit to Joe and Helen's winter home in Sonoita to talk about the possibility of building a new visitor center on the escarpment. Although that particular vision never materialized, the existing headquarters building was expanded to provide additional offices and a library. Ultimately, the visitor center was enlarged and the Acopian Center was built to accommodate interns and the research program.

"When I left Hawk Mountain early in 1990 to return to Alaska to work for the State of Alaska on the restoration program following the Exxon *Valdez* oil spill, Joe wrote in the June 1990 issue of the *Hawk Mountain News*:

> 'We will all miss Stan. We wish him the best, and we know that the
> day is not far off when we will be proud to say "We knew him when..."'

"I am not sure that I ever fulfilled his prediction, but I am content to know we both had an impact on the future of Hawk Mountain.

"Joe's legacy at Hawk Mountain is huge. His association with the sanctuary was rooted in its early days. He led the transition to a modern nonprofit organization ready to compete for resources and influence in a more crowded environmental field. It was all done while preserving the character of the mountain and honoring the past. Of course, Joe did it with quiet, firm leadership, a twinkle in his eyes and a certain style which is hard to describe. I still miss him dearly and always will."[80]

A memorial from James Brett, curator of Hawk Mountain Sanctuary: "We came to know one another as Joseph and James.

"We are persuaded that a thread runs through all things: all worlds strung on it, as beads and men and events and life come to us only because of that thread. For me, for many, I suspect, Joseph was part of that thread. So too, as that thread has run through each of us, there has been woven the fabric, and those who came to know and love him can be privileged to wear Joseph's coat.

"Odd that he has left now – or timely. I think he sensed it would be soon. Vague migratory longings seemed to spring up – longings which would, of late, find fulfillment in reflection and contemplation. I sensed it for some time. Instincts, sensations, inclinations bequeathed to him by heredity were awakened, took shape and asserted themselves with imperious authority. Last week he hugged me and, with those deeply penetrating eyes said 'Goodbye,' and I knew it was. The time had come when with dignity he quietly burst out of the prison of his pain and could now roam about at liberty in another space.

"And what a mark he has left. Certainly in the genius of his wonderful children, in the hundreds of friends around the world and so, too, in his beloved Hawk Mountain that, together with Helen, he so faithfully nurtured and guided for a quarter of a century. He was to pass on the president's baton soon, but he didn't really ever want to do that. And he took it along. In a wonderful essay, entitled 'The Way to Rainy Mountain,' N. Scott Momady wrote, 'Once in his life a person ought to concentrate his mind upon the remembered earth, I believe. He ought to give himself up to a particular landscape in his experience, to look at it from as many angles as he can, to wonder about it, to dwell upon it. He ought to imagine that he touches it with his hands at every season and listens to the sounds that are made upon it. He ought to imagine creatures there and all the faintest motions of the wind. He ought to recollect the glare of noon and all the colors of the dawn and dusk.' How adequately those words serve to sum up Joseph's feelings for his mountain.

"It's time to say our goodbyes, and this is an especially painful goodbye, but his enormous energy and glowing spirit will serve to lessen the pain and our remembrances of Joseph will help us reconcile his passing through the days ahead. I choose to paraphrase the words of Rachel Carson from *Under the Sea*, 'He wheeled out over the bay in a wide circle, flashing white wing bars. He returned crying loudly as he passed over the flats where his progeny were still running and, probing at the edge of the curling wavelets, he turned his head to the wind and was gone.'

"Farewell, Joseph. Farewell, friend." [81]

––

Joseph Alexander Taylor, his son and my brother, eulogized: "Father loved his family, especially Mother, whom he met when he was seventeen and to whom he was married for fifty-three years, his children – Ann, Mary, brother Hank and me – his grandchildren and his step-grandchildren. He never played favorites. He seemed to love each one of us separately, individually.

"As children, we were all imbued with birds. Birds were an integral part of our parents' lives which, in turn, became part of ours. There was always something flying about worth noting. Surrounded by Audubon prints, stuffed birds and bird feeders, we were accustomed to Father spending many weekends wandering the local woods and ponds with fellow birders. We were aware of the bird 'alerts,' the annual counts, and their yearly birding trips, but did not participate with them.

"Father was a man of few words, at least with us, his children. In fact, growing up, we saw him very little. Weekends, he had handyman projects, his rose garden, his bonsai collection, his tropical and marine fish, his double-crostics – all solitary hobbies. And dogs! He had so many over the years, he couldn't remember them all.

"He was great at consoling people in time of need. If you were ever hugged by him, it was something hard to forget. I remember shortly after my brother died, I met him by accident at the top of the backstairs at 590. I burst into tears, and he was there for me, wrapping his strong arms around me.

"After he retired in 1969, Father devoted his energies to the nonprofit world, pursuing his avid interest in birds, other wildlife and the preservation of the environment. He served as president of Hawk Mountain Sanctuary for twenty-six years, was a founder of the American Birding Association and, over the years, participated in many ways in numerous conservation organizations.

"Father admired creativity of all kinds whether applying oils with a brush to canvas, carving stone with a chisel, melting steel rod into sculpture, or simply putting pen to paper. He was a busy man. One of his favorite preoccupations was pouring over maps in preparation for a trip somewhere. And it didn't matter if it was a trip he and Mother were taking or one of mine!

"Always focused on the future, Father's courage was formidable; his imagination boundless – whether it was booking the new trans-Canadian railway, planning the enlarged headquarters at Hawk Mountain, designing their large butterfly garden or overseeing the creation of the lake at Parrish Road.

"I think that for Father, God was everywhere, in every living thing. I think he saw himself, he felt himself, a part of nature. 'Lovely' was the word he used when the spring was new; when the butterfly landed; when the hoar frost bit. His gentleness with the natural world belied the intensity with which he loved it.

"The summer before he died, Father and I were on a short walk outside their home. He spotted a dead chickadee on the grass beside us. He reached down, picked it up and held it in his hand for a long moment. Then, he walked to the edge of the field and placed it carefully in the tall grass. Without a word we walked on.

"The night that Father died, my wife Sheila had a dream. She dreamt we were following Father up the path to the North Lookout at Hawk Mountain. He was dressed in a white coat with a brown collar. When we reached the summit, he spread his wings and took off. He'd become an eagle soaring into the radiant sunlight."[82]

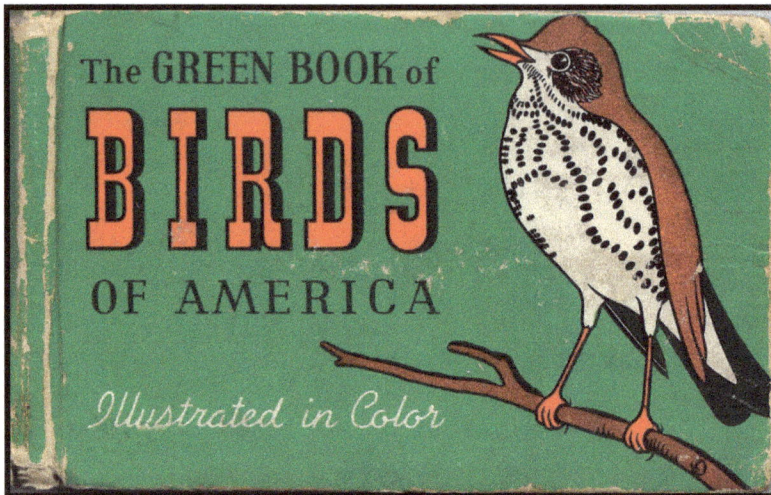

Joe's first pocket field guide
Whitman Publishing Company, Racine, Wisconsin, 1931

GRATITUDE

Impetus for this compilation began while I was reading Wallace Stegner's Pulitzer Prize winning novel *Angle of Repose* in which the protagonist is compiling a biography of his grandmother, a western pioneer. Her determination to eschew the shackles of her traditional upbringing and forge an entirely different life, reminded me of my father's similar life-changing quest.

Armed with numerous research materials, I began to review the articles about and by Joseph William Taylor which I had collected since the 1960s. With the accord of my Taylor siblings Mary and Joseph, *BORN TO BIRD* began to take form. Detailed editorial revisions by my daughter Alyssa Taylor Wendt, line-editing by my sister Mary and astute commentary by my friends Sally Sommer and Robbie Brada created an integrated text for birders and non-birders alike. I am truly grateful for all their critical work.

My thanks to Laurie Goodrich at Hawk Mountain Sanctuary for allowing me to gather my father's archival photographs and acknowledge my sincere appreciation to Eleonore and John Herman who drove me to collect them. I am indebted to Gregory Neise at the American Birding Association who provided articles which augmented my collection and to my father's birding friends who penned reminiscences of their experiences with him.

If I had told my father about this book when he was alive, he probably would have quipped, "Nonsense! Wrong season!" echoing what he was told by his own father when he identified the Golden-crowned Kinglet in their barberry hedge. I believe, however, this is exactly the right season for *BORN TO BIRD*.

Ann Taylor
2022

NOTES

1. Mackey, Kitty, "The 600: An Elite Birders' Flock," *Town and Country*, October, 1975
2. Starr, Mark, "Joe Taylor, Bird World's Babe Ruth," Upstate Magazine, *Democrat and Chronicle,* Rochester, New York, April 8, 1974
3. Weidensaul, Scott, "Joe Taylor," *Bird Watcher's Digest*, Vol. 14, No. 6, July/August 1992.
4. Ibid. Starr, Mark.
5. Taylor, Ann, "Helen Taggart Taylor," *All of Us, a biographical history of John Jacob Bausch and his descendants from 1930 to 1978*, 1978.
6. Anonymous, "Contemporary Audubon Comes to Key West," *Key West Citizen*, Key West, Florida, March 24, 1972.
7. King, Floyd, *Democrat and Chronicle*, Rochester, New York, May 16, 1954.
8. Taylor, Joseph W., "What's in a Name*," Democrat and Chronicle*, Rochester, New York, December 17, 1972.
9. Snyder, Courtney, Photograph of North Lookout, Hawk Mountain Sanctuary, with permission from Discover NEPA, August, 2022.
10. Zaslowsky, Dyan, "The Flight of the Raptors," *New York Times,* New York, New York, September 20, 1992.
11. Anonymous, "At Home with Joe and Helen Taylor," *Hawk Mountain News*, Hawk Mountain Sanctuary, Kempton, Pennsylvania, Number 77, Fall 1992.
12. Taylor, Joseph W., "Hawk Mountain: The First Fifty Years," *Birding,* Vol. XVI, Number 6, December, 1984.
13. Oresman, Stephen B., e-mails to the author, October 7 and 24, 2021, with permission.
14. Taylor, Joseph W., "President's Report," *Hawk Mountain News*, Hawk Mountain Sanctuary, Kempton, Pennsylvania, Number 74, Winter 1991.
15. Taylor, Joseph W., "President's Report," *Hawk Mountain News*, Hawk Mountain Sanctuary, Kempton, Pennsylvania, Number 76, Summer 1992.

16. Taylor, Joseph W., "The Long View," *Hawk Mountain News*, Hawk Mountain Sanctuary, Kempton, Pennsylvania, Number 77, Fall 1992.

17. Rochester Museum and Science Center, Citation, 1968

18. Taylor, Joseph W., "A Preview of May and June," *Democrat and Chronicle*, Rochestet, New York, April 16, 1969.

19. Taylor, Joseph W., "Success Tale for Starling – Too Bad," *Democrat and Chronicle*, Rochester, New York, November 12, 1969.

20. Taylor, Joseph W., "Geese Symbol of the Wild," *Democrat and Chronicle*, Rochester, New York, October 31, 1971.

21. Taylor, Joseph W., "Carried Away with Spring," *Democrat and Chronicle*, Rochester, New York, June 1, 1975.

22. Taylor, Joseph W., "Gray Jay Shows No Fear," *Democrat and Chronicle*, Rochester, New York, September 17, 1969.

23. Taylor, Joseph W., "A Day with Juncos," *Democrat and Chronicle*, Rochester, New York, November 5, 1969.

24. Taylor, Joseph W., "The Joy of Freeing Two Owls," *Democrat and Chronicle*, Rochester, New York, January 28, 1970.

25. Taylor, Joseph W., "Delightful Floating Bog," *Democrat and Chronicle*, Rochester, New York, June 18, 1971.

26. Taylor, Joseph W., "Higgins Lake Background for Many Songs," *Democrat and Chronicle*, Rochester, New York, August 8, 1972.

27. Taylor, Joseph W., "Ausable – River to the Past," *Democrat and Chronicle*, Rochester, New York, August 27, 1969.

28. Taylor, Joseph W., "Birds' Extinction Could be Natural," *Democrat and Chronicle*, Rochester, New York, August 1, 1976.

29.. Taylor, Joseph W., "Silent Summer," "Pinewords," *Pinewoods Camp Newsletter*, Higgins Lake, Michigan, August 12, 1992.

30. Taylor, Joseph W., "Birding Good on Island," *Democrat and Chronicle*, Rochester, New York, October 15, 1969.

31. Taylor, Joseph W., "Black-Polls Lose Caps," *Democrat and Chronicle*, Rochester, New York, October 22, 1969.

32. Taylor, Joseph W., "Heath Hills Unique on Nantucket," *Democrat and Chronicle*, Rochester, New York, October 29, 1969.

33. Taylor, Joseph W., "Cramped Bermuda, Still Beautiful," *Democrat and Chronicle*, Rochester, New York, June 18, 1969.

34. Taylor, Joseph W., "Bermuda's Beauty," *Democrat and Chronicle,* Rochester, New York, June 25, 1969.

35. Taylor, Joseph W., "The Bermuda Petrel – A Story of Romance," *Democrat and Chronicle,* Rochester, New York, July 2, 1969.

36. Taylor, Joseph W., "The Enchanting Galapagos," *Democrat and Chronicle,* Rochester, New York, May 21, 1969.

37. Taylor, Joseph W., "Galapagos: Lava Caves, Giant Black Lizards," *Democrat and Chronicle,* Rochester, New York, May 28, 1969.

38. Taylor, Joseph W., "Wildlife Thrives in African Park," *Democrat and Chronicle,* Rochester, New York, May 13, 1970.

39. Taylor, Joseph W., "A Reminder of Home in East Africa," *Democrat and Chronicle,* Rochester, New York, May 20, 1970.

40. Taylor, Joseph W., "Rugged splendor – Birds Vary in Size, Color," *Democrat and Chronicle,* Rochester, New York, April 29, 1970.

41. Taylor, Joseph W., "Guacharos of Trinidad," *Democrat and Chronicle,* Rochester, New York, June 4, 1972.

42. Taylor, Joseph W., "A Day with the Trinidad Wildlife," *Democrat and Chronicle,* Rochester, New York, June 11, 1972.

43. Taylor, Joseph W., "Down a Trace in Trinidad," *Democrat and Chronicle,* Rochester, New York, June 18, 1972.

44. Taylor, Joseph W., "Battle Against Pesticides," *Democrat and Chronicle,* Rochester, New York, April 23, 1969.

45. Taylor, Joseph W., "Danger: Dieldrin," *Democrat and Chronicle,* Rochester, New York, July 23, 1969.

46. Taylor, Joseph W., "The Destruction of the Redeemed," *Democrat and Chronicle,* Rochester, New York, August 20, 1969.

47. Taylor, Joseph W., "All Pesticides Harm Wildlife," *Democrat and Chronicle,* Rochester, New York, August 26, 1970.

48. Taylor, Joseph W., "The Fight to Save Bald Eagle," *Democrat and Chronicle,* Rochester, New York, December 3, 1978.

49. Taylor, Joseph W., "Mysteries of Avian Behavior," *Democrat and Chronicle,* Rochester, New York, November 11, 1979.

50. Taylor, Joseph W., "Let's Do Our Bit for Endangered Species," *Democrat and Chronicle,* Rochester, New York, November 25, 1973.

51. Taylor, Joseph W., "A Sea Eagle Swoops, Soars," *Democrat and Chronicle,* Rochester, New York, July 16, 1978.

52. Schroeder, Dennis, Carving of an Eskimo Curlew, with permission, September 1, 2022.

53. Brown, John W., "Rochesterian Joins '600 Club' Birders," *Times Union*, Rochester, New York, 1972.

54. Taylor, Joseph W., "Listing – The Games Birders Play. Is 700 possible?," *Birding,* Volume 2, Number 4, July-August 1970.

55. Adams, Marjorie Valentine, "Have you started your list?," *National Wildlife*, June-July 1975, Volume 13, Number 4.

56. Keith, Stuart, "700 in North America: A New Birding Landmark! Joe Taylor Does It!," *Birding*, Volume 4, Number 3, May-June 1972.

57. Brown, John W., "Top Birdwatcher to be Watched," *Times Union*, Rochester New York, 1972.

58. Starr, Mark. " Mr. Taylor Would Go Miles & Miles..." *Wall Street Journal*, New York, New York, September 11, 1974.

59. Kasper, Ed, photographs for *Sports Illustrated*, Volume 50, Number 19, May 7, 1979.

60. Gammon, Clive, "The Great Bird Bash," *Sports Illustrated*, Volume 50, Number 19, May 7, 1979.

61. Taylor, Joseph W., "Birding by Learjet – but No Record," *Democrat and Chronicle,* Rochester, New York, May 27, 1979.

62. Oresman, Stephen B., with permission, 2021.

63. Taylor, Joseph W., "Canada Geese in Oak Orchard," *Democrat and Chronicle,* Rochester, New York, April 10, 1972.

64. Taylor, Joseph W., "Monogamy of Geese," *Democrat and Chronicle,* Rochester, New York, November 18, 1979.

65. Ibid. Weidensaul, Scott

66. Balch, Lawrence G., "Joseph W. Taylor 1914–1992," *Birding*, Volume XXIV, Number 6, December 1992.

67. Taylor, Joseph W., "Birdwatcher's Paradise on Forty Acres of Land," *Democrat and Chronicle*, Rochester, New York, July 9, 1969.

68. Jones, Eleanor, "Needlepoint a New Hobby for this Bird-Watcher*," Honeoye Falls Times*, Honeoye Falls, New York, October 7, 1976.

69. Gaimbrone, Jean, "The Taylors Bring Outdoors Inside," *Times Union*, Rochester, New York, May 5, 1970

70. Smith, Andy, "Area Birder 'Retires,'" *Democrat and Chronicle*, Rochester, New York, January 4, 1981

71. Taylor, Joseph W., "About Sonoita," March 7, 1992

72. Taylor, Joseph W., "Birds Enjoy Phoenix Sun," *Democrat and Chronicle,* Rochester, New York, March 19, 1972

73. Taylor, Joseph W., "Birds Slowly Coming Back," *Democrat and Chronicle*, Rochester, New York, May 7, 1978

74. Brockner, Winston William, "'Win' Brockner Remembers Joe Taylor," *New York Birders Newsletter*, Volume 21, Number 4, Federation of New York State Bird Clubs, December, 1992.

75. Peterson, John M. C., "Joseph W. Taylor," *High Peaks Audubon Newsletter*, Volume 20, Number 6, November-December 1992.

76. Goodrich, Laurie, with permission, 2022.

77. Brown, Jr., Carl W., "Taylor's Spiriit to Linger," *Reading Eagle*, Reading, Pennsylvania, October 5, 1992.

78. Wright, Minturn, with permission, 2021.

79. Gill, Frank, with permission, 2021.

80. Stenner, Stanley, with permission, 2022.

81. Brett, James, curator, "Tribute to Joseph Taylor," Hawk Mountain Sanctuary, September 29, 1992.

82. Taylor, Joseph Alexander, "A Son's Reflections," September 29, 1992.

INDEXES

BIRDS

PERSONAL REFERENCES

WILDLIFE ORGANIZATIONS